KU-269-190

Financial Development and Economic Growth

British Association for the Advancement of Science books

Series Editor: **David Reisman**

Titles include:

Charles A. E. Goodhart (*editor*)
FINANCIAL DEVELOPMENT AND ECONOMIC GROWTH
Explaining the Links

Frank Hahn (*editor*)
THE MARKET: Practice and Policy

Douglas Hague (*editor*)
THE MANAGEMENT OF SCIENCE

Phyllis Deane (*editor*)
FRONTIERS OF ECONOMIC RESEARCH

Aubrey Silberston
TECHNOLOGY AND ECONOMIC PROGRESS

Alan Williams (*editor*)
HEALTH AND ECONOMICS

R. D. Collison Black (*editor*)
IDEAS IN ECONOMICS

Kenneth Boudling (*editor*)
THE ECONOMICS OF HUMAN BETTERMENT

Roy Jenkins (*editor*)
BRITAIN AND THE EEC

R. C. O. Matthews (*editor*)
ECONOMY AND DEMOCRACY

Jack Wiseman (*editor*)
BEYOND POSITIVE ECONOMICS?

Lord Roll of Ipsden (*editor*)
THE MIXED ECONOMY

British Association for the Advancement of Science books
Series Standing Order ISBN 0–333–71461–X
(*outside North America only*)

You can receive future titles in this series as they are published by placing a standing order. Please contact your bookseller or, in case of difficulty, write to us at the address below with your name and address, the title of the series and the ISBN quoted above.

Customer Services Department, Macmillan Distribution Ltd, Houndmills, Basingstoke, Hampshire RG21 6XS, England

Financial Development and Economic Growth

Explaining the Links

Edited by

Charles A.E. Goodhart
London School of Economics and Political Science
UK

Editorial matter and selection and Chapter 7 © Charles A.E. Goodhart 2004
Chapter 4 © Erik Berglof and Patrick Bolton 2004
Remaining chapters © Palgrave Macmillan Ltd 2004

All rights reserved. No reproduction, copy or transmission of this
publication may be made without written permission.

No paragraph of this publication may be reproduced, copied or transmitted
save with written permission or in accordance with the provisions of the
Copyright, Designs and Patents Act 1988, or under the terms of any licence
permitting limited copying issued by the Copyright Licensing Agency, 90
Tottenham Court Road, London W1T 4LP.

Any person who does any unauthorized act in relation to this publication
may be liable to criminal prosecution and civil claims for damages.

The authors have asserted their rights to be identified
as the authors of this work in accordance with the Copyright,
Designs and Patents Act 1988.

First published 2004 by
PALGRAVE MACMILLAN
Houndmills, Basingstoke, Hampshire RG21 6XS and
175 Fifth Avenue, New York, N.Y. 10010
Companies and representatives throughout the world

PALGRAVE MACMILLAN is the global academic imprint of the Palgrave
Macmillan division of St. Martin's Press, LLC and of Palgrave Macmillan Ltd.
Macmillan® is a registered trademark in the United States, United Kingdom
and other countries. Palgrave is a registered trademark in the European
Union and other countries.

ISBN 1–4039–2066–4

This book is printed on paper suitable for recycling and made from fully
managed and sustained forest sources.

A catalogue record for this book is available from the British Library.

Library of Congress Cataloging-in-Publication Data
    Financial development and economic growth : explaining the links /
edited by Charles A.E. Goodhart.
        p. cm. – (British Association for the Advancement of Science books)
Papers from the 2003 meeting of the British Association for the
Advancement of Science, Section F (Economics).
    Includes bibliographical references and index.
    ISBN 1–4039–2066–4 (cloth)
        1. Finance – Congresses. 2. Economic development – Congresses.
3. Financial institutions – Congresses. I. Goodhart, C. A. E. (Charles Albert
Eric) II. British Association for the Advancement of Science. Section F
(Economics) III. Series.

HG173.F4894 2004
332—dc22   2004043622

10 9 8 7 6 5 4 3 2 1
13 12 11 10 09 08 07 06 05 04

Printed and bound in Great Britain by
Antony Rowe Ltd, Chippenham and Eastbourne

Contents

List of Tables

List of Figures

Preface

Professor T. M. Rybczynski

One of the oldest interdisciplinary bodies offering the opportunity to discuss important issues – issues already important or about to be recognised as important – has been the British Association for the Advancement of Science. Since 1831 it has provided a forum for the presentation of papers examining work accomplished or under way in a number of areas of learning. It has encouraged a wide debate on the complex problems to which they draw attention. Among the disciplines represented has been that of economics which has been organised as Section F. An account of the way Section F has developed and the contribution it has made is contained in the paper by Professor David Reisman published below. Professor Reisman is a former Recorder of the Section and has for many years been a member of the small group responsible for the Section's work. As pointed out by the author, the work of Section F has involved participation in the annual conference at which valuable papers were presented and the 'big' issues of the day discussed.

It has been the policy of the Section to invite a distinguished President drawn from the world of letters or the world of affairs to present the main paper on the theme of the year. The theme is then developed further by other eminent speakers. As is shown in the list at the end of this booklet, the Presidents of the Section include the names that form the backbone of the history of economic thought in Britain. They have played a pivotal part in economic policy-making in Britain in the last one hundred and sixty years and are still doing so today. It is indeed no exaggeration to say that Section F has been the nursery of economic thought in the UK.

The long tradition is continuing. It is the hope of the Committee that, by being unique in character, by being able to take a detached and dispassionate view of various issues, Section F will in the future make a still more valuable and important contribution to the advancement of economics and to the solution of urgent and important social problems.

The policy of Section F makes it unique both in the scope of its work and its interdisciplinary contribution. It is the contention of the Section and its officers that complex problems are well approached in a dispassionate manner before a wide forum such as that provided by the British Association.

Foreword

The theme of the 2003 meeting of the British Association for the Advancement of Science was 'Sustainable Growth'. I had been asked, and agreed, to be President of the Economic Section of the B.A. (Section F), and my main field of expertise has been Monetary Economics. Put these two together, and a natural subject for our own Section was 'Financial Development and Economic Growth'.

I was fortunate to persuade a world-class group of authors in this field to contribute papers. The quality of their work was such that it seemed right to publish them altogether, thereby returning to a prior and long-standing tradition whereby Macmillan/Palgrave has published the proceedings of Section F, the last being in 1999, when *Public Choice Analysis of Economic Policy* (eds) A. Chrystal and R. Pennant-Rae was published.

In that book there was a short introductory 'History of Section F', and, with the kind permission of its author, David Reisman, we have decided to re-publish this.

I am not going to provide a lengthy summary of the respective chapters, but it might be helpful for me to explain why I chose this ordering. Patrick Honohan's (World Bank) chapter, on 'Financial Development, Growth and Poverty: How Close are the Links?', comes first because it gives a clear and excellent overview on current positive views on the importance of financial development for contributing to sustainable economic growth. This is naturally followed by the chapter by Panicos Demetriades and Svetlana Andrianova (Leicester University), on 'Finance and Growth: What We Know and What We Need to Know', since they cover the same general ground, but from a considerably more sceptical viewpoint.

The third chapter is by Stijn Claessens (University of Amsterdam) and Luc Laeven (World Bank) on 'Competition in the Financial Sector and Growth: A Cross-country Perspective'. They use an innovative empirical methodology, devised by Rajan and Zingales (1998), to explore the relationships between banking system competition and development and economic growth.

The fourth chapter is by Erik Berglof (Stockholm Institute of Transition Economics) and Patrick Bolton (Princeton). Their chapter on 'The Great Divide and Beyond: Financial Architecture in Transition' has also been published in the *Journal of Economic Perspectives* (16(1), Winter 2002: 77–100), and we are grateful for permission to reprint. This deals with the problems faced in transition economies in establishing a well-functioning financial system and the effects of that on growth and economic advancement more widely.

The fifth chapter, by Beatriz Armendáriz (Harvard) and Jonathan Morduch (NYU), on 'Microfinance: Where do we Stand?', covers recent innovations in microfinance, the institutions that deliver financial services to low-income individuals. They focus on four such innovations; the use of 'progressive lending', the flexible treatment of collateral, the emphasis on women as customers, and the promotion of clients' savings.

The penultimate chapter is by Phil Davis (Brunel) on the subject of 'Financial Development, Institutional Investors and Economic Performance'. In the previous chapters much of the focus is on the role of banks, or bank-like micro-finance lenders. Phil switches the emphasis to the role of institutional intermediary investors, such as pension funds, insurance companies and mutual funds in encouraging savings, allocating resources and enhancing growth.

The final chapter, on 'Money, Stability and Growth', is my own. The earlier papers generally deal with the influence of financial intermediation on economic growth. I look at an even more fundamental issue, which is the importance of the institution of money itself in enabling economic development, and in particular the triangular relationship between good governance, monetary stability and economic growth.

Notes on Contributors

Beatriz Armendáriz, de Aghion is a Lecturer in Economics at the Department of Economics of Harvard University. She is currently on leave from the Department of Economics of University College London where she is a tenured Senior Lecturer in Economics. Prior to her current positions at Harvard University and University College London, she has been an Associate Visiting Professor at the Department of Economics at the Massachusetts Institute of Technology, a Lecturer at the London School of Economics, and Visiting Fellow at the University of Toulouse. Armendáriz de Aghion has written a number of articles on Microfinance, including 'On the Design of a Credit Agreement With Peer Monitoring' in the *Journal of Development Economics*, "Peer Group Formation In An Adverse Selection Model" (joint with Christian Gollier) in *The Economic Journal*, 'Microfinance Beyond Group Lending' (joint with Jonathan Morduch), in the *Journal of Economics of Transition*, and 'Development Banking' in the *Journal of Development Economics*. She is currently writing a book with Jonathan Morduch titled *The Economics of Microfinance* for MIT Press. Armendáriz de Aghion grew up in Chiapas, Mexico, where she founded the first Grameen-style replication in 1996.

Svetlana Andrianova is a lecturer in Economics at the University of Leicester with research interests in contract and game theory, political economy and financial development. She holds an undergraduate degree in applied mathematics and mechanics from Moscow State University (Lomonosov), and completed her postgraduate studies in economics at the Universities of Cambridge (PGDip), Staffordshire (MA), Keele and South Bank (PhD).

Erik Berglof is Director of the Stockholm Institute of Transition Economics (SITE), Professor at the Stockholm School of Economics, and President of the Center for Economic and Financial Research (CEFIR) in Moscow. He is also a Programme Director of the transition and development program at the Centre for Economic Policy Research (CEPR) in London, a Fellow at the European Corporate Governance Institute in Brussels, and Director of the bankruptcy task force of the Initiative for Policy Dialogue at Columbia University. He is on the editorial board of the *Review of Finance, Economics of Transition*, and *Journal of Comparative Economics*. He has served as Special Advisor to the Prime Minister of

Sweden, on several government commissions and EU-related panels, and as a consultant to the international financial institutions. Erik Berglof's academic work focuses mainly on corporate governance, financial development, and political economy.

Patrick Bolton is the John H. Scully 1966 Professor of Finance and Economics at Princeton University. Professor Bolton has both a PhD in Economics and a M.Sc. in Mathematical Economics and Econometrics from the London School of Economics. He is a Fellow of the Econometric Society, a Fellow of CEPR and NBER, and the European Corporate Governance Institute. He is Co-organizer of the European Summer Symposium in Economic Theory at the Studienzentrum, Gerzensee, Switzerland. He is a member of the Editorial Board of the *Journal of Financial Intermediation*, and a previous member of the Editorial Boards of *Econometrica, Review of Economic Studies, Annales d'Economie et de Statistique* and *Economic Policy*. He is a Managing Editor of the *Journal of the European Economic Association* and a former Managing Editor of the *Review of Economic Studies*. Professor Bolton's main research interests are in Contact Theory, Corporate Finance, Political Economy and Industrial Organization.

Stijn Claessens Stijn Claessens is Professor of International Finance Policy at the University of Amsterdam. Prior to this, he taught at New York University business school and worked at the World Bank. At the World Bank, Mr Claessens has provided advice and participated in missions to emerging markets in Latin America, East Asia and the transition economies. His principal role was to help governments develop strategies for external debt restructuring and asset-liability management; and to provide advice on financial sector restructuring and reform. His research on international finance issues has been published in the *Journal of Financial Economics, Journal of Finance* and *Quarterly Journal of Economics*. He is on the Editorial Board of the *World Bank Economic Review* and an associate editor of the *Journal of Financial Services Research*. He is also a fellow of the *CEPR*. His current research interests are enterprise and financial sector restructuring in transition economies and developing countries; sovereign asset-liability and risk management; corporate governance and capital market development; and internationalization of financial services.

E. Philip Davis is Professor of Economics and Finance at Brunel University, West London and a Visiting Fellow at the National Institute for Economic and Social Research. Davis is also an associate member of the Financial Markets Group at the London School of Economics, an Associate Fellow of the Royal Institute for International Affairs and a Research Fellow of the Pensions Institute at Birkbeck College, London. Davis left Oxford University in 1980, and was employed by the Bank of England up till 2000 except for two spells on secondment, to the Bank for International Settlements in 1985–87, and in 1993–97 to the European Monetary Institute and its successor, the European Central Bank. Davis has published widely in the fields of pensions, institutional investment, euromarkets, banking, corporate finance, financial regulation and financial stability. He has published five books including 'Pension Funds, Retirement-Income Security and Capital Markets, an International Perspective' Oxford, 1995 and "Institutional Investors" with Benn Steil, published by MIT Press in early 2001.

Panicos Demetriades is Professor of Financial Economics and Head of the Department of Economics at the University of Leicester. He has published widely in the area of financial development, focussing on causality issues using time-series methods, and policy questions such as financial liberalisation. He has acted as Consultant to the World Bank and Speaker for the Economic Development Institute of the Bank. He holds a PhD in Economics from the University of Cambridge and BA and MA degrees from the University of Essex.

Charles Goodhart, CBE, FBA is Deputy Director of the Financial Markets Group at the London School of Economics. Until his retirement in 2002, he had been the Norman Sosnow Professor of Banking and Finance at LSE since 1985. Previously, he had worked at the Bank of England for seventeen years as a monetary adviser, becoming a Chief Adviser in 1980. In 1997 he was appointed one of the outside independent members of the Bank of England's new Monetary Policy Committee until May 2000. Earlier he had taught at Cambridge and LSE. Besides numerous articles, he has written a couple of books on monetary history; a graduate monetary textbook, *Money, Information and Uncertainty* (2nd ed. 1989); two collections of papers on monetary policy, *Monetary Theory and Practice* (1984) and *The Central Bank and the Financial System* (1995); and several other studies relating to financial markets and to monetary policy and history. In his spare time he is a sheep farmer (loss-making).

Patrick Honohan is a Senior Financial Policy Advisor in the World Bank. Previously he was Economic Advisor to the Taoiseach (Irish Prime Minister) and spent several years as Professor at the Economic and Social

Research Institute, Dublin, and at the Central Bank of Ireland. Dr Honohan, who is a graduate of the London School of Economics and University College Dublin, has published widely on issues ranging from exchange rate regimes and purchasing-power parity, to migration, cost-benefit analysis and statistical methodology. Based in Dublin, he is also a member of the Royal Irish Academy, a Research Fellow of the Centre for Economic Policy Research, London and a Research Associate of Trinity College, Dublin.

Luc Laeven is a Financial Economist at the World Bank. He has partici-pated in several financial and private sector operations of the World Bank, focusing on the development of banking systems and corporate sectors. His research focuses on international banking and corporate finance issues and has been published in several books and academic journals, including the Journal of Finance, the Journal of Money, Credit, and Banking, Financial Management, the Journal of Financial Intermediation, the Journal of Banking and Finance, the Journal of Financial Services Research, the Journal of Comparative Economics, and the World Bank Economic Review. His current research interests are in the areas of bank governance, financial development and access to finance. He studied at Tilburg University, the University of Amsterdam and the London School of Economics.

Jonathan Morduch is Associate Professor of Public Policy and Economics at New York University. He is currently Chair of the United Nations Steering Committee on Poverty Measurement. In 2002–03 was an Abe Fellow at the University of Tokyo. Prior to joining NYU, he taught on the Economics faculty at Harvard University, was a National Fellow at the Hoover Institution at Stanford University, and was a MacArthur Foundation Research Fellow at Princeton University. His research on risk, financial markets, and poverty and inequality has been published in the Review of Economic Studies, Economic Journal, Journal of Econometrics, Journal of Development Economics, and Journal of Public Economics. A new book on The Economics of Microfinance (co-authored with Beatriz Armendariz de Aghion) will be published by the MIT Press in early 2005. His current research is on the political economy of foreign aid and the economic foundations of social investment.

The History of Section F

D.A. Reisman
University of Surrey

The first meeting of the British Association for the Advancement of Science was held in York, at the Yorkshire Philosophical Society, in 1831. Modelling itself on the German Science Association (founded in 1822), the new body was imbued both with a belief that the future lay with pure and applied science and a fear that Britain was already beginning to lag behind. Charles Babbage, a pioneer of the automatic calculating machine and Professor of Mathematics at Cambridge, was instrumental in the formation of the BA. He had represented British science at the 1828 meeting of the German Association in Berlin and had seen for himself the need for British technology not to lose out to 'Made in Germany'.

By the time of the 1833 (Cambridge) meeting of the BA, Babbage had decided that, as well as the more traditionally scientific disciplines of Physics, Chemistry, Geology, Zoology and Geography, there was a need for a Statistics Section that would show how quantitative inquiry could throw light on economic and social problems. His proposal for an additional Section – Section F – was supported by Malthus (then in the last year of his life) and by Richard Jones (Malthus's successor to the first-ever British Chair in Political Economy, at the East India College, Haileybury). Both of them were inductivists who were critical of the Ricardian vice of theory without evidence.

The foundation of Section F owed something to the presence of the distinguished Belgian statistician, Quételet, at the Cambridge meeting: Quételet had brought some papers on social statistics with him and had been unable to find a Section that wanted to discuss them. The foundation of Section F owed at least as much to the fact that the President of the BA in 1833, Professor Adam Sidgwick, could be persuaded that the new Section would be able to deal in facts without enflaming the passions in a troubled period, halfway between the Peterloo Massacre and the 'Hungry Forties'. Sidgwick, while approving of the new Section, nonetheless felt moved to give it a word of warning: 'Our meetings have been essentially harmonious, only because we have kept within our proper boundaries, confined ourselves to the laws of nature, and steered clear of all questions in the decision of which bad passions could have any play. But if we transgress our proper boundaries, go into provinces not belonging to us, and open a door of communication with the dreary world of politics, that instant will the foul Demon of discord find his way into our Eden of Philosophy.' Other physical scientists would no doubt have preferred to shut out the new Section altogether.

The first meeting of the Statistical Section was held in 1834: the first President was not Babbage, but Sir Charles Lemon. Babbage was the second President, albeit the President under whom (in 1835) the initial F was finally adopted. In 1856 the title of the Statistics Section was changed to the Section of Economic Science and Statistics. In 1948 Section F became the Economics Section. The title may have changed, but not so the focus. Section F has a tradition of applied papers dealing with policy-orientated subjects. It has never been, and never sought to be, at the coal-face of theoretical economics.

Initially the President of Section F (elected on an annual basis and nowadays not normally eligible for a second term) tended to be a civil servant, a politician or a statistician. Nassau Senior in 1860 had a background in academic economics and so did Thorold Rogers in 1866 and W. S. Jevons in 1870. In general, however, it was only from the 1880s that the typical President was an academic economist. One consequence was the variable standard of the early papers presented (the 1858 paper on the race and language of the gypsies is believed to have been deficient in both economics and statistics), together with a civil service eclecticism in the choice of topics (consider the following, from the 1860 programme: 'On the Economical Results of Military Drill in Popular Schools'). In 1860 Nassau Senior argued that the Section should in future confine itself within the boundaries set by the division of labour: 'Within the strict limits of economic science and statistics', he observed pointedly, 'a large field is open to us'.

In 1877 Francis Galton, founder of eugenics, wrote to the Council of the BA on behalf of the Physical sciences to recommend (unsuccessfully) that Section F be abolished: 'The general verdict of scientific men would be that few of the subjects treated fall within the meaning of the word "scientific" ', he said. He subsequently repeated his charge of 'unscientific' and 'unsuitable' in the *Journal of the Royal Statistical Society*. John Kells Ingram, using his presidential Address to spring to the defence of the Section, only succeeded in drawing attention to the extent to which political economy, pre-Marshall, was badly divided into conflicting schools. Criticising Ricardo for abstraction and Senior for narrowness, Ingram in 1878 called for an interdisciplinary approach to the Comte-like study of social development: 'What appears to be the reasonable suggestion, is that the field of the Section should be enlarged, so as to comprehend the whole of Sociology.' If the Section was under attack in its first half-century, then the reason is likely to have been the well-publicized disagreements between the approaches at least as much as the questionable standard of some at least of the early papers presented.

Some of the early papers were, however, serious and thoughtful. Few could have been more subversive of the orthodox assumptions than was Jevons's 'Notice of a General Mathematical Theory of Economy', read to the BA at Cambridge in 1862. Mathematical, marginalist, abstract, deductivist, Jevons's paper could have been the manifesto of neoclassical economics that Jevons's book, *The Theory of Political Economy*, was to be in 1871. The very fact that Jevons accompanied his paper on demand-led valuation with a second paper on trade cycles ('On the Study of Periodic Commercial Fluctuations') could have done much to establish his name as a economic theoretician with a sound grasp of economic statistics. Section F, sadly, was to let the discipline down on that occasion, and Jevons (who forgave the Section sufficiently to become its President in 1870) was bitter about the neglect: 'The year' he wrote in his diary in 1862, 'has seen my theory of economy offered to a learned society and received without a word of interest or belief.... This year had taken much youthfulness out of me.' Time limits no doubt counted against good discussion; and so did the presence at the BA of what Henry Sidgwick was later to call 'certain familiar bores'. Besides that, membership of the BA was open to the public, as it has always been. Business people, interested professionals, outsiders of all kinds have always given discussion at the BA freshness and breadth that is less common when experts swap techniques with specialists. The mix can, however, also mean that complicated departures are not rewarded with the in-depth exchange of views that would today take place at a Royal Economic Society conference. Whatever the reasons (and Jevons's own reluctance to attend the BA in person was undoubtedly one of them), the fact is that the Section in 1862 did less than justice to one of the more important of its early papers.

By the 1880s, the Section was becoming more and more of a forum for scholarship. The high standard of its Presidents did much to accelerate the transition – RH Inglis Palgrave (1883), Henry Sidgwick (1885), Robert Giffen (1887), Francis Ysidro Edgeworth (1889), all saw to it that standard of debate was kept high. Edgeworth had previously been Recorder of the Section (1887, 1888) and was later to be one of the few Presidents to be offered a second term (1922). Edgeworth's first

Presidential Address was entitled 'Mathematical Reasoning and Political Economy' it showed that Jevons's love of abstraction lived on in the economic theories of his Hampstead friend and former neighbour. His second Presidential Address was on the subject of 'Equal Pay to Men and Women for Equal Work'.

In 1890, in the year of the *Principles*, the President was none other than the economist of the moment, the professor who had unified the discipline. Alfred Marshall at Leeds spoke on the theme of 'Some Aspects of Competition'. Averse to the pure waste of zero-sum salesmanship, he looked back on his visits to the protected markets of Germany in 1871, the United States in 1875, to draw the general lesson that competition is usually in the public interest and its restriction on balance is not. The economists of the English Historical School were more sympathetic to the dynamic efficiency of the giant organization: economic nationalists, advocates of a protective tariff, they looked to the State for more than simply the correction of a market failure. Marshall's Cambridge colleague, Herbert Foxwell, was one of their number: the Recorder of Section F from 1882–88, Foxwell in 1888 read to the Section at Bath his important paper on 'The Growth of Monopoly, and its Bearing on the Functions of the State', in which he reached the conclusion (a very unusual one in the British economics of the late-nineteenth century) that, for all its attendant evils, monopoly had 'enormous advantages' nonetheless. Foxwell (who lived on until 1936) never became President of Section F. Nor incidentally, did Lionel Robbins or Richard Stone among university-based economists, Hugh Dalton or Robert Hall from Westminster and Whitehall. As the profession has expanded, so the Section has had to recognise that not every eminent economist in Britain will be able to at some time to be its President.

Marshall in 1890 was an especially active President who, styling himself the spokesman for the Section, convened the meeting at University College, London, at which the British Economic Association, now the Royal Economic Society, was created. He carried forward into the recommendations he made for the new Association at least two features which had long been distinctive of the older one: the membership was to be open-ended and no single approach was to be the official orthodoxy. As if to prove that Marshall's trust in the Section had not been misplaced, the Section in 1891 made William Cunningham his successor. Simultaneously Vicar of Great St Mary's, Cambridge, and Professor of Political Economy at Kings College, London, Cunningham was a member of the Historical School and a critic of Ricardian-Marshallian deductivism. The title of his Presidential Address suggested that he was planning to open an English *Methodenstreit* in support of the sociologists and statisticians who were more than sceptical about the claims of pure theory. The title may have suggested war – 'The Comtist Criticism of Economic Science' – but the advice was that the future lay with peace and collaboration: 'We shall perhaps come to hope that each of the rival schools of economists may furnish a contribution which is a real aid to the advance of the study.'

Section F at an early stage decided that it wanted to conduct research-projects of its own as well as to run conferences. Something like 25 research-projects were undertaken in the first century of its existence. In 1872 a Section committee recommended the adoption of the metric system. In 1879 the Section put forward reforms in the Patent Laws which were subsequently taken over by the Government. In 1889 a committee reported on how best to measure the variations in the value of money: Edgeworth, Foxwell, Giffen, Marshall, Palgrave and Sidgwick had all been among its members. In the First World War the Section continued its tradition of public service through commissioned research: committees were set up to report on 'Fatigue from an Economic Standpoint', on 'Effects of War on Credit, Currency and Finance', and on 'Replacement of Men by Women in Industry'.

The conferences themselves show that the Section was keen to invite eminent academics who would contribute their scholarship to issues of contemporary interest. Thus Walras gave a paper in 1887 on monetary problems and Hobson addressed the Section in 1894 on pay and productivity. Also in 1894 Irving Fisher gave a paper on bimetallism. In 1896 there was Clément Juglar on 'Les Crises Commerciales', in 1906 Wicksell on interest and prices, in 1907 Ramsay MacDonald on 'The Labour Legislation of the Australian States'. In 1920 Clapham spoke on 'Europe after the Great Wars, 1816 and 1920'. In 1923 Beveridge attacked Keynes on population and unemployment. In 1927 Joseph Schumpeter visited the Section to speak on 'The Instability of Capitalism'. In 1928 Allyn Young took as the topic of his Presidential Address the hotly debated question of economies of scale and the forward-falling supply-curve. His paper, 'Increasing Returns and Economic Progress', was to become a standard reference in Marshallian economics.

The Section has never shied away from the big issues. Nor, indeed, has it failed to attract the big names. Shaw gave a paper on 'The Transition to Social Democracy' (1888). Sidney Webb spoke on 'Economic Heresies of the London County Council' (1894) and Edwin Cannan on population (1931). In 1959 John Jewkes addressed the Section on the costliness of science: he suggested that its incessant advancement might put a strain on the nation's scarce resources. In 1983 Kenneth Boulding addressed the Section on human betterment: he exhorted economists not to underestimate ethics or to neglect evolution. Other familiar names that have spoken to Section F include Patrick Minford, Roy Hattersley, Alec Cairncross, Wassily Leontief, James Meade, Joan Robinson, Ralph Ball – and Florence Nightingale.

The Section since the Second World War has occasionally experimented with inter- and multidisciplinary sessions organised jointly with other Sections (most commonly Engineering and Sociology) in the Association: as 15 full Sections plus two Sub-Section are represented at the Annual meeting, the opportunity to collaborate is obviously a persuasive argument for exploring common territory. A more important innovation has, however, been the practice of inviting the President to structure his programme around a single issue or theme. First adopted in 1953 – the President was Paish and the topic was 'Uncertainty and Business Decision' – the result has been a series of conferences concentrating explicitly on a named subject: public finance, the EEC, the mixed economy and technological change are some of the themes that have given unity to F's proceedings. From 1966 until 1996 – the President in 1966 was Shackle and the title of the volume was *On the Nature of Business Success* – the Section published (the editor was always the President for the year) the papers presented to its annual conference. The Section F series includes *Conflicts in Policy Objectives*, edited by Nicholas Kaldor (Blackwell, 1971), *The Economics of Tolerable Survival*, edited by Max Gaskin (Croom Helm 1981), *Technology and Economic Progress*, edited by Aubrey Silberston (Macmillan 1989), and *The Economics of Wealth Creation*, edited by R.J. Ball (Edward Elgar 1992). In addition, selections of Section F papers from the earlier years of 1860–1960 have been published by Duckworth as *Essays in Economic Method* (1962) and *Essays in the Economics of Socialism and Capitalism* (1964), both edited by R.L. Smyth. For many years the Presidential Address to Section F was automatically published in the *Economic Journal*. That said, it is not the purpose of Section F to duplicate the technical aspirations of the Royal Economic Society and its *Economic Journal*. What Section F seeks to do is something different – to stimulate informed discussion in the wider community on the present-day issues to which the useful economist has the most to contribute.

Presidents of Section F (Economics) of the British Association for the Advancement of Science

1834	Sir Charles Lemon, FRS	1865	Lord Stanley, MP, FRS
1835	Charles Babbage, FRS	1866	Prof J.E.T. Rogers
1836	Sir Charles Lemon, FRS	1867	M.E. Grant-Duff, MP
1837	Lord Sandon	1868	Samuel Brown
1838	Col W.H. Sykes, FRS	1869	Sir Stafford H. Northcote, MP
1839	Henry Hallam, FRS		
1840	Lord Sandon	1870	Prof W. Stanley Jevons
1841	Lieut-Col W.H. Sykes, FRS	1871	Lord Nevons
1842	G.W. Wood, MP	1872	Prof Henry Fawcett, MP
1843	Sir C. Lemon, MP	1873	W.E. Forster
1844	Lieut-Col W.H. Sykes, FRS	1874	Lord O'Hagen
1845	Earl Fitzwilliam, MA, FRS	1875	James Heywood, FRS
1846	G.R. Porter, FRS	1876	Sir George Campbell, MP
1847	Travers Twiss, DCL, FRS	1877	Earl Fortescue
1848	J.H. Vivian, MP, FRS	1878	Prof J.K. Ingram
1849	Lord Lyttleton	1879	G. Shaw Lefevre, MP
1850	The Very Rev John Lee, DD	1880	G.W. Hastings, MP
1851	Sir John P. Boileau, FRS	1881	M.E. Grant-Duff, MP, FRS
1852	The Archbishop of Dublin	1882	G. Sclater-Booth, MP, FRS
1853	James Heywood, MP, FRS	1883	R.H. Inglis Palgrave, FRS
1854	Thomas Tooke, FRS	1884	Sir Richard Temple
1855	R. Monkton Miles, MP, DCL	1885	Prof H. Sidgwick
1856	Lord Stanley, MP	1886	J.B. Martin
1857	The Archbishop of Dublin	1887	Robert Giffen
1858	Edward Baines	1888	Lord Bramwell
1859	Colonel Sykes, MP, FRS	1889	Prof F.Y. Edgeworth
1860	Nassau W. Senior	1890	Prof Alfred Marshall
1861	William Newmarch, FRS	1891	Prof W. Cunningham
1862	Edwin Chadwick	1892	Sir C.W. Fremantle
1863	William Tite, MP, FRS	1893	Prof J.S. Nicholson
1864	William Farr, MD, DCL, FRS	1894	Prof C.F. Bastable

1895	L.L. Price	1938	Sir R.F. Harrod
1896	L. Courtney, MP	1939	Prof H.O. Meredith
1897	Prof E.C.K. Gonner	1947	Sir D.H. Robertson
1898	J. Bonar	1948	Sir H.D. Henderson
1899	H. Higgs	1949	Sir Alexander Gray
1900	Major P.G. Craigie	1950	Prof G.C. Allen
1901	Sir R. Giffen	1951	Prof R.G. Hawtrey
1902	E. Cannan	1952	Prof D.T. Jack
1903	E.W. Brabrook	1953	Prof F.W. Paish
1904	Prof William Smart	1954	E.A.G. Robinson
1905	Rev W. Cunningham	1955	Prof J.R. Hicks
1906	A.L. Bowley	1956	Prof Gilbert Walker
1907	Prof W.J. Ashley	1957	Prof J.E. Meade
1908	W.M. Acworth	1958	Prof A.J. Brown
1909	Prof S.J. Chapman	1959	Prof John Jewkes
1910	Sir H. Llewellyn Smith	1960	Prof R.S. Sayers
1911	W. Pember Reeves	1961	Sir C.F Carter
1912	Sir H.H. Cunynghame	1962	Prof W.B. Reddaway
1913	Rev P.H. Wickstead	1963	Prof T. Wilson
1914	Prof E.C.K. Gonner	1964	Prof B.R. Williams
1915	Prof W.R. Scott	1965	Prof E. Victor Morgan
1916	Prof A.W. Kirkaldy	1966	Prof G.L.S. Shackle
1919	Sir Hugh Bell	1967	Prof A.R. Prest
1920	Dr J.S. Clapham	1968	Prof E.M. Hughes-Jones
1921	W.L. Hichens	1969	Sir Alec Cairncross
1922	Prof F.Y. Edgeworth	1970	Lord Nicholas Kaldor
1923	Sir W.H. Beveridge	1971	G.D.N. Worswick
1924	Sir William Ashley	1972	Prof Joan Robinson
1925	Miss Lynda Grier	1973	Prof H.G. Johnson
1926	Sir Josiah Stamp	1974	Prof K.J.W. Alexander
1927	Prof D.H. Macgregor	1975	Rt Hon Aubrey Jones
1928	Prof Allyn Young	1976	Prof Wassily Leontief
1929	Prof Henry Clay	1977	Prof E.E. Nevin
1930	Prof T.E. Gregory	1978	Prof Wilfred Beckerman
1931	Prof E. Cannan	1979	Prof Max Gaskin
1932	Prof R.B. Forrester	1980	Lord Roll of Ipsden
1933	Prof J.H. Jones	1981	Prof Jack Wiseman
1934	H.M. Hallsworth	1982	Rt Hon Roy Jenkins
1935	Prof J.G. Smith	1983	Prof Kenneth Boulding
1936	Dr C.R. Fay	1984	Prof R.C.O. Matthews
1937	Prof P. Sargant Florence	1985	Prof R.D.C. Black

1986	Prof Alan Williams	1995	R. Pennant-Rea
1987	Prof Aubrey Silberston	1996	Prof J. Kay
1988	Prof Phyllis Deane	1997	Prof A. Atkinson
1989	Sir Douglas Hague	1998	Prof Sir J. Mirrlees
1990	Prof Frank Hahn	1999	Prof D. Hendry
1991	Sir R.J. Ball	2000	Prof Amartya Sen
1992	Lord M. Peston	2001	Prof Stephen Nickell
1993	Sir Samuel Brittan	2002	Prof Angus Deaton
1994	Prof A.J. Culyer	2003	Prof Charles Goodhart

Recorders of Section F (Economics) of the British Association for the Advancement of Science

Note: before 1901 the Recorder was not identified separately from the other members of the Committee

1901	E. Cannan	1930	R.B. Forrester
1902	A.L. Bowley	1931	R.B. Forrester
1903	A.L. Bowley	1932	Dr K.G. Fenelon
1904	A.L. Bowley	1933	Dr K.G. Fenelon
1905	A.L. Bowley	1934	Dr K.G. Fenelon
1906	Prof S.J. Chapman	1935	Dr K.G. Fenelon
1907	Prof S.J. Chapman	1936	Dr K.G. Fenelon
1908	Prof S.J. Chapman	1937	Dr P. Ford
1909	Dr W.R. Scott	1938	Dr P. Ford
1910	H.O. Meredith	1939	Prof P. Ford
1911	Dr W.R. Scott	1947	Prof P. Ford
1912	Dr W.R. Scott	1948	Prof P. Ford
1913	Dr W.R. Scott	1949	E.D. McCallum
1914	Prof A.W. Kilkaldy	1950	E.D. McCallum
1915	Prof A.W. Kilkaldy	1951	E.D. McCallum
1916	Miss Ashley	1952	E.D. McCallum
1919	C.R. Fay	1953	E.D. McCallum
1920	C.R. Fay	1954	J.K. Eastham
1921	Prof H.M. Hallsworth	1955	J.K. Eastham
1922	Prof H.M. Hallsworth	1956	J.K. Eastham
1923	Prof H.M. Hallsworth	1957	J.K. Eastham
1924	Prof H.M. Hallsworth	1958	J.K. Eastham
1925	R.B. Forrester	1959	R.L. Smyth
1926	R.B. Forrester	1960	R.L. Smyth
1927	R.B. Forrester	1961	R.L. Smyth
1928	R.B. Forrester	1962	R.L. Smyth
1929	R.B. Forrester	1963	R.L. Smyth

1964	Prof E.M. Hughes-Jones	1984	Dr D.A. Reisman
1965	Prof E.M. Hughes-Jones	1985	Prof B. Corry
1966	Prof E.M. Hughes-Jones	1986	Dr D. Mair
1967	R. Shaw	1987	Dr D. Mair
1968	R. Shaw	1988	Dr D. Mair
1969	R. Shaw	1989	Mr P. Simpson
1970	A.F. Peters	1990	Mr P. Simpson
1971	A.F. Peters	1991	Mr P. Simpson
1972	A.F. Peters	1992	Mr P. Simpson
1973	A.F. Peters	1993	Prof D. Mair
1974	A.F. Peters	1994	Prof D. Mair
1975	A.F. Peters	1995	Prof A. Chrystal
1976	E.J. Cleary	1996	Prof A. Chrystal
1977	E.J. Cleary	1997	Prof A. Chrystal
1978	E.J. Cleary	1998	Prof P.N. Sinclair
1979	Dr D.A. Reisman	1999	Prof P.N. Sinclair
1980	Dr D.A. Reisman	2000	Prof P. N. Sinclair
1981	Dr D.A. Reisman	2001	Prof P.N. Sinclair
1982	Dr D.A. Reisman	2002	Prof A.W. Mullineaux
1983	Dr D.A. Reisman	2003	Prof A.W. Mullineaux

1
Financial Development, Growth and Poverty: How Close are the Links?

Patrick Honohan

1 Introduction and summary

Among the most striking empirical macroeconomic relationships uncovered in the past decade is the apparently causal link between financial development and economic growth. This chapter begins (Section 2) with a brief account of the key methodological elements underlying this discovery.

A second generation of empirical cross-country models recognized that, while financial depth and average GDP growth represent useful starting points for the measurement of cause and effect (input and output), neither is comprehensive nor fully satisfactory.

On the output side, while average growth rates remain by far the most studied, there has also been more emphasis on the quality of growth in terms not only of volatility, but also income distribution, both of which are crucial to sustainability. Section 3 contributes to this emphasis presenting new evidence on the question of whether finance-intensive growth is pro-poor.

Regarding the input side, financial depth remains central in empirical analysis despite its severe shortcomings whether as a cross-country or time series measure of financial development. Section 4 illustrates these shortcomings in a brief examination of four contrasting country cases (China, Korea, Russia and the United Kingdom). Recognizing these difficulties, second generation research has widened the focus on the input side to include *structural* characteristics of finance, such as the relative importance of banks and securities markets and *infrastructural and institutional* prerequisites, such as the legal and informational environment as well as the regulatory style. Use of data on these dimensions has allowed a richer interpretation of the processes by which financial development impacts wider economic conditions. Section 5 suggests drawing on some of these second generation findings to construct a more comprehensive composite indicator of financial development, using complementary institutional characteristics.

2   The scale of banking and the rate of growth

Of course rich countries have big banking systems, but whoever thought it was a causal link? Until about ten years ago, most of those working in money and banking believed that monetary policy was only good for preserving stability. Using money to drive growth was like pushing on a string.

True, there was a 1970s 'money and growth' literature which argued essentially that by manipulating the rate of inflation the government could correct an underinvesting economy by inducing a change in the private savings ratio. But that was an era in which it was somewhat less than respectable for economists to think that economic policy could alter economic *growth rates* on a sustained basis. Once full employment was achieved, all that could be hoped for was for growth in productivity to augment labour growth. A higher propensity to save out of income would result in a more capital-rich economy, but one which, with diminishing marginal returns to capital, would eventually settle down at the same growth rate as before – driven by productivity. And productivity was not something that most economists felt comfortable talking about.

Instead of seeking to manipulate long-term growth rates, students of growth theory in that era were concerned instead to design policy that would ensure that the economy would select the long-term equilibrium growth path with the appropriate level of capital – not overinvesting (like Soviet Russia), and not underinvesting (like, perhaps, Britain in those days). Here's where that manipulative use of money through the inflation tax, to ensure sufficient saving, could come in.

But for most purposes, money and finance were seen as something that could go wrong, plunging the economy into a disequilibrium of involuntary unemployment as had occurred in the 1930s, and seemed to be re-emerging in the 1970s with the collapse of the Bretton Woods system and the oil crises. Avoiding crises seemed to be the main task of financial policy.

What changed? It is an interesting vignette of intellectual history. First, as more and more data accumulated on national economic growth rates across the world, it became evident that there were large and sustained differences in average growth rates between different countries. This tended to cast some doubt on the usefulness of models that had nothing to say about what might explain such differences. Then theoretical advances emphasizing increasing returns to scale and spillovers from investment in education and technology brought it home to economists that their analytical tools could be useful in analyzing market behavior that could influence the rate of growth of economies on a permanent basis. The intellectual liberation resulting from these theoretical advances – and the availability of cross-country data – unleashed a tidal wave of international cross-sectional growth regressions (for a survey see Easterly, 2001). Each researcher had his or her favorite explanatory variables, many of them mutually correlated, and each (if advanced on its own) seeming to provide a considerable explanatory power. But the theories couldn't all be right.

In an important contribution Levine and Renelt (1992) showed that the data could not discriminate between most of the alternatives. The volume of investment and the level of education provision seemed to be about the only economic variables robust to the inclusion of alternative candidates. Not that the other variables were necessarily irrelevant, but they were too closely correlated among each other to be able to tell which was the driving force and which was merely tagging along. A researcher coming with a strong prior belief about any of some two dozen causal variables could find confirmation in the data, but what such a researcher could not do was refute an opponent who believed that another of the collection of supposed causal variables was instead the truly significant one. Levine and Renelt seemed to put paid to the prospect that a robust causal variable would be found.

Then, unexpectedly, from the apparent wreckage of most cross-country growth studies, a neglected variable bubbled to the surface. Almost uniquely, financial depth, when tested in the same way, proved to survive. The discovery was made by King and Levine (1993). Over night, the finance and growth literature was relaunched along an entirely new dimension.

The subsequent literature has been a large one, which I will not attempt to review here. For me its conclusions are summarized in two charts. The first one I call *post hoc ergo propter hoc*, because, in itself, its force is no stronger than that. Nevertheless, it is suggestive that the mean GDP growth rate over the next 35 years of country groups sorted by financial depth is so clearly ranked (Figure 1.1). King and Levine's 1993 papers of course went well beyond that. One of their main goals,

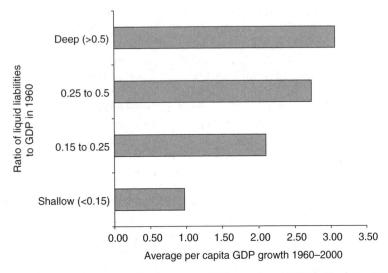

Figure 1.1   post hoc ergo propter hoc, mean GDP growth rate 1960–95 of country groups sorted by 1960 financial depth

as mentioned, was to show that this correlation survived the process of controlling for other candidate variables for explaining growth.[1] And it does, whether we look at contemporaneous or initial (1960) data on financial depth.

The other chart (Figure 1.2) draws on a later paper by Levine, with Loayza and Beck (2000), which is my favourite from this literature, because of the persuasive way it deals with another problem: that of reverse causality (endogeneity). After all, perhaps *post hoc ergo propter hoc* is not enough (especially if we look at shorter periods than 30 years). Perhaps persistently rapid-growth countries call forth deeper financial systems: if so, then observing a deep financial system in such a country may not be telling us anything about the power of finance to generate growth. The standard way of dealing with this problem in econometrics requires the use of instrumental variables, that is, variables correlated with financial depth, but not otherwise linked to GDP growth. Employing, in the causal regressions, the predicted value of a country's financial depth from a regression using such instruments removes the potential reverse causality bias. Finding valid and strong instrumental variables is easier said than done, but LLB employs a recently discovered fact, namely that countries which have inherited variants of English common law tend to have deeper financial systems than those whose

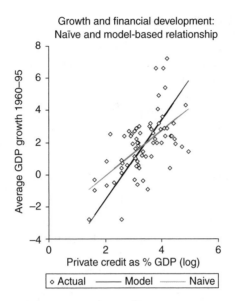

Figure 1.2 Modeling the effects of reverse causality

legal inheritance is from the Napoleonic code or the distinct German and Scandinavian traditions that are recognized. These legal origins date so far back as to exclude the possibility of feedback from recent growth processes, which helps ensure that they are valid instruments.[2]

Figure 1.2 shows the scatter of financial depth and growth rates in the LLB sample. Two lines are plotted. One is drawn by me as a naïve simple regression, and as such potentially contaminated not only by reverse causality, but by the omission of other causal factors. The other line, marked 'model' is the projection of the multivariate relationship estimated by LLB. I learn two striking facts from this figure. First, the relationship is not a very close one: much of the variation in growth is due to other causes. And if a country moved from the lowest decile of financial depth (13 per cent) to the highest (75 per cent) it could expect to improve its growth rate by a lot (over 4 per cent in this model) all other things being equal, but there are pairs of countries with a smaller financial depth difference (30 percentage points) but a growth difference more than twice as great. Second, the modeled impact of finance on growth is much stronger than the naïve regression would have indicated. That is to say, the combined effect of reverse causality and omitted variables bias is to mask rather than to exaggerate the effect.[3]

3   Not mainly for the rich

Aggregate economic growth is, of course, the key to economic prosperity of rich and poor alike, and the finding that financial development contributes to it must inform policy that seeks to achieve a reduction in global poverty.

Yet for some observers emphasizing finance seems to be getting the wrong end of the stick. Noting such characteristics as the high salaries paid on average in the financial sector, these observers suppose that if the financial sector prospers, this may mean a deterioration in the distribution of income: more for well-paid investment bankers, not much for their drivers or cleaners. Rajan and Zingales (2003b) cite Tom Wolfe's novel *The Bonfire of the Vanities* as illustrative of the widely held view that finance benefits only, or mainly, the rich. If this casual prejudice was borne out in reality then one would become somewhat ambivalent about relying on financial development as a priority instrument for tackling poverty in developing economies.

But, as Rajan and Zingales note, a healthy financial system can be a powerful anti-monopoly tool, providing the lubrication for the emergence of competitors that can undermine the power of incumbent firms, and the means for poor households and small-scale producers to escape the tyranny of exploitative middle-men. In contrast, the undeveloped financial system, in their words, can be 'clubby, uncompetitive and conservative'. If so, financial development *could* be pro-poor. But is it?

To be sure, financial development promotes growth, and we have extensive evidence that growth worldwide has been a powerful mechanism for reducing poverty. Furthermore, the lowest quintile shares in the national rate of growth. To use the terminology of fiscal policy, growth is neither progressive nor regressive: it is – on average – neutral (Dollar-Kraay, 2002). That means that the rich get more dollars from every increment of growth than do the poor, and that no improvement can be expected in relative poverty from the growth process per se, but it also means that absolute poverty declines.

But the Dollar-Kraay results do not amount to saying that 'a rising tide raises all boats' The tidal analogy is quite imperfect. Of the many drivers of growth it could still be that financial development is regressive. This indeed is the prediction of the widely cited model of Greenwood and Jovanovic (1990). They argue that getting involved in the financial sector and benefiting from the screening and risk pooling that it offers requires an initial set-up cost (either of participating in the group that establishes financial infrastructure, or eventually paying an access charge to those who have done so). Poor households will not be in a position to incur this cost, and will not find it worthwhile even to set aside savings for this outlay, hence falling even further behind in the distribution of wealth.

The regressiveness prediction of Greenwood and Jovanovic has not been borne out in the empirical literature. Specifically, Li *et al.* (1998) found that financial depth entered strongly and significantly as a contributor to lower inequality (Gini index) and raise the average income of the lower 80 per cent of the population.[4] The reasoning suggested by Li, Squire and Zou is that better financial development should alleviate credit constraints for poorer households, allowing them to make productive investments, for example in human capital. (They also note that the household Gini for wealth index in the past should also predict inequality of investment – though in that case it is perhaps easy to think of multiple paths through which past wealth inequality persists in predicting current income inequality.)

Inequality and poverty incidence are not, of course, the same thing, especially if we measure poverty in absolute terms, such as the share of the population earning less than $1 a day. Nor does analysis of the growth of the average income of the bottom quintile directly address the impact of financial development on poverty. Indeed, there appears to have been comparatively little reported empirical cross-country research on the possible impact of financial development on absolute poverty ratios.

Apparent gaps in the empirical literature often reflect the absence of significant and robust empirical relationships. Yet, in this case, there are already intriguing indications from cross-country evidence that finance may be surprisingly effective in reducing poverty.

One contribution employing indirect but highly suggestive evidence suggesting a pro-poor dimension to finance-rich growth comes from the study of Dehejia and Gatti (2002), who study child labor, well known to be a correlate of poverty.[5] Using a panel of countries at five or ten-year intervals, and controlling for the level of GDP per capita and other expected causes, they find that the incidence of child labor seems to be affected on a cross-country basis by the degree of financial depth. That this might reflect the enhanced ability of deep financial sectors to insulate poor households from shocks is further suggested by the fact that the impact of national income volatility on child labor is insignificant if analysis is confined to the countries with deep financial systems.

The problems of reverse causality which plague the empirical analysis of the causal role of finance and growth may be less severe when it comes to exploring a causal role for finance in poverty. After all, only a small fraction of aggregate financial assets are held by the poor, so poverty rates are very unlikely to influence financial depth in a significant manner. Anyway, although it is rarely possible to exclude the possibility of reverse causality altogether, we will proceed on the basis that assuming its absence is likely to be better than working with weak instruments.

Thus, the way is open to a fairly straightforward approach to seeing if there might be a possible causal link. Accordingly, drawing on a cross section of some 70-odd developing countries[6] for which poverty data is available, we now show that a striking empirical relationship seems to emerge: deep financial systems appear to be associated with lower poverty.

The major determinant of variations in poverty incidence across developing countries is, not surprisingly, the mean level of GDP per capita: an unevenly divided small cake leaves more people hungry than a large one. As shown in Equation 1.A of Table 1.1, this variable alone explains 47 per cent of cross-country variation in absolute poverty (share of population below $1 a day). The point estimate implies that a 10 per cent increase in mean per capita income translates into a 1.6 percentage point reduction in absolute poverty. Naturally, the way in which this income is distributed also matters: for example, calculating the mean income of the bottom 90 per cent of the population (by subtracting the income earned by the top 10 per cent income earners) greatly improves the fit – the RSQ now is 54 per cent (Equation 1.B). Interestingly – and I am not aware that this has been commented on in the literature – the income share of the top 10 per cent also contributes to explaining cross-country poverty variance (likely because it also predicts a higher share for the *non*-poor that are in the lower 90 per cent).[7] Anyway with this addition, the RSQ is up to 58 per cent (Equation 1.C).

Now it's time to add in the financial variables. Starting with the standard non-government ("private") credit variable. Here we prefer to exclude three countries which are outliers in a cross-country regression of credit on inflation and per capita GDP – their data for non-government credit is more than three standard errors away from the regression line.[8] One is Panama, an offshore center, the other two are Thailand and China. (We will return to China below, observing that most Chinese "non-government" credit is to state-owned or controlled firms). With the remaining data, a striking negative coefficient is observed in the regression explaining poverty (Equation 1.D). The additional variable improves the fit to 64 per cent. Taken literally – and we should not do this except as a rough indication of the size of the effect – the estimates

Table 1.1 Poverty and financial depth: core results (Dependent variable: $1 per day poverty ratio)

Equations:	1.A		1.B		1.C		1.D		1.E		1.F	
	Coeff.	t-stat	Coeff.	t-stat	Coeff.	t-stat	Coeff.	t-stat	Coeff.	t-stat	Coeff.	t-stat
Constant	152.0	**9.0	229.8	**9.9	184.4	**7.3	164.9	**6.3	184.3	**7.6	152.1	**5.8
GDP per cap (log)	−16.6	**7.8										
GDP per cap lower 90% (log)			−17.3	**9.0	−15.3	**8.2	−13.4	**6.7	−15.4	**8.6	−11.9	**5.8
Share of top 10%					0.635	**3.4	0.708	**3.8	0.671	**3.7	0.709	**3.8
Private credit							−0.260	**2.5				
Private credit residual									−0.353	**3.2	−0.354	**3.3
Inflation											−0.096	*2.4
R-squared / NOBS	0.462	73	0.535	73	0.601	73	0.636	71	0.652	70	0.663	70
Adjusted R-squared	0.454		0.529		0.590		0.620		0.636		0.642	
SE of regression	15.8		14.7		13.7		13.3		13.0		12.9	
Log likelihood	−304.2		−298.8		−293.2		−282.6		−277.1		−276.0	

Notes: ** and * indicate significance at the 1% and 5% levels, respectively.
Cross section excluding China, Panama and Thailand.

imply that a ten percentage point in the ratio of private credit to GDP should (even at the same mean income level) reduce poverty ratios by 2.5 to 3 percentage points.

This finding suggests that the theories which argue that financial development can help the poor may have some bite. The balance-sheet size of even a well-developed banking system will be adversely affected by inflation, as is repeatedly confirmed in the literature. Allowing for this either by including inflation as an additional regressor, or by substituting the residual in a regression of credit on per capita GDP and inflation,[9] takes account of this. In both cases credit remains highly significant. (Equations 1.E, 1.F).

Since politico-institutional characteristics can affect financial development as they can affect other aspects of economic conditions, as a robustness check, we included each of the omnibus governance variables included in the World Bank's database (Kaufman, Kraay and Zoido-Lobatón, KKZ, 1999; Kaufman, Kraay and Mastruzzi, 2003) as additional regressors. None were significant at the 95 per cent level, and the credit variable retained its significance. (Table 1.2)

(Using the higher poverty threshold of $2 a day gives broadly similar results, though not quite as strong an effect of credit; see Tables 1.3, 1.4).

So much for the banking dimension to finance. How about capital markets? Their development has been shown to be equally important for growth. Do they also contribute to a greater lowering of poverty than implied by their effect on growth? The answer is that apparently they do not. Adding stock market capitalization and/or market turnover to the basic equation does not significantly alter fit or the other coefficients and the new variables are not significant. Nor does bank concentration appear to be a significant contributor (Table 1.5).[10]

The empirical correlation which we have detected is suggestive, rather than conclusive evidence that emphasizing financial development is benign in regard to poverty in that it is more likely to reduce poverty than the average pro-growth initiative. But the analysis is at too aggregative a level to be fully convincing. Additionally, the ways in which financial development is being measured, based mainly on size, are clearly rather weak ones.

4   The pitfalls in measuring financial development with banking depth – country cases

The focus so far here, as in much of the early literature, has been on banking depth as the main measure of financial development. But when

Table 1.2 Poverty and financial depth: the role of institutions (Dependent variable: $1 per day poverty ratio)

Equations:	1.A		1.B		1.C		1.D		1.E	
	Coeff.	t-stat	Coeff.	t-stat	Coeff.	t-stat	Coeff.	t-stat	Coeff.	t-stat
Constant	194.7	**6.1	186.9	**6.8	191.4	**7.4	194.1	**6.5	185.5	**6.2
GDP per cap lower 90% (log)	−16.2	**6.9	−15.6	**7.8	−16.0	**8.3	−16.2	**7.1	−15.5	**7.0
Share of top 10%	0.649	**3.4	0.666	***3.6	0.666	***3.6	0.649	***3.5	0.669	***3.6
Private credit residual	−0.368	**3.2	−0.361	***3.1	−0.364	***3.3	−0.371	***3.3	−0.355	***3.1
Institutions (KKF)	2.14	0.5	0.716	0.2	1.82	0.8	2.01	0.6	0.243	0.1
Which institution	Corrupt		Govteff		Regqual		Regqual		Rulelaw	
R-squared / NOBS	0.654	70	0.652	70	0.656	70	0.654	70	0.652	70
Adjusted R-squared	0.632		0.631		0.635		0.633		0.631	
SE of regression	13.1		13.1		13.1		13.1		13.1	
Log likelihood	−276.9		−277.0		−276.7		−276.9		−277.1	

Notes: ** and * indicate significance at the 1% and 5% levels, respectively.
Cross section excluding China, Panama and Thailand.

Table 1.3 Poverty and financial depth: alternative poverty threshold (Dependent variable: $2 per day poverty ratio)

Equations:	1.A		1.B		1.C		1.D		1.E		1.F	
	Coeff.	t-stat	Coeff.	t-stat	Coeff.	t-stat	Coeff.	t-stat	Coeff.	t-stat	Coeff.	t-stat
Constant	215.1	**9.4	313.5	**9.7	269.4	**7.3	251.3	**6.4	266.6	**7.3	233.3	**5.9
GDP per cap (log)	-21.8	**7.6										
GDP per cap lower 90% (log)			-22.4	**8.4	-20.6	**7.6	-18.9	**6.3	-20.4	**7.6	-16.8	**5.4
Share of top 10%					0.639	*2.3	0.714	*2.5	0.666	**3.7	0.701	*2.5
Private credit							-0.232	1.5			-0.355	*2.1
Private credit residual									-0.355	**3.2		
Inflation											-0.110	1.8
R-squared / NOBS	0.439	75	0.492	75	0.527	75	0.547	73	0.552	72	0.663	72
Adjusted R-squared	0.431		0.485		0.514		0.527		0.532		0.642	
SE of regression	22.1		21.0		20.4		20.4		20.1		20.0	
Log likelihood	-337.6		-333.9		-331.2		-321.5		-316.2		-315.4	

Notes: ** and * indicate significance at the 1% and 5% levels, respectively.
Cross section excluding China, Panama and Thailand.

Table 1.4 Poverty and financial depth: institutions at the alternative threshold (Dependent variable: $2 per day poverty ratio)

Equations: Dependent variable:	1.A Pov2		1.B Pov2		1.C Pov2		1.D Pov2		1.E Pov2	
	Coeff.	t-stat	Coeff.	t-stat	Coeff.	t-stat	Coeff.	t-stat	Coeff.	t-stat
Constant	267.6	**5.5	273.2	**6.6	273.1	**6.9	311.1	**6.9	255.6	**5.6
GDP per cap lower 90% (log)	−20.5	**5.8	−20.9	**6.8	−20.9	**7.1	−24.0	**7.0	−19.6	**5.8
Share of top 10%	0.663	*2.3	0.654	*2.3	0.659	*2.3	0.566	*2.0	0.686	*2.4
Private credit residual	−0.357	*2.1	−0.373	*2.1	−0.365	*2.2	−0.427	*2.5	−0.337	1.9
Institutions (KKF) Which institution	0.21 Corrupt	0.0	1.65 Govteff	0.3	1.43 Polstabl	0.4	1.65 Regqual	1.6	−2.17 Rulelaw	0.4
R-squared / NOBS	0.552	72	0.553	72	0.553	72	0.569	72	0.553	70
Adjusted R-squared	0.525		0.526		0.527		0.543		0.526	
SE of regression	20.2		20.2		20.2		19.9		20.2	
Log likelihood	−316.2		−316.1		−316.0		−314.8		−316.1	

Notes: ** and * indicate significance at the 1% and 5% levels, respectively.
Cross section excluding China, Panama and Thailand.

Table 1.5 Poverty and other dimensions of financial development (Dependent variable: $1 per day poverty ratio)

Equations:	5.A		5.B		1.C		1.D	
	Coeff.	t-stat	Coeff.	t-stat	Coeff.	t-stat	Coeff.	t-stat
Constant	189.5	**6.5	212.3	**6.6	203.9	**6.7	213.7	**6.0
GDP per cap lower 90% (log)	−15.5	**7.7	−15.6	**7.2	−16.5	**7.4	−16.2	**6.8
Share of top 10%	0.617	**3.3	0.666	*2.3	0.523	**2.7	0.649	*2.3
Private credit residual	−0.368	**3.1	−0.361	**2.9	−0.329	**2.9	−0.371	*2.6
Bank concentration							−3.62	0.3
Stock market capitalization	−4.86	0.6	4.66	0.5			4.72	0.5
R-squared / NOBS	0.638	68	0.669	46	0.671	45	0.673	45
Adjusted R-squared	0.615		0.636		0.638		0.622	
SE of regression	12.9		11.0		11.1		11.3	
Log likelihood	−267.9		−172.9		−169.4		−169.2	

Notes: ** and * indicate significance at the 1% and 5% levels, respectively.
Cross section excluding China, Panama and Thailand.

one considers the likely channels through which a more developed financial system likely helps promote growth and reduce poverty, it becomes evident that, though useful and readily available, banking depth is unlikely to be a wholly reliable summary indicator. Indeed, financial development itself is a proxy for what we really are interested in, which is some measure of the quantity and quality of financial services that households, firms, and governments received in total (as well as which part of this they get from domestic financial service providers – the decline in this share is likely to attenuate the link between domestic finance and growth).

Current theories about these channels of effect emphasize that four key functions of finance are central: mobilizing savings (thereby creating concentrations of capital that allow exploitation of economies of scale); allocating capital (helping judge where returns are most likely to be obtained); monitoring the use of loanable funds by entrepreneurs; and transforming risk by pooling and repackaging it (cf. Levine, 1997). When put this way, it becomes less surprising that legal structures may have a role in determining the scale and the efficiency of finance (making them so useful as econometric instruments), given that the intertemporal contracts that underlie each of these functions need to be actively supported by a legal and judicial system. Regulatory and information infrastructures in the economy may also evidently be important. Also, it becomes evident that summarizing the development of a financial system by a single measure of the scale of its banking is not likely to fully capture variations in the degree and effectiveness with which it performs these functions. Nor has the literature neglected these points.

Thus, if we are to speak of financial development contributing to growth, the concept of development we have in mind must be far more subtle and complex than simply size. Indeed size measures can be quite misleading in a number of ways which will now be illustrated by reference to several specific country experiences.

China   Among large countries, China has the deepest banking system of all (bar a few places like Luxembourg which are important offshore centers and the scale of whose banking system is based on the export of financial services). The ratio of China's bank deposits to GDP is still rapidly growing – the M2 to GDP ratio now exceeds 170 per cent. And we know that China's economy has been growing very rapidly for the past couple of decades. Yet China's banking system does not normally receive the accolade for having importantly contributed to this rate of growth. Instead, commentators like Lardy (1998) point to the quasi-fiscal use of China's banking system as a means of keeping afloat state-controlled enterprises: at a time when rapid liberalization of the Chinese economic system had left many enterprises – no longer able to function profitably on the basis of policy-influenced relative prices that were very different to those of the world economy – high and dry. China's state-controlled banks – and that accounts (one way or another) for more than 95 per cent of the system, had responded by advancing the needed funds to these enterprises on the basis of public interest. These were not the engines of growth – though it could be argued that keeping them going offered a degree of political and social insulation to the process of adjustment to a more coherent set of market prices that *was* an essential prerequisite of growth. As a result of this practice, non-performing loans at the Chinese banks rose very rapidly in the late 1990s and the government has already had to make special provisions to ease the burden on the banks.

China is, of course, a vast country of contrasting economic structures. Provincial level data exploiting this variation offers another opportunity for applied econometricians to test their favorite theories. In a recent working paper Genevieve Boyreau-Debray (2003) has examined the banking depth and growth relationship across 26 Chinese provinces. Interestingly, and perhaps not surprisingly, she finds the opposite relationship to that found cross-countries. The provinces with the greatest banking depth are the provinces which have been growing more slowly (Figure 1.3). (Boyreau-Debray does examine some other aspects of the financial environment: e.g. greater diversity in provincial finance does seem to help growth).[11]

The Chinese case does not only raise the question of measurement: it also confronts us with the challenge of explaining just why China could have done so very well in terms of growth this past quarter century with a financial system that, though deep, has not been performing the theoreticians functions of a market-driven financial system to any considerable extent. Undoubtedly, there is a financial dimension here, namely the scale of investible resources: if the Chinese savings ratio averaged over 35 per cent for two decades, these savings have certainly built up the stock of capital in China. Just as with other East Asian miracles, I think it's fair to say Chinese growth can be largely attributed to the accumulation of capital and the successful shift in the application of available labour away from subsistence agriculture to higher productivity activities using this capital.

This helps us understand better how to view the role of finance in growth. You can get a long way *without* a state of the art financial system. Even if available savings are not allocated to the most effective

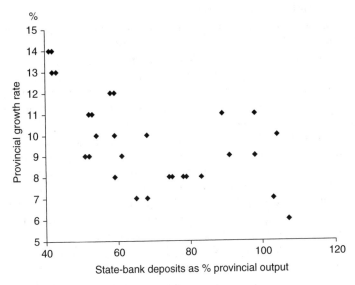

Figure 1.3 China: provincial banking depth and growth

enterprises, the sheer volume of capital accumulation (even if not the most appropriate or best-judged design), combined with the huge productivity gain from shifting workers from subsistence agriculture to the modern economy allows very rapid growth. At the same time, for all the rapid growth that China has had, it is still not at the global production frontier. Per capita income is still less than $1000 measured at market prices, and less than $5000 measured at purchasing power parities.[12] Even the higher figure puts it into the same class (only) as Eritrea, Macedonia, Algeria or Peru. Still a long way to go to match Korea, say (with its PPP per capita income at $18 000): it will need a better financial system to get to the frontier.

Russia A more dramatic example of the way in which banking depth can be misleading comes from the former Soviet Union countries, where deposit growth through the 1980s left them with deep banking systems as it appeared. The ratio of M2 to GDP in Russia in 1990 was 81 per cent. But here the holding of bank deposits was distorted by a number of features, including the widespread rationing (why spend your bank deposits if there is nothing to buy). Indeed, the true value of bank deposits was much lower in that price-controls held prices of consumer goods far below their market-clearing values. If valued at market-clearing prices, aggregate bank deposits were much smaller, and (though output figures were also somewhat flattered by the artificial prices), the true money to GDP ratio was surely much smaller. In the event, rapid inflation fuelled by the printing press following price liberalization soon made the initial stock of bank deposits in Russia almost worthless. Russians were slow to return to trusting their banking system, which remained small, and collapsed again in the exchange rate and debt default crisis of 1998. Even today, the Russian banking system does very little of the classic activities for which the theoreticians would have us look. A decade after the collapse of the old system, by end-2000, the M2/GDP ratio had recovered, but only to 22 per cent. Three-quarters of household deposits are with the state-owned Sberbank, which accounts for over a quarter of the total banking system and still lends more than half of its resources to the state. It is evident that Russia did not have what we would regard as a developed financial system when it had a high M2/GDP ratio and it does not have one now.

A feature common to Russia and China is that much of the banking resources were being lent to the public sector either as part of a plan (pre-reform Russia)[13] or in a vestigial survival of plan-type allocation. The use, by econometricians like Levine, of lending to the private sector as a better measure than simply M2 or total credit is one way of getting around this problem.

Britain and Korea   One further dimension must be mentioned to complete the catalogue of shortcomings of monetary aggregates as measures of financial development. Let me do this by way of two examples: United Kingdom and Korea. In deference to our hosts today, I will begin with the British data. Figure 1.4 shows a time series of money (wide money as measured in *International Financial Statistics*) and bank credit to the private sector each deflated by GDP. The series end in 1980 because of a major change in data definitions that year; but the series is long enough to show some interesting and, to observers of UK monetary policy, well-known features. The first of these is the declining monetary depth throughout the 1950s.[14] High monetary depth was clearly not a sufficient condition for sustaining rapid growth in the Britain of the 1950s. On the other hand, the share of private credit in GDP does start to grow fairly steadily from 1958 on and this coincides with a period of higher average GDP growth in the 1960s; but before we get too excited about a possible correlation look what happens at the beginning of the 1970s: a huge credit boom followed by a crash. Of course the crash is mainly related to the first oil crisis, but somewhat exacerbated by the collapse of a property bubble that had been fuelled by credit.[15] This experience points to a myriad of other considerations that need to be

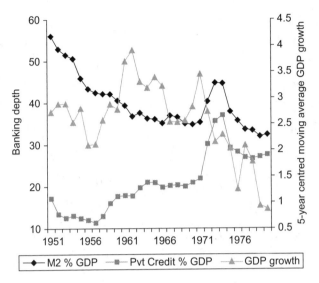

Figure 1.4 United Kingdom: money and growth 1951–80

brought into the picture in any particular instance, and especially over the short- to medium-term, to determine the relation between financial aggregates and growth: microeconomic policies on credit; wider macroeconomic stabilization issues; business cycle effects.

The case of Korea reinforces these points, especially in regard to the vulnerabilities that can be created by the high leverage and weakened creditworthiness associated with credit booms. The Korean experience of the 1960s and 1970s could be seen as – and I think are – part of the positive feedback interaction between monetary deepening and a strengthening of the economic structure. But if we look at the last 20 years, the Korean data seems to show a negative association between banking depth and growth. This is especially so if we take the conventional base of the core banks – the so-called deposit money bank of *International Financial Statistics*. Here the rapid acceleration in monetary depth of the late 1990s seems to coincide with the collapse in growth rates. (See Figure 1.5) But such a sharp break in trend as we see at 1996–97 alerts the applied economist to the likelihood that something else is happening in the background that (even if there is no change in the statistical definitions used to construct the series – and there is none here) alters the interpretation or representativeness of the series. Indeed, something was going on and – interestingly it was a phenomenon which confused

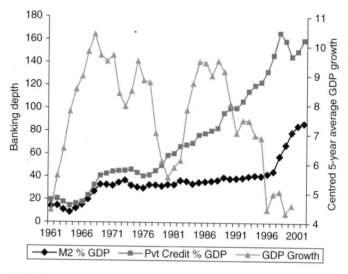

Figure 1.5   Korea: money and growth

Korean policy-makers at the time, pulling some statistical wool over their eyes and blinding them to an impending disaster. As is explained by Cho (2001), Korean financial institutions and their customers, maneuvering around both macroeconomic policy (including monetary targets) and prudential controls, began to employ forms of credit which were off the balance sheets of the commercial banks. Monetary aggregates – based on the balance sheets of the banks – were reassuringly stable, and prudential warning bells remained silent even as rapid increases in corporate leverage, especially short-term indebtedness, heightened the vulnerability of the entire economy. Adding back in the credit issued by near-banks[16] shows the true evolution of credit in Korea: a steady and rapid rate of increase until the crisis. The effect of the adjustment is to reinforce the appearance: rapid credit growth precedes a crisis. And this is, of course, a fairly universal observation (Honohan, 1997; Demirgüç-Kunt and Detragiache, 2001, etc.).

Another message of the Korean and UK experience is the increasing slipperiness of the data as the financial sector increases in complexity and scale. We saw how crucial the dividing line between commercial banks and nearbanks was for interpreting the scale of Korean intermediation. Rolling forward the UK data reveals several huge changes in the measured aggregates (both increases and decreases) as statistical conventions were revised over the years from 1980 to try to keep appropriate track of financial innovations. Between 1986 and 1987, the definition of bank deposits was revised, bringing the measured ratio in *IFS* of M2 (money plus quasi-money) to GDP from 46.8 per cent in 1986 to 80.5 per cent the following year. How can cross-country comparisons be relied upon if even within a country two acceptable definitions of monetary depth can be so widely differing for consecutive years? As a rule of thumb, I suggest that any country which has a monetary depth of 100 per cent has already satisfied the minimum scale criterion for having reached the frontier in financial development: a necessary condition, but not a sufficient one.

So, in summary, several drawbacks have been noted to the use of banking aggregates as proxies for overall financial development. Monetary depth will be a misleading indicator of financial development (i) if the savings so mobilized are being monopolized by the state. That is not to say that the liquidity and money transmission services being provided by narrow banking systems are of no importance, but they are arguably simpler to achieve: the hugely important credit dimension cannot be neglected. Turning to private credit, an issue of quality arises: if (ii) expanded too rapidly or too much, credit creates risks both microeconomic (poor judgement on the allocation of credit) and macroeconomic (excessive leverage creates linked vulnerabilities to various adverse shocks).

Two other quantitative bank-related measures of financial development have been proposed and I mention them here for completeness. Neither is unproblematic. First is the value-added of the banking sector as measured in the national income and expenditure accounts.[17] To the extent that the value-added does represent the contribution of the sector to GDP, it would appear to be a potentially good measure. In particular, if the prices charged and profits received indicate social value provided, then it may take us beyond the aggregates. However, it is largely an input-based measure in an environment often characterized by lack of competition, and one in which many of the social benefits of intermediation may not be captured by the intermediaries. Protection and lack of competitiveness in the financial system is likely to increase unit costs and profitability, thereby expanding this measure while holding the effectiveness of the system well below its potential.

The other bank-related measure is one of efficiency: interest rate spreads or margins.[18] This potentially disposes of the problem of uncompetitive systems, but is very partial in its focus: scale has fallen out altogether. Also, since interest spreads vary widely depending on the credit and maturity risks, as well as the monitoring costs that are involved, they may be considered exceptionally problematic in a cross-country comparison.

Scale and activity of equity and bond markets

Though bank-dominated financial systems remain the norm in developing countries, increasing emphasis has been placed in recent years on the development of securities markets (mainly for debt and equities, though the growth of derivatives markets has been especially rapid). A comprehensive statistical view of financial system development clearly needs to take these markets into account also and this has been done largely with the use of aggregates such as total market capitalization, and the liquidity of the stock market as measured by the turnover ratio. Some studies suggest that market activity, as measured by the turnover ratio predict growth (Levine and Zervos, 1998; Beck and Levine, 2004).[19]

However, attempts to judge the relative success of economies with large banking systems and those with large or active stock exchanges have so far proved, in my reading, inconclusive (cf. Demirgüç-Kunt and Levine, 2001). It seems that countries have done rather well with a wide variety of relative bank- and market-intensities. Perhaps each of these advanced countries has seen an adaptation of its financial structure to accommodate both the particular needs of its nonfinancial sectors and the differing inherited legal, administrative and informational infrastructures.

5   Using data on infrastructures to construct a composite indicator of financial development

Indeed, intriguingly, what is found consistently across many studies is that the functioning of financial markets is more effective where certain governmental, informational and legal pre-conditions are also present. In this section we consider how such findings could be drawn upon to help construct a more balanced and comprehensive measure of financial development that captures these additional dimensions.

Perhaps a *caveat* is not out of order here. We have also seen how similar variables have been employed as econometric *instruments* for banking depth in the finance and growth literature. But a variable cannot logically both be a valid instrument and an appropriate component in a composite financial development indicator. After all, a valid instrument must have its effect on the dependent variable (growth in the case above) only through the variable being instrumented. Its exclusion from the main causal regression must be justified. In devising a composite indicator, care should be taken to avoid being trapped in a contradiction where we assert that a particular environmental or infrastructural variable has a direct effect, and in addition rely on the results of some study where it has been employed as an instrument.[20]

Bearing this caution in mind, but forging bravely ahead, let me assert as a stylized summary of the literature that legal, regulatory and informational infrastructures do have a strong impact on the degree to which particular financial structures (banking systems of a certain depth, stock markets of a certain level of activity) are actually effective in delivering the benefits which we would like to see: long-term growth, insulation, access to SME and microenterprises, poverty reduction. Some of these infrastructures may also have an independent direct effect.

If infrastructures are crucially important components of financial development, it seems that a summary measure of financial development should include these in some way. In the remainder of the paper I would like to sketch an approach to devising a composite indicator, and offer a preliminary examination of whether it would make much difference in practice as compared with conventional size-based measures of financial development.

We can picture the situation as a multiple input, multiple output situation at the center of which the measured structures x_i of the financial system sit: influenced by the infrastructural inputs z_j, influencing the outputs y_k. Other factors w_l will also be relevant. Examples of structures: banking depth, stock market turnover; example of infrastructures: legal system, quality and style of regulation, informational infrastructures; examples of output: GDP growth, stability of output, employment and poverty. If the process can be written:

$$y_k = f^*_k(x, z, w) = f_k(g_k(x, z), w) \tag{1}$$

then we can think of the function g_k as capturing the contribution of finance (structure and infrastructure) to the output k. An overall objective function $W(y)$ may be postulated to aggregate the outputs. Then the marginal contribution of a financial structure variable x_i to the objective function W can be written

$$\frac{dW}{dx_i} = \sum_k W_k f_{k1} g_i = \sum_k \frac{\partial W}{\partial y_k} \frac{\partial f_k(g_k(x, z), w)}{\partial g_k} \frac{\partial g_k(x, z)}{\partial x_i} \tag{2}$$

If f is linear in its two components, then this expression will be independent of the other non-financial factors w.

In a linear approximation then, a composite financial development indicator would be a weighted average of the various components:

$$D = a + \sum_i b_i x_i + \sum_j c_j z_j \quad \text{where } b_i = \sum_k W_k f_{k1} g_{ki}; \ c_j = \sum_k W_k f_{k1} g_{kj}$$

So much for the algebra. Let me illustrate with some examples which will serve to illustrate the diversity of the data sources being employed in the recent literature to dig behind the aggregates and try to uncover the mechanisms that are at work in linking finance to wide economic goals.

I will take three particular infrastructural dimensions: legal, regulatory and ownership, and look at just a handful of papers which illustrates the way in which these infrastructures interact with the financial system itself in influencing outputs along – again – three major dimensions, growth, stability and distributional aspects.

Legal infrastructures

In their highly influential 1997 and 1998 papers, La Porta *et al.* (LLSV) assembled a database on the major distinguishing characteristics of legal systems in different countries as they impact financial contracts and control. In essence the major distinctions lie in the relative protection that is provided to a firm's managers, controlling shareholders and other insiders as against outsider financiers including both creditors and minority shareholders. Fairly systematically, the relative protection formally granted correlates with the degree of development of the relevant market. Stronger shareholder rights are, on a cross-country basis, associated with a greater number of listed firms and with higher stock market capitalization; stronger creditor rights are associated with a higher level of bank credit and bond finance.[21, 22]

Looking behind the national aggregates to the performance of individual firms, Beck, Demirgüç-Kunt and Maksimovic (2002) draw on a recent survey of some 4000 firms – small and large – in 54 countries which were asked for their perception of financing, legal and corruption constraints to their growth. The responses allow one to pinpoint where in the economy these constraints are biting. Uniformly, while all sizes of firms report constraints, it is the smaller firms whose growth is being more affected by a given level of self-reported constraint. Disappointingly, the answers to more detailed questions on the specific nature of the constraint (eleven specific questions about legal constraints, for example) fail to predict firm growth rates, making it difficult to draw detailed inferences on what are the most damaging legal difficulties.[23] Interestingly the main explanatory power comes from comparing average experience across countries: the within country variation in self-reported legal (and other constraints is not highly correlated with individual firm performance). Thus (even though the systemwide "law and order" variable from the abovementioned KKZ database does not add much explanatory power to the self-reported legal constraints in predicting differences in firm growth), it does seem to be cross-country differences in legal conditions that matter rather than just the idiosyncratic experiences varying from firm to firm.[24]

Regulatory

If the content of the law may be less important than the fact that it is enforced, an argument can be made that the opposite is true for prudential regulation. Practitioners of regulation typically see the regulators as disinterested technocrats for whom the only requirements are adequate legal powers and sufficient skilled resources. However, the wider perspective of the economic analyst points to self-serving or politically biased regulatory performance. And the informational and skill requirements for the effective pursuit of some regulatory strategies is simply beyond reach in most countries, with the result that the damaging side effects of regulatory capture and rent-seeking may be incurred without any compensating gain in stability. The World Bank's extensive survey of regulatory practice in 107 countries (a second wave has recently been conducted) allows the impact of regulatory style on financial stability and financial development to be assessed quantitatively. Barth, Caprio and Levine (BCL, 2002) *et al.*, find that the regulatory choices made on some three dozen different dimensions tend to cluster into one of two styles, which they term the 'grabbing hand' and the 'helping hand'. The interventionist 'grabbing hand' approach relies heavily on discretionary official supervision of bank activities; the 'helping hand' approach empowers market discipline by, for example, ensuring information disclosure, and removing discretion that could turn into excessive forbearance. Perhaps unsurprisingly (given the loaded terminology) they proceed to show that helping hand policies work better for promoting bank development, performance and stability – at least in the sense of limiting the frequency of systemic banking failures and reducing non-performing loans. But the less discretionary approach may come at a cost in terms of amplifying short-term fluctuations, as shown in evidence presented by Caprio and Honohan (2003).

Ownership (government and foreign)

A third infrastructural characteristic (overlapping to be sure with the regulatory classification above) relates to ownership. If Government decides to take a large ownership share in the banking system, or to exclude foreign-owned banks systematically from a large share in the system, will financial sector performance improve or diminish? A growing literature has studied these issues with generally market-friendly findings. The cross-country findings by La Porta *et al.* (2002), showing that a higher degree of state ownership was associated with lower financial sector development, lower growth and lower productivity, and a higher risk of crises have been confirmed by several subsequent studies (including Barth *et al.*, 2002).

The case of foreign ownership is more highly contested, given the widely observed tendency for the typical foreign-owned bank to lend to larger firms, and the fear that their commitment to the host country might be limited, with the result that they might have a greater tendency to exit in a downturn. However, data-based findings (surveyed by Clarke *et al.*, 2002[25]), suggest that these concerns are over done and that entry of foreign banks tends to improve the efficiency and stability of the financial system. Even small firms report easier access to finance in systems with larger foreign bank penetration (as is shown by Clarke *et al.*, 2001, using the 400-firm database mentioned above).

Numerical implications

Drawing from these studies, we may propose an extended set of measures of financial development, combining not only scale and competitive efficiency, but also the presence of these major infrastructural preconditions. Unfortunately, a metastudy of the existing literature based on the framework outlined in (1) and (2) above is not altogether straightforward.

For one thing, there does not seem to be any existing discussion in the literature on the policy weights to be assigned to the different components of outturns (the W_k). Much of the literature seems to proceed as if growth were the only objective, but this surely cannot be so. Aggregate national fluctuations cannot easily be insured, so the second moment must be of some relevance. Likewise the poverty dimension may be important if, as has been suggested by the empirical evidence provided above, some policy approaches are more effective in reducing poverty than others, conditional on growth. Finally, it is likely that growth at the production frontier (attained in advanced economies) has somewhat different determinants than growth which is mainly a convergence to that frontier. If they embody new technology, access by new firms to finance may be even more important for growth at the frontier than away from it. For the present then, the literature does not tell us much about how to value these different components, which we need to do according to equation (2) above.

The second difficulty is a more practical one, namely that the various empirical studies have not all been set up to closely conform with equation (1). Different variables are used on both sides of the equation and so forth. So arriving at an acceptable summary is a task which, though not insurmountable, has not yet been accomplished.

But we can already begin to see whether the composite indicator has the potential to be substantially different from the size-based measures. Could it, for example, result in a considerable reordering of the international league table of financial development.

As an initial illustration along these lines, we took the developing countries already examined in the poverty exercise above and assembled data on (i) governance and legal institutions (KKZ and LLSV data) (ii) regulatory approach (BCL data) and ownership (also from BCL). The same indicators are not always available for all countries, indeed, for only 17 of the poverty countries are they all available. Table 1.6 (panel A) shows that pairwise the indicators are not highly correlated among themselves or with the size and activity measures (Table 1.6 shows the correlations on the basis of the common sample, those based on the much larger maximal samples are broadly similar). Even when aggregated in an ad hoc manner[26] to three sub-aggregates the correlations are all moderate (panel B). This suggests that re-ranking is quite possible depending on the weights used.

Indeed, Figure 1.6 illustrates the contrast for about 20 countries, using an aggregate of (i), (ii) and (iii) as a preliminary non-size composite. Countries substantially above or below a 45-degree line would be re-ranked by an index that combined the size and non-size data. The way in which re-ranking would occur can be seen by rotating the chart to the right: the angle of rotation indicating the relative weight on the non-size component. It can be seen in particular that China, which as mentioned has the largest banking system as a share of GDP, would lose this title with quite a moderate weight (0.3) on the the non-size composite (when both are normalized to zero mean and unit variance).

Further work will be needed to fill out the data set and choose weights in a systematic manner.

Table 1.6 Correlations matrix: size, activity and institutional variables

Panel A: individual series

	PVTCRED GDP	MKTCAP	Turn over	BNK CONC	Property Rights	Mean KKZ	Official PC	CAPIndex PC	Restrict PC	Private IndexPC	Foreign Owned	State Owned
Private credit % GDP	1.00	0.52	-0.23	-0.06	0.18	0.58	-0.12	-0.02	-0.30	0.37	0.12	-0.21
Market capitalization % GDP	0.52	1.00	-0.03	0.31	0.38	0.58	-0.72	0.19	-0.34	0.44	-0.17	-0.17
Market turnover % GDP	-0.06	0.31	0.12	1.00	0.02	-0.04	-0.49	0.24	0.25	-0.22	-0.11	0.36
Bank concentration	-0.23	-0.03	1.00	0.12	-0.27	-0.15	-0.15	0.07	0.01	0.02	-0.44	0.58
Property rights	0.18	0.38	0.02	-0.27	1.00	0.66	-0.09	0.12	0.01	0.01	0.06	-0.09
Governance (mean KKZ)	0.58	0.58	-0.04	-0.15	0.66	1.00	-0.28	0.17	-0.19	0.07	0.28	-0.12
Official regulation	-0.12	-0.72	-0.49	-0.15	-0.09	-0.28	1.00	-0.40	0.21	-0.03	0.33	0.23
Capital requirements	-0.02	0.19	0.24	0.07	0.12	0.17	-0.40	1.00	-0.13	-0.09	0.18	-0.10
Line of business restrictions	-0.30	-0.34	0.25	0.01	0.01	-0.19	0.21	-0.13	1.00	-0.37	-0.04	0.39
Market discipline	0.37	0.44	-0.22	0.02	0.01	0.07	-0.03	-0.09	-0.37	1.00	-0.31	-0.15
Foreign owned banks (%)	0.12	-0.17	-0.11	-0.44	0.06	0.28	0.33	0.18	-0.04	-0.31	1.00	-0.23
State owned banks (%)	-0.21	-0.17	0.36	0.58	-0.09	-0.12	0.23	-0.10	0.39	-0.15	-0.23	1.00

Panel B: sub-aggregates

	PVTCREDGDP	PHINST	PHREG	PHOWN
Depth	1.00	0.49	0.45	0.11
Institutions	0.49	1.00	0.38	0.15
Regulation	0.45	0.38	1.00	-0.11
Ownership	0.11	0.15	-0.11	1.00

Notes: For the individual series, the mnemonics in the column headings are as in the sources. MeanKKZ is the mean of the six KKZ governance indexes. The sub-aggregates in panel B are computed as follows: Depth is PVTCREDGDP; Institutions is Average of normalized PropertyRights and MeanKKZ; Regulation is the algebraic sum of OfficialPC, CAPIndexPC, RestrictPC and PrivateIndexPC: all except the last with minus sign; Ownership is ForeignOwned minus State Owned.

Source: Based on data in Barth *et al.*, 2002; Kaufmann *et al.*, 2003; Levine *et al.*, 2000; *International Financial Statistics*.

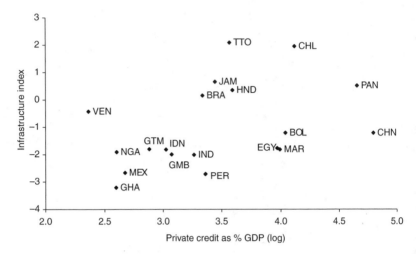

Figure 1.6   Depth and infrastructure: China added, outliers omitted

6   Conclusion

Probing financial development by means of cross-country regressions has greatly enriched our understanding of the processes most likely to be at work. The apparent importance of financial development for contributing to sustainable economic growth has been underlined. Second generation models have probed additional dimensions of both cause (finance) and effect (sustainable economic development). We have shown that finance-intensive growth (at least as measured by banking depth) is empirically associated with lower poverty ratios. On the other hand, depth alone is an insufficient measure of financial development, and we have suggested an approach to defining a more comprehensive summary statistic, drawing on results in the literature.

Notes

1. Such as initial income level, education, government spending, inflation, trade openness, measures of political liberties and law and order.
2. A third requirement for validity, that the instruments have no independent causal effect on GDP growth, is not easily tested. The well-known over-identification tests do not fully test this, contrary to what many authors seem to believe.
3. The finance–growth relationship continues to be studied, and even challenged, as in, for example, Favar (2003), who fails to find significant coefficients on finance in instrumented growth regressions. At bottom the main

problem is typically one of weak instruments: OLS estimates still indicating causality. Such negative findings are not sufficient to revise the main line view that finance causes economic development based, as it is, not only on the studies cited but on a wide range of cross-country studies, including those based on firm-level, industry-level and state-level evidence (see World Bank, 2001, and the papers cited therein).

4. The first result is subjected to more robustness tests than the second, where the financial depth variable is correlated with other variables measuring overall development or per capita income.
5. Though some research suggests that it may not reduce schooling by as much as is often thought.
6. Note that the finance and growth studies typically study both rich and poor countries. Poverty shares in the advanced countries are all measured at essentially zero for these international cut-off lines of $1 and $2 a day.
7. Though the Gini coefficient does not enter significantly. Alternative specifications using the share of the top 20 per cent, or the bottom 10 or 20 per cent, are inferior in fit. Results from including alternative aspects of the distribution as explanatory variables are reported in Table 1.7.
8. Results for the full sample are reported as Table 1.1 a. (alternate)
9. This auxiliary regression is reported in Table 1.8.
10. Once again the $2 a day threshold gives similar results (not shown).
11. Most of the international (cross-country) studies exclude the Chinese data for one stated reason or another.
12. The PPP measure is better for judging living standards; perhaps less good for assessing convergence to international levels of productivity.
13. Even if lending is to the private sector, heavy involvement of the state in allocating this credit can have much the same effect as if credit was simply going to the state. This is the underlying rationale for the use by some researchers of the ratio of central bank assets to total banking assets as a supplementary banking indicator of financial development.
14. Essentially this was the working off of an inherited over-liquid situation created by war-time borrowing. The problem was addressed by the famous Radcliffe Report of 1958.
15. The credit boom had been unleashed to be a relaxation for quantitative credit controls.
16. The 'Other Banking Instititutions' of *International Financial Statistics*. There may be a slight overstatement here in that some bank credit received by non-bank financial institutions is double-counted; but this is small.
17. There are some important technical issues here related to the allocation of banking margins – the so-called 'imputed service charge'.
18. Spreads are measured by subtracting one interest rate from another; margins by expressing net interest receipts of an intermediary as a percentage of total assets or some other relevant aggregate.
19. Personally I have some doubts that the turnover ratio is simply capturing churning; is it not likely that instead it is acting as a proxy for the degree of genuine reliance on the stock market for financing. Markets in which there is little trading of the listed shares are likely to be those in which the share of corporate outsiders in ownership is also low, and that the stock market may not therefore be performing much of a governance function.

Table 1.1(a) Poverty and financial depth (Alternate data set: including China, Panama and Thailand. Dependent variable: $1 per day poverty ratio)

Equation:	1.A Coeff.	1.A t-stat	1.B Coeff.	1.B t-stat	1.C Coeff.	1.C t-stat	1.D Coeff.	1.D t-stat	1.E Coeff.	1.E t-stat	1.F Coeff.	1.F t-stat
Constant	152.8	**9.2	230.8	**10.2	186.1	**7.5	174.4	**6.8	187.8	**7.7	165.8	**6.4
GDP per cap (log)	-16.7	**8.1										
GDP per cap lower 90% (log)			-17.4	**9.3	-15.5	**8.5	-14.3	**7.3	-15.6	**8.7	-13.2	**6.7
Share of top 10%					0.629	**3.4	0.655	**3.5	0.625	**3.4	0.646	**3.5
Private credit							-0.134	**1.9			-0.185	*2.5
Private credit residual									-0.184	*2.5		
Inflation											-0.081	*2.1
R-squared / NOBS	0.467	76	0.541	76	0.605	76	0.625	74	0.634	73	0.643	73
Adjusted R-squared	0.460		0.534		0.594		0.609		0.618		0.622	
SE of regression	15.5		14.4		13.5		13.3		13.2		13.1	
Log likelihood	-315.3		-309.7		-304.0		-294.7		-289.9		-288.9	

Notes: ** and * indicate significance at the 1% and 5% levels, respectively.
Cross section: all available countries.

Table 1.7 Poverty and financial depth: additional distributional variables (Dependent variable: $1 and $2 per day poverty ratios)

Equation: Dependent variable:	2.A Pov1		2.B Pov1		2.C Pov1		2.D Pov2		2.E Pov2		2.F Pov2	
	Coeff.	t-stat	Coeff.	t-stat	Coeff.	t-stat	Coeff.	t-stat	Coeff.	t-stat	Coeff.	t-stat
Constant	182.7	**5.5	146.5	**2.5	181.4	**7.3	269.6	**5.4	102.7	1.2	264.4	**7.2
GDP per cap lower 90% (log)	−15.4	**8.4	−15.3	**8.3	−15.3	**8.4	−20.5	**7.5	−20.1	**7.7	−15.3	**7.5
Share of top 10%	0.668	**3.2	0.950	*2.2	0.373	0.7	0.672	*2.3	2.005	**3.3	0.300	0.4
Share of second 10%	0.090	0.1	1.228	0.6			−0.182	0.1	5.197	1.8		
Share of lowest 10%			3.175	0.7					15.16	*2.5		
Gini (hdr)					0.270	0.6					0.690	0.5
Private credit residual	−0.353	**3.2	−0.369	**3.3	0.353	**3.2	−0.354	*2.1	−0.369	*2.6	0.356	**2.1
R-squared / NOBS	0.652	70	0.655	70	0.654	70	0.552	72	0.590	72	0.554	72
Adjusted R-squared	0.631		0.628		0.633		0.525		0.559		0.527	
SE of regression	13.1		13.2		13.1		20.2		19.5		20.2	
Log likelihood	−277.1		−276.8		−276.9		−316.1		−312.9		−316.0	

Notes: Pov1 (2) are the $1 ($2) per Day Poverty Ratios.
** and * indicate significance at the 1% and 5% levels, respectively.
Cross section excluding China, Panama and Thailand.

Table 1.8 Predicted financial depth (auxiliary regression) (Dependent variable: private credit as share of GDP)

Equation:	7.A		7.B	
	Coeff.	*t*-stat	Coeff.	*t*-stat
Constant	55.1	*2.5	−41.6	**2.7
GDP per cap (log)	11.1	**4.0	8.82	**4.5
Inflation	−0.175	**2.9	−0.123	**3.0
R-squared / NOBS	0.226	75	0.269	72
Adjusted *R*-squared	0.205		0.248	
SE of regression	21.3		14.6	
Log likelihood	−334.2		−293.8	

Notes: 7.A includes all countries; 7.B excludes China, Panama and Thailand.
** and * indicate significance at the 1% and 5% levels, respectively.

20. There has to be some question as to whether some of the institutional variables that have been employed as instruments really do satisfy the necessary exclusion criteria: as mentioned above this is not something that is easily tested.

21. These papers have led to an explosion of research refining and deepening the results. For example, Emre Ergungor (2002) shows that it is mainly in common law countries that creditor rights explain variations in banking sector development (and he also explains why this should be expected).

22. An ongoing debate concerns the primacy of legal origin and geographic endowments in creating the environment for subsequent financial and wider economic development. Using a sample of 70 former colonies, Beck, Demirgüç-Kunt and Levine (2003a) find evidence for both hypotheses. However, it is initial endowments that are more robustly associated (than legal origin) with financial intermediary development and they also explain more of the cross-country variation in financial intermediary and stock market development than does legal origin. But this debate does not affect the validity of legal origin as an instrument. Just why legal origin should matter is discussed by Beck, Demirgüç-Kunt and Levine (2003b), perhaps because some legal traditions do a better job at defending private interests against the state, or perhaps (and what evidence there is favors this one) law in some traditions is better able to adapt itself to varying commercial conditions. Political – and as such time-varying – influences from interest groups on the policies determining financial development are emphasized by Rajan and Zingales (2003a).

23. Details of the self-reported financing constraints are more informative in this regard: high collateral requirements, banking bureaucracy, high interest rates, need for the borrower to have a special connection with the bank, and 'banks lack money to lend' all correlated with firm growth.

24. Note a hidden assumption here, namely that defining good-for-finance legal systems is unproblematic. We already highlighted the fact that different legal

systems attach different priorities to the main players. Most writers on this topic assume that enforcement of creditor rights is the key thing, but a respectable theoretical proposition can be made to the effect that lenience in this regard might encourage entrepreneurship: however, the empirical evidence, including that cited here, seems to argue against such a soft proposition. In developing countries policy discussion focuses as much (or more) on the judicial and administrative enforcement of the law as on how to tilt the legal protections in law: few would disagree with the importance of enforcement.

25. See also Levine (2002) confirming in a striking way the favorable impact of foreign banks on bank spreads. More widely, the role of competition in improving performance but potentially adding to vulnerability is examined in the papers presented at a World Bank conference in Washington DC in April 2003, see http://www.worldbank.org/research/interest/confs/bank_concentration.htm.

26. Essentially by normalizing and adding together, with algebraic sign corresponding to the literature's consensus on the direction of impact on growth.

References

Barth, James R., Gerard Caprio, Jr and Ross Levine. (2002), 'Bank regulation and supervision: What works best?' World Bank Policy Research Working Paper 2733, forthcoming *Journal of Financial Intermediation* (BCL).

Beck, Thorsten, Asli Demirgüç-Kunt and Ross Levine. (2003a), 'Law and finance: Why does legal origin matter?', World Bank Policy Research Working Paper 2904, October 2002, forthcoming *Journal of Comparative Economics* 31: 653–75.

Beck, Thorsten, Asli Demirgüç-Kunt and Ross Levine. (2003b), 'Law, endowments and finance', forthcoming, *Journal of Financial Economics* 70: 137–81.

Beck, Thorsten, Asli Demirgüç-Kunt and Vojislav Maksimovic. (2003), 'Financial and legal constraints to firm growth: Does size matter?' World Bank Policy Research Working Paper 2784, February 2002.

Beck, Thorsten and Ross Levine. (2004), 'Stock markets, banks and growth: Panel evidence', *Journal of Banking and Finance* 28: 423–42.

Boyreau-Debray, Genevieve. (2003), 'Financial intermediation and growth: Chinese style', World Bank Policy Research Working Paper 3027.

Caprio, Gerard, Jr and Patrick Honohan. (2003), 'Banking policy and macroeconomic stability: An exploration' in William C. Hunter, George G. Kaufman and Michael Pomerleano (eds), *Asset Price Bubbles: The Implications for Monetary, Regulatory, and International Policies*, Cambridge, MA: MIT Press, pp. 337–60.

Cho, Yoon Je. (2001), 'The role of poorly phased liberalization in Korea's financial crisis', in Gerard Caprio, Patrick Honohan and Joseph E. Stiglitz (eds), *Financial Liberalization: How Far, How Fast?* New York: Cambridge University Press.

Clarke, George, Robert Cull and Maria Soledad Martinez Peria. (2001), 'Does foreign bank penetration reduce access to credit in developing countries? Evidence from asking borrowers', World Bank Policy Research Working Paper 2716.

Clarke, George, Robert Cull, Maria Soledad Martinez Peria and Susana M. Sánchez. (2002), 'Bank lending to small businesses in Latin America: Does bank origin matter?', World Bank Policy Research Working Paper 2760, January 2002.

Dehejia, Rajeev H. and Roberta Gatti. (2002), 'Child labor: The role of income variability and access to credit in a cross section of countries', World Bank Policy Research Working Paper 2767.

Demirgüç-Kunt, Asli and Enrica Detragiache. (1999), 'Financial liberalization and financial fragility', in Boris Pleskovic and Joseph E. Stiglitz (eds), *Proceedings of the 1998 World Bank Conference on Development Economics*, Washington, DC.: World Bank.

Demirgüç-Kunt, Asli, and Ross Levine. Eds. (2001), *Financial Structure and Economic Growth*. Cambridge, MA: MIT Press.

Dollar, David and Aart Kraay. (2001), 'Growth is good for the poor', World Bank Policy Research Working Paper 2587.

Easterly, William. (2001), *The Elusive Quest for Growth*, Cambridge, MA: MIT Press.

Emre Ergungor, Ozgur. (2002), 'Legal traditions; financial intermediaries; financial markets; comparative financial systems; investor protection', Federal Reserve Bank of Cleveland. Working Paper 0101R.

Favara, Giovanni. (2003), 'An empirical reassessment of the relationship between finance and growth', *IMF Working Paper* 03/123.

Fuchs, Michael. Ed. (2002), *Building Trust: Developing the Russian Financial Sector*, Washington DC.: The World Bank.

Greenwood Jeremy and Boyan Jovanovic. (1990), 'Financial development, growth and the distribution of income', *Journal of Political Economy* 98 (5,1): 1076–107.

Honohan, Patrick. (1997), 'Banking system failures in developing and transition countries: Diagnosis and prediction', BIS Working Paper No. 39.

Kaufmann, Daniel, Aart Kraay and Pablo Zoido-Lobatón. (1999a), 'Aggregating governance indicators', World Bank Policy Research Working Paper No. 2195, Washington, DC. (KKZ)

Kaufmann, Daniel, Aart Kraay and Massimo Mastruzzi. (2003), 'Governance matters III: Governance indicators for 1996–2002', World Bank Policy Research Working Paper.

King, Robert G. and Ross Levine. (1993a), 'Finance and growth: Schumpeter might be right', *Quarterly Journal of Economics* 108(3): 717–37.

La Porta, Rafael, Florencio López-de-Silanes, Andrei Shleifer and Robert W. Vishny. (1997), 'Legal determinants of external finance', *The Journal of Finance* 52(3): 1131–50.

———. (1998), 'Law and finance', *Journal of Political Economy* 106 (6): 1113–55. (LLSV)

La Porta, Rafael, Florencio López-de-Silanes, and Andrei Shleifer. (2002), 'Government ownership of commercial banks', *Journal of Finance* 57(1): 265–301.

Lardy, Nicholas. (1998), *China's Unfinished Economic Revolution*, Washington DC: The Brookings Institution.

Levine, Ross. (2002), 'Denying foreign bank entry: Implications for bank interest margins, Presented at *Central Bank of Chile Conference*, Santiago, December (2002). (http://www.bcentral.cl/eng/studiesandpublications/conferences/annual/pdf/ross_levine.pdf).

Levine, Ross and David Renelt. (1992), 'A sensitivity analysis of cross-country growth regressions', *The American Economic Review* 82(4): 942–63.

Levine, Ross. (1997), 'Financial development and economic growth: Views and agenda', *Journal of Economic Literature* 35: 688–726.

Levine, Ross, Norman Loayza, and Thorsten Beck. (2000), 'Financial intermediation and growth: Causality and causes', *Journal of Monetary Economics* 46(1): 31–77.

Levine, Ross, and Sara Zervos. (1998), 'Stock markets, banks, and economic growth', *American Economic Review* 88(3): 537–58.

Li, Hongyi, Lyn Squire and Heng-fu Zou. (1998), 'Explaining international and intertemporal variations in income inequality', *Economic Journal* 108(1): 26–43.

Rajan, Raghuram G. and Luigi Zingales. (2003a), 'The Great Reversals: The politics of financial development in the 20th century', forthcoming, *Journal of Financial Economics* 69: 5–50.

Rajan, Raghuram G. and Luigi Zingales (2003b), *Saving Capitalism from the Capitalists*, New York: Crown Business.

Temple, J.R.W. (1998), 'The new growth evidence', *Journal of Economic Literature* 37. 112–156.

World Bank. (2001), *Finance and Growth: Policy Choices in a Volatile World*, New York: Oxford University Press.

2
Finance and Growth: What we Know and What we Need to Know

P. Demetriades and S. Andrianova

1 Preliminaries

In modern economies finance underpins virtually every economic transaction that takes place. When we go to the supermarket, we usually pay using credit or debit cards issued by commercial banks (or the supermarkets themselves). Even when we pay using cash, we have to first find an ATM in order to withdraw the necessary bank notes. The banking system, which includes commercial banks as well as the central bank (the Bank of England in the United Kingdom), provides the payments system which makes economic exchange possible. It is hard to imagine what economies would look like without 'money' – broadly defined as anything that is used in exchange for goods and services and the settlement of debt. Besides providing the means of payment, which underpins all economic transactions, the financial system provides a link between current and future output and consumption. When we borrow from a bank to buy a car, we are essentially bringing forward consumption against future income. This is made possible because financial intermediaries, like banks, raise funds from surplus units (those economic agents whose income is greater than their current expenditure) and pass them on as loans to deficit units (those economic agents whose income is less than their current expenditure). Without the financial system, which facilitates such inter-temporal transfer of resources, all consumption would have to be financed from current income. Similarly, firms would not be able to raise capital to finance investment in plant and equipment unless they already had accumulated enough profits in previous years. Many profitable, socially beneficial, investment opportunities – for example, the creation of new firms and innovation – would simply not take place.

Since the financial system is at the core of modern economies, the proposition that finance is essential for economic growth – the change in output from one year to the next – is therefore in some sense almost a trivial one. It may therefore come as a surprise to non-economists that there is a very large and growing body of academic literature that discusses the (seemingly rather obvious) relationship between finance and growth. However, there are very good reasons why this literature exists, other than career progression of many academics! The main reason can be traced back to pre-1970s economics literature, which, by and large, takes finance for granted. Traditional 'neoclassical' economics, taught in most mainstream microeconomics courses throughout the world, does not explicitly address the role of finance in consumption or investment decisions. It implicitly assumes that finance is 'neutral'; that is to say it does not make any difference whatsoever to economic decision making.[1]

Neoclassical consumer and producer theory analyses consumption and investment decisions without explicit reference to finance. In static models of consumption (i.e. models where time is not explicitly analysed), households choose the bundle of goods and services that maximises their utility subject to a single-period income constraint, without any explicit reference to the payments system. Similarly, in this type of model, firms maximise profit by choosing the optimal level of inputs and output, again without any explicit reference to money or finance. By their very nature, such models are not capable of addressing the role of money and finance, since money and finance are both linked to inter-temporal decision-making. However, even when inter-temporal models are used to analyse consumption and investment decisions over time, the traditional neoclassical approach has been to treat money and finance in a superficial manner, usually by assuming – often implicitly – that there is a 'perfect capital market', in which economic agents can borrow or lend as much as they wish to maximise their respective objective functions. In practice, this assumption translates into having a single interest rate that is used to discount to the present all future income or expenditure streams. In the neoclassical theory of investment, the source of finance does not matter in determining the level of investment; bank loans, bonds, retained earnings, stock issues all have the same cost. Similarly, neoclassical consumer theory assumes that households face no borrowing constraints, that is, they can borrow or lend as much as they like at the same interest rate. We all, of course, know that there are hundreds of different interest rates on the market, when we wish to borrow (or lend), and that searching to find the best rate does take time. Sometimes when we think we have found the best rate, we fill in all the necessary application forms, and the lender may well decide to decline the application. Meanwhile, we have incurred substantial *transaction costs* in terms of both the fees we may have paid and the time we have wasted. This is, of course, a rather superficial criticism of neoclassical consumer theory. The conclusions of the model may not be fundamentally altered even if we explicitly allow for transaction costs – thus to ignore them may be an acceptable simplification. A more fundamental criticism is that allocation decisions themselves may change when we relax the assumption of perfect capital markets. If a consumer is refused credit, then her consumption decision may well change – she may not buy the car she intended to, which, has implications for the firm that produces cars. Similarly, if a firm cannot raise capital, an investment opportunity may go unexploited. Or it may be exploited by a competitor in a different country, so that even if the firm was to 'save-up' to carry out this investment, by the time it is able to do so, the project may no longer be profitable. Thus, finance may well 'matter' in a very fundamental sense. This can have profound implications, not only in terms of explaining why some countries grow faster than others but also in terms of the validity of some of the most fundamental axioms of mainstream (neoclassical) economics, on which many generations of economic students have been educated. For example, the so-called 'First Theorem of Welfare Economics', which states that the 'competitive economy is Pareto-efficient' (that is to say no one could be made better of without making someone else worse of), is derived from a model that has no role for money and no role for finance.[2]

Once we relax the assumption of 'perfect capital markets', many interesting questions arise, including what the sources and implications of financial market imperfections might be. We have already touched on one imperfection, namely 'transaction costs'. We have also touched upon what may be at the root of transaction costs when we said that it takes time for consumers to find out about the various interest rates on the market. The key to understanding finance – banks, capital markets, money, prudential regulation of financial markets and institutions – is indeed the understanding of the information problems that are associated with financial decision making by firms, households and financial institutions. In the last 30 years or so, a very large body of academic literature has emerged on the economics of information, much of which specifically focuses on finance. Take, for example, the information problems associated with borrowing and lending decisions. Information is usually distributed asymmetrically (shared unequally) between borrowers and lenders. This gives rise to two problems: adverse selection and moral hazard. Adverse selection occurs before a transaction takes place and in the case of loans it refers to the selection of bad credit risks.[3] Moral hazard occurs after a loan is granted and refers to the incentive of the borrower to act in a way that is not acceptable to the lender (if they knew about it), typically taking on excessive risk since this increases the probability of default. Between them, adverse selection and moral hazard can explain much of what we see in the financial system and can also provide a justification for some forms of government intervention, such as prudential regulation and supervision of financial institutions. They can also explain why banks exist in the first place. In a nutshell, banks can be efficient forms of organisation able to address the adverse selection and moral hazard problems in the credit market, mainly through screening and monitoring of potential borrowers. Information problems are also at the heart of theoretical models that try to explain the relationship between finance and growth (e.g. Bencivenga and Smith 2000).

Once it is accepted that what goes on in (imperfect) financial markets can make a difference to economic decision making and, consequently, to the allocation of resources, then an in-depth study of various aspects of the relationship between finance and growth begins to make a lot of sense. Different types of finance, by addressing information problems in various ways, can result in differences in both the volume and pattern of investment (e.g. those with short-term payoffs versus those with long-term payoffs), as well as the productivity of physical and human capital. In any sensible economic model, these are important channels of economic growth. Additionally, it also becomes legitimate to study government policies towards the financial system: should, for example, governments own banks, should they provide central banking services, should they control capital flows or even interest rates, should they stipulate capital or reserve requirements for banks, should they regulate stock markets, and, if so, how, and so on. Since information problems are at the heart of financial decision making, it is also not unreasonable to argue that the relationship between finance and growth may in part depend on how successfully the financial system manages to address information problems. An economy with a well-functioning financial system that manages to address the variety of adverse selection and moral hazard problems adequately, is likely to enjoy high rates of investment, and to have a highly productive capital stock. In contrast, an economy with a financial system that fails to effectively address information problems is likely to exhibit high levels of uncertainty, low and unproductive investment and low growth, as well as financial instability.

In order to unravel what we know about the relationship between finance and growth and highlight areas where we need to know more, we will embark on a selective (and somewhat idiosyncratic) review of relevant academic, mainly empirical, literature. We will focus particularly on policy issues, importantly financial liberalisation, government ownership of banks and prudential regulation. As we shall see, this literature is not free from controversy, indeed one could argue it is full of contentious issues! This should perhaps not be surprising. We are dealing with an area of economics where policy issues are abundant (e.g. financial liberalisation, financial globalisation), and where a lot is at stake, in both developed and developing countries. We will certainly attempt to provide an objective assessment of various points of view. However, it is left to the reader to decide the extent to which we succeed in doing so.

This chapter is structured as follows. Section 2 provides a review of mainly empirical literature on the finance–growth nexus, which draws on a number of influential cross-country studies, as well as on a variety of studies that focus on individual countries through time. Section 3 discusses likely obstacles to financial development, including financial repression, government ownership of banks, legal factors and political economy constraints. Finally, Section 4 summarises and concludes.

2   The empirical relationship between finance and growth

As already argued, in modern market economies the financial system underpins virtually all economic transactions. A positive association between measures of financial sector development and economic growth (or real GDP) is, therefore, a very basic first test of the finance–growth relationship. Indeed, this question has preoccupied the empirical literature on finance and growth for quite some time. The main conclusion that has emerged on this question by early as well as more recent studies is that there is indeed an association in the data both across countries and within countries, over time, even though the relationship is neither linear nor very precise.[4]

The more contentious issue in this literature has been not whether this positive association exists in the data but what is the direction of causality between these two variables. Specifically, does financial development cause economic growth or does it simply follow growth generated elsewhere in the economy? Applied economists approach causality-type questions using the notion of 'Granger causality', which utilises the concept of statistical predictability. If variable X helps predict the future time path of variable Y, then it is said that X Granger-causes Y. Without getting too philosophical, this is of course not quite the same as true causality: if a variable helps predict another variable it does not necessarily mean it causes it. It may well be the case that there is another variable, Z, that is the true cause of both Y and X, but X responds more quickly to Z than Y. Hence Granger-causality may just mean that X is a leading indicator of Y. Thus, even if we find that financial development helps predict future economic growth (in the Granger-sense), it does not necessarily follow that it causes it. However, this need not concern us too much, for the following reason. Conceptually, financial development is, at best, a facilitator of economic growth, rather than its ultimate true cause. Its true cause has to be sought in the real sector: the creation of new ideas, the discovery of natural resources or of alternative ways of using existing resources, product innovation, technological progress and so on. Finance is, of course, essential in ensuring that new ideas are translated into new products and services, natural resources are exploited, and that new products and technologies materialise. A well-functioning financial system is one that enables the real economy to fully exploit such new opportunities. Thus, we could interpret Granger-causality from financial development to economic growth as a basic second test that a healthy, well-functioning, financial system must normally be able to pass.

What if we don't find Granger-causality running from financial development to economic growth but we find reverse causality, that is, from economic growth to financial development? This is usually pretty bad news, assuming of course that we trust our econometric procedures and data (e.g. we are confident that the variables we have used to measure financial development are the appropriate ones – more on this below). Financial development is, of course, expected to follow economic growth elsewhere under most circumstances, since when the real economy grows, there should be more savings coming into the financial system, which will allow it to extend new loans and so on. But a well-functioning financial system is also expected to lead economic growth. Thus, we would normally expect to see bi-directional causality between finance and growth, sometimes known technically as a feedback relationship.

If there is no Granger causality from finance to growth, a number of factors could be at play. One possibility is that funds are being diverted to non-productive activities due to micro-economic inefficiencies in the banking system. If the banks are not able to solve informational problems very well, because the problems themselves are either very severe or because their screening and monitoring systems are not effective, they may end up financing low quality projects or may avoid funding long-term projects altogether, focusing on projects with shorter-term payoffs. An alternative explanation is political interference in the banking system that may channel funds into unproductive projects (e.g. building weapons of mass destruction or financing white elephant projects that generate rents for government officials). Reverse causality may also indicate fundamental macroeconomic problems, such as a high degree of political or economic uncertainty, including high and unpredictable inflation.[5] Under these circumstances, financial savings may not be channelled into new investment because firms, domestic and foreign, are simply not willing to invest when the future is highly uncertain. Thus, a country's financial savings might be channelled into foreign banks and may well end up financing growth in other countries. A final, related but more innocuous, explanation of reverse causality, is that the financial system under consideration is either an international or a regional centre of finance, and may therefore have a weak relationship with domestic economic growth (e.g. Hong Kong, London or New York).

One of the most influential papers in recent literature that examines the relationship between financial development and economic growth is King and Levine (1993). Utilising data on 77 countries for the period 1960–89, King and Levine consider a variety of indicators of financial development, mostly ratios of aggregates measuring the size of the financial system relative to GDP, and 3 growth indicators (average growth rate of real GDP per capita, average growth rate of capital stock per capita and a measure of total factor productivity). They estimate a cross-country growth regression of the form:

$$g_i = a + bFD_i + cZ_i + u_i,$$

where g_i is the growth rate of country i averaged over the period 1960–89, FD_i is the level of financial development of country i, Z_i is a vector of other possible determinants of economic growth, such as initial income, education, inflation, openness to trade, political uncertainty and so on, and u_i is a statistical error term.

They find that the coefficient of DEPTH (the indicator of FD defined as the ratio of liquid liabilities to GDP in the equation above), is 2.4 and highly significant statistically. In his recent review of the literature on finance and growth, Levine (2003) suggests that raising DEPTH from the mean of the slowest growing quartile of countries to the mean of the fastest growing quartile, would have increased growth by almost 1 per cent per year. Over a 30-year period, this is a lot of growth! Levine, does, however, admit that these calculations ignore causality and the issue of how to increase DEPTH. In another set of regressions, King and Levine replace *FD* by its level in 1960, in an attempt to isolate the causal influence of financial development on economic growth. The effect remains positive and significant, which allows the authors to conclude that financial development helps predict long-run growth.

There are a number of problems with the interpretation of the King and Levine (1993) results, some of which Levine (2003) alludes to, including the difficulty in establishing causality in cross-country data sets and the measures of financial development utilised. Additionally, when dealing with cross-country data sets, one is, at best, dealing with the average effects of financial development. This is fine, assuming the relationship does not vary considerably across countries. However, if it is driven by one or two 'outliers' – not uncommon in cross-country growth regressions – these results would be meaningless for non-outlier countries from a policy perspective. Moreover, it is frequently the case that these results are sensitive to the specification of the equation; changing the control variables, *Z*, could well affect the statistical significance of *b*, making any results difficult to interpret. These problems led a number of authors to examine the finance–growth relationship using time-series data on individual countries. Time-series data allow the use of appropriate statistical procedures, such as cointegration, to test for the existence of long-run relationships; they also allow the use of statistical procedures that can shed light on the causality between two or more variables in both the long-run and the short-run. Their main limitation, however, is that the time-series that we have at our disposal are not sufficiently long to allow a very high degree of confidence in the estimates.[6] Demetriades and Hussein (1996), is one of the earlier studies in recent literature that adopts the time-series approach for a reasonably large and diverse set of countries. These authors use data from 16 countries that were not highly developed in 1960, for the period 1960–90. They find a stable long-run relationship between indicators of financial development and real per capita GDP in 14 countries. However, the direction of causality varies considerably across countries. Alarmingly, while they find bi-directional causality in seven countries, they find clear evidence of reverse causality in six cases (El Salvador, Greece, Pakistan, Portugal, South Africa and Turkey). Odedokun (1996) also reports different effects of finance on growth in different countries. Even more disturbing results are found by De Gregorio and Guidotti (1995), who report a negative relationship between financial development and growth in 12 Latin American countries during 1950–85.

Thus, according to time-series studies, one size does not seem to fit all in the case of the finance–growth relationship. Rioja and Valev (forthcoming) examine this issue more closely using panel techniques and data from 74 countries and suggest that there are three distinct regions of financial development. The effects of financial development on growth vary across the three. In the low region, which mostly contains very poor countries, increases in financial development have no statistically significant effect on growth. In the intermediate region, financial development changes are most effective in promoting growth. In the high region, additional financial development has positive, albeit smaller effects.

Many of the empirical studies on the finance–growth nexus have utilised indicators that are primarily focused on the development of the banking system, such as the ratio of liquid liabilities or private credit to GDP. More recently, there has been an explosion of studies that use broader measures of financial development, particularly those including the development of stock markets. This is partly justified by the growth of stock markets around the world, particularly in emerging market economies, which makes any study of the finance–growth nexus incomplete if it does not consider the contribution to growth that stock markets might have. Efficient stock markets, like well-functioning banking systems, could play a complementary role in financing investment to that of banks, and may also help to exercise corporate control through mergers and acquisitions. If stock markets are (informationally) efficient, that is, stock prices truly reflect the expected future profitability of companies, resources flow to the most efficient and productive companies, which are then able to implement their investment plans. On the other hand, if stock prices are excessively volatile and are prone to speculation, bubbles, and price manipulation, then stock markets may be unable to contribute to growth or may even have negative effects by compounding economic uncertainty (Singh 1997).

Some studies using cross-country growth regressions find that stock markets have large positive effects on growth, in addition to banks (Levine and Zervos 1998). However, the causality issue is difficult to address in these studies. Moreover, it is now known that some of these results are driven by outliers; when the East Asian 'tigers' are excluded from the sample the nature of the results is altered substantially.[7]

For these reasons, a number of authors have resorted to time-series methods, even though this means that fewer countries can be examined. Arestis, Demetriades and Luintel (2001), henceforth ADL, is one such study. These authors utilise time-series data and methods to examine the causality between stock markets, banks and real GDP. Because time-series techniques are data intensive, data limitations dictate that they focus on five advanced countries: the United Kingdom, the United States, Germany, France and Japan. ADL find a relatively strong long-run relationship between the three variables in Germany, France and Japan, where they find that stock markets have made a significant contribution to growth in addition to banks, albeit of a much smaller magnitude (ranging from 1/3 to 1/7 of that of banks). Interestingly, they also find that the link between financial development and growth in the United Kingdom and the United States is statistically weak and, if anything, exhibits reverse causality. ADL suggest that their results are consistent with the view that bank-based financial systems, such as those of Germany and Japan, may be better able to promote long-run economic growth than capital-market based ones. They acknowledge, however, that the results may to some extent reflect the international character of the UK and the US financial systems, which may well result in a weaker relationship between domestic GDP and their respective, internationally oriented, financial systems.

Beck and Levine (2004) utilise panel data techniques, which exploit both the cross-section and time-series variation in data, to examine the role of stock markets alongside that of banks on economic growth. Their data set includes 40 countries over 1975–98. They find that stock market liquidity (the total value of shares traded relative to market capitalisation), is positively related to subsequent GDP growth. In their regressions, they control for banking sector development using a credit-based measure, which is also found to have a positive, larger, influence. Once again, their estimated coefficients suggest that the influence of both banks and stock markets on growth is quite large. However, while panel data techniques offer a very good way to increase sample sizes and to exploit data variation, they may suffer from other limitations. For instance, averaging over 5-years per country, as Beck and Levine do, is unlikely to be sufficient to remove business-cycle influences from the data. This means that the estimated relationships may not capture the underlying long-run relationships very well and may well suffer from econometric problems, including dynamic heterogeneity,[8] resulting in biased estimates (Pesaran and Smith 1995).

Thus, it is still difficult to draw out any reliable policy implications from cross-country or panel regressions, and those conclusions that we may draw from time-series studies for individual countries cannot easily be generalised. With increasing data availability it may be possible to utilise panels that use observations that have been averaged over ten years instead of five, which is clearly preferable. Confidence in the results obtained from time-series studies will also increase, once we are able to have samples that span 40 or even 50 years, especially if these data are available in quarterly frequencies. There is, therefore, considerable scope for further work in this area, especially in order to increase the degree of confidence in the results that we already have or, indeed, to check their robustness.

To summarise, there is now a voluminous empirical literature on the relationship between financial development and economic growth, using different methodologies, different data sets, and a variety of indicators, which this section has briefly and selectively reviewed. What we do know from this literature is that there is, with few exceptions, a positive long-run association between financial development and economic growth, as measured either by the long-run growth rate or the level of per capita GDP. What we are less sure about is the causal nature of the estimated relationships between growth and finance. We need to have a lot more results, using larger data sets and better econometric methods, before we can conclude with a reasonable degree of confidence that finance leads economic growth in every country in the world. Meanwhile, results indicating reverse causality need not be dismissed, just because they do not agree with the 'one-size fits all' approach. These results could be very useful for policy makers (domestic and international), since they may suggest some underlying structural problems such as political interference in the financial system, cronyism, corruption, political uncertainty and such others. A final conclusion that we would like to draw is that, irrespective of the direction of causality between finance and growth found in empirical studies, a better understanding of the factors that promote financial development – in a broader sense than perhaps may be suggested by various indicators – is likely to shed light on the mechanisms and policies that may promote economic growth. Even in the cases where we observe reverse causality in the data, promoting financial development in the sense of identifying and fixing what is wrong in the financial system, is likely to result in more growth, even if it doesn't necessarily lead to higher values of the financial development indicators. There should therefore be little doubt that better, if not more, finance is likely to result in more growth.

3   Promoting financial development

In understanding what factors may promote financial development, it is instructive to ask an almost equivalent question: what are the obstacles to financial development, where it has not occurred? To this end, we review relevant literature under the following four themes: (i) financial repression and liberalisation, (ii) government ownership of banks, (iii) legal factors and (iv) political economy constraints.

Financial repression and liberalisation

The early literature on financial development (McKinnon 1973, Shaw 1973), highlights ill-conceived government interventions, like interest rate ceilings, high reserve requirements and directed credit programmes, as the main source of financial underdevelopment. These controls were dubbed 'financial repression'. Controls on capital flows have also frequently been included among such interventions, even though a growing number of authors (Arestis and Demetriades 1999, Stiglitz 2000) now acknowledge that these may occasionally have a stabilising influence.

McKinnon and Shaw argued that ceilings on deposit and/or lending rates, because of high inflation rates, frequently resulted in negative real rates of interest, which discouraged saving and created an excess demand for investable funds. The volume of investment declined when real interest rates were too low and so did the productivity of capital, since when real interest rates are low, low-productivity investment projects may become profitable. The problem was frequently exacerbated by governments that interfered in credit allocation, which aimed at allocating credit to 'priority sectors', frequently a euphemism for cronyism and corruption. In addition, governments imposed excessively high reserve requirements on banks, usually at low or even zero interest rates, in order to finance their own deficits cheaply. These reserve requirements, however, acted as a tax on the banking system, resulting in further depression of deposit rates, thereby creating greater disincentives for financial saving. Removing interest rate ceilings, reducing reserve requirements and abolishing priority lending – freeing the domestic financial system from such government distortions – was seen as critical in delivering financial development and consequently, more growth. For a time, this became the mantra of the IMF and the World Bank, whose officials prescribed (and frequently imposed) financial liberalisation to many developing countries.

The reality of financial liberalisation in the 1970s and early 1980s, was, however, very different from what was predicted by the financial repression literature. Real interest rates soared to unprecedented levels (sometimes in excess of +20 per cent), as a result of fierce competition for funds and excessive risk-taking by firms and banks themselves.

Speculation flourished and when borrowers were unable to pay their debts, many banks failed and governments were forced to (re-)nationalise them, resulting in very large fiscal costs. Instead of more growth, there was more unemployment. Instead of more prosperity there was more poverty. Instead of a better, more developed, financial system there were failed banks that had to be rescued by the government. In a classic paper entitled 'Good-bye financial repression, hello financial crash', Diaz-Alejandro (1985) provides a first attempt at analysing the failure of financial liberalisation in Latin America. Subsequent analysis of what went wrong in the first wave of financial reforms (Villanueva and Mirakhor 1990) highlights adverse preconditions, such as macroeconomic instability (large fiscal deficits and high inflation), exacerbated moral hazard problems and inadequacies in banking supervision. McKinnon (1991) suggests that incorrect sequencing of reforms was at the root of the problem. He suggests that financial liberalisation should be preceded by real sector reforms, including privatisation of state enterprises, aimed at ensuring that relative prices adequately reflect economic scarcities. He also advocates reducing deficits and inflation before embarking on reforms, to remove any price distortions that may be associated with high inflation. Finally, adequate regulation and supervision of banks is necessary in order to contain moral hazard problems in the banking system. McKinnon also argues that domestic financial liberalisation (i.e. interest rate deregulation and lowering of reserve requirements) should precede liberalisation of capital flows, with restrictions on long-term flows, such as FDI, being lifted first while those on volatile short-term flows being lifted last.

Adverse selection and moral hazard problems are exacerbated in the aftermath of interest rate liberalisation, especially when banks are not sufficiently well capitalised. Under-capitalised banks have incentives to take excessive risks, especially if they are protected by government safety nets (deposit insurance or 'too big to fail' policies). It is often believed that such safety nets encourage banks to behave imprudently, since they allow them to benefit from a one-way (unfair) bet against the government. By making speculative loans at very high interest rates they stand to make very large profits, assuming of course that the borrowers do not default. If the borrowers do default, the bank will not suffer the full cost of these defaults if it is bailed out by the government. Even if the bank is allowed to fail, the depositors may not suffer if they are protected by deposit insurance. Thus, depositors have no incentives to monitor bank managers when they are protected by deposit insurance. Bank shareholders have no incentive to monitor bank managers either when they don't have much capital at stake. In the extreme, bank shareholders may even benefit from the gambling behaviour by the managers, if they have little or no capital at stake (i.e. when the bank has little or no net worth). In such circumstances it may be in their interests to instruct bank managers to gamble (with taxpayers' money) – this is sometimes known as 'gambling for resurrection' (Llewellyn 1999).

A number of papers provide empirical evidence that substantiates the uncanny relationship between financial liberalisation and financial crises. Demirgüç-Kunt and Detragiache (1999) analyse the determinants of the probability of banking crises in 53 countries during 1980–95. They find that financial liberalisation has a very large and statistically significant positive effect on the probability of banking crisis, even after controlling for many other possible determinants of banking crises. The magnitudes are quite startling: the probability of a banking crisis increases up to five times following financial liberalisation. The increase in this probability is lower in more developed economies or when institutional quality is high. Their institutional quality indicators include law and order, bureaucratic delay, contract enforcement, quality of bureaucracy and corruption. The authors argue that the influence of financial liberalisation on financial fragility works its way through reduced bank franchise values. Financial liberalisation intensifies competition, which reduces the value of a banking license to shareholders and exacerbates moral hazard in the form of excessively risky lending. They also present evidence which suggests that while financial liberalisation has a positive effect on financial development, banking crises have a negative effect. They find that the two effects offset each other in countries that liberalise from a position of positive real interest rates, while in those that started from a repressed position the effect of financial liberalisation on financial development outweighs that of the banking crisis. They conclude by arguing in favour of gradual financial liberalisation, to be accompanied or preceded by institutional development.

Kaminsky and Reinhart (1999) in their empirical analysis of the 'twin' – banking and currency – crises find that financial liberalisation and/or increased access to international capital markets have played a major role in the first phase of such crises. Specifically, they examine the empirical regularities and the sources of 76 currency crises and 26 banking crises. They find that banking and currency crises are closely linked in the aftermath of financial liberalisation, with banking crises beginning before currencies collapse. Currency collapse exacerbates the problems in the banking system further, making the 'twin crises' a lot more severe than crises that occur in isolation. Financial liberalisation or increased access to international capital markets fuel the boom phase of the boom-bust cycle that precedes crises. This phase is associated with increased access to financing and the formation of asset price bubbles. The bust is attributed to overvalued exchange rates, declining exports, and a rising cost of credit, both of which create vulnerabilities in the financial system. The authors see the draconian reductions in reserve requirements that accompany financial liberalisation as one of the main factors that trigger lending booms. They also suggest that high interest rates result in increased risk taking, in line with earlier literature. The authors conclude by arguing that there is a compelling case for strength-ening banking regulation and supervision to 'allow countries to sail smoothly through the perilous waters of financial liberalization'. And that the Asian crisis of 1997–98, like earlier crises 'remind us that capital inflows can on occasion be too much of a good thing' (p. 496).

Stiglitz (2000) offers further insights into the Asian financial crisis of 1997–98, as well as on other recent crises, including Russia and Latin America, drawing on his experience as Chief Economist of the World Bank. He suggests that premature financial and capital market liberalisation – in the sense of not first putting in place an effective regulatory framework – was at the root of these crises. He also suggests that global economic arrangements are fundamentally weak. Stiglitz's analysis highlights some of the difficulties that the sequencing literature has in explaining the East Asian crisis, which ensued soon after these countries liberalised their financial systems. By conventional definitions, these countries had good economic policies and sound financial institutions. They did not have fiscal deficits, they enjoyed very high growth rates for long periods and their inflation rates were low. Their macroeconomic fundamentals were (or at least appeared to be) very strong. They were also thought to have reasonably respectable systems of banking regulation and supervi-sion (World Bank 1993). Stiglitz emphasises the destabilising influence of short-term capital flows in his analysis, arguing that 'there is not only no case for capital market liberalization, [   ] there is a fairly compelling case *against* full liberalization' (p. 1076). His analysis of why capital mar-ket liberalisation produces instability, not growth, identifies the follow-ing fallacy in the pro-liberalisation arguments, namely that 'financial and capital markets are essentially different from markets for ordinary good and services'. He points out that capital and financial markets are 'information-gathering' markets, which means that standard results for competitive markets derived from models with perfect information are not applicable. He also argues that capital flows are pro-cyclical, therefore the argument that the opening of capital markets would allow diversification and enhance stability is deficient. Finally, he challenges the notion that any destabilising effects emanating from capital account liberalisation are transitory, while the benefits are permanent, by alluding to a vast econometric literature,[9] which suggests that shocks to output can be long-lasting. The debate has now shifted, Stiglitz argues, to the type of interventions that might be necessary in order to stabilise short-term capital flows, rather than their desirability as such, with these actions being endorsed by the IMF itself.

Stiglitz (1999) elaborates on the weaknesses of the institutional financial architecture, which amplify the destabilising effects of financial liberalisation. Specifically, he highlights the role of the tight monetary policies recommended by the IMF to Asian crisis countries, in the aftermath of the crisis. These policies, which were aimed at stabilising exchange rates, had the opposite effect, Stiglitz argues. This was because high interest rates raised the probability of corporate bankruptcies. This, in turn, made international lenders more reluctant to renew or rollover their loans to highly leveraged East Asian corporations. This highly contentious issue was for a time at the centre of a major argument between Joseph Stiglitz and his counterpart at the IMF, Stanley Fischer. There have been several attempts to address this question, many of these by World Bank and IMF economists. These have resulted in two different sides of the argument. However, a major empirical issue that needs to be tackled when addressing this question is that in any reasonable economic model interest rates and exchange rates are simultaneously determined. Hence, identifying the effects of policy tightening is extremely difficult. Caporale *et al.* (forthcoming) exploit the heteroskedasticity properties in the relevant time-series for these variables in order to identify the system. Using a bivariate econometric model, they find that while tight monetary policy helped to defend the currencies concerned during tranquil periods, it had the opposite effect during the Asian crisis.

A number of authors continue, however, to propagate the benefits of financial liberalisation, focusing primarily on the effects of capital account liberalisation on stock returns and the cost of equity capital, using event studies. Bekaert and Harvey (2000), for example, measure how (capital account) liberalisation has affected the equity return-generating process in 20 emerging markets. They use a variety of methods to determine liberalisation dates, including official liberalisation dates, dates of first issues of country funds or American Depository Receipts (ADRs), which may signal a change in access to international capital markets, and econometric methods to identify structural breaks in the series. They find that dividend yields decline after liberalisations, but the effect is always less than 1 per cent on average. They also find that there is no significant impact of liberalisation on unconditional volatility. In a series of other studies (see Bekaert and Harvey (2003) for a review), they challenge Stiglitz's critique of capital account liberalisation, dubbing as 'odd' the whole discussion concerning increased volatility. They review evidence which suggests that the ratio of investment to GDP increases following liberalisation, while the ratio of consumption to GDP does not increase. Durham (2000), however, finds that many of the results in this literature are sensitive to (i) alternative liberalisation event dates and (ii) conditioning on other determinants of stock returns suggested by the literature on stock market anomalies.

Evidence from time-series studies on the effects of financial liberalisation on financial development is mixed. While it is quite common to find that the real interest rate has a small positive effect on financial development, there is also evidence to suggest that the direct effects of 'repressive' policies on financial development are sometimes positive and quite large. Demetriades and Luintel (2001) provide time-series evidence from South Korea – one of the fastest growing economies in the world – in which an index of financial repression is found to have a large positive effect on financial development. They explain this finding by arguing that the Korean banking system behaved like a cartel when interest rates were deregulated. Using a monopoly-bank model they show that mild repression of lending rates increases the amount of financial intermediation.[10] It is also worth noting that domestic financial liberalisation in South Korea was not followed by financial instability. The Korean crisis occurred well after domestic interest rates were liberalised; it followed the opening up of short-term capital flows, which destabilised the banking system. In sharp contrast to their findings on South Korea, in an earlier study of the Indian banking system Demetriades and Luintel (1997) find that financial repression had large negative effects on financial development, over and above the retarding influence of low real rates of interest. The difference in results is attributed as reflecting institutional differences and differences in the severity of repression. While mild financial repression may turn out to have positive effects under certain conditions, severe financial repression is likely to result in financial under-development not only due to large negative real interest rates, but also because of other disincentive effects.

The conclusion that we wish to draw from the above discussion is that the case for financial liberalisation promoting financial development and growth is far from proven. More often than not, financial liberalisation has been associated with severe bouts of financial and economic instability. Moreover, this association is not coincidental, it is well documented in the empirical literature and there are sound theoretical reasons to expect it, emanating from financial market imperfections. These imperfections and associated moral hazard problems can, nonetheless, be contained by a sound institutional infrastructure. An effective system of financial regulation and supervision would ensure that banks have adequate risk management systems and that bank shareholders are penalised if banks take excessive risks. Capital requirements that accurately reflect risk-taking by banks are one mechanism for achieving this. Increased transparency regarding banks' risk management systems, as well as increased disclosure concerning exposure to large risks, can help to increase market discipline on bank managers and may well contain such risk taking. Institutions such as contract enforcement and the rule-of-law also matter, since they have implications for the protection of investors' property rights,[11] which are crucial in determining investor confidence in the financial system, as well as for the effective implementation of financial regulation and supervision.

Government ownership of banks

Another form of government intervention in the financial system that may have implications for financial development and growth, and the one that has attracted considerable attention in recent literature, is government ownership of banks. Government owned (henceforth 'state') banks provide an effective means for politicians to influence the allocation of credit, allowing them to support firms and enterprises that may further their political interests. This view, known as the 'political view' of state banks, has a clear policy implication: privatising state banks can improve the efficiency of credit allocation and, consequently, can have positive effects on the quality and quantity of investment. Privatisation of government-owned banks is also likely to promote financial development, since private banks would be in a better position to attract funds into the banking system than inefficient state-owned banks.

La Porta *et al.* (2002) examine the relationship between government ownership of banks, financial development and economic growth using a cross-country data set. They find that government ownership of banks is negatively correlated with both financial development and growth. The estimated coefficients are quite large: they suggest that a 10 per cent reduction in the share of banking assets owned by the government is associated with an increase in growth by 0.25 per cent per annum.

Assuming that the relationships are causal, the clear policy implication is that the privatisation of government-owned banks would yield very large benefits in terms of additional financial development and economic growth. La Porta *et al.* also report bi-variate regressions that suggest that government ownership of banks is higher when institutional indicators, including property rights and government efficiency, are weak. This highlights the possibility of reverse causation: if government ownership of banks is the result of institutional weaknesses, then lower growth rates and financial under-development may be the result of the same institutional weaknesses. Thus, privatising state banks without addressing the institutional deficiencies that brought them about may not have the positive effects of growth predicted by La Porta *et al.* (2002).

Andrianova *et al.* (2003), henceforth ADS, provide further insights into the relationship between institutions, state banks and financial development using a locational model of banking in which there are two types of private banks – 'honest' and 'opportunistic' – and a state bank. Private banks are assumed to offer more competitive interest rates to depositors than the state bank. In the absence of deposit-contract enforcement problems they are therefore always preferred by depositors. However, if deposit contract enforcement is weak and the number of opportunistic banks is large, then some depositors would prefer to place their savings in the state bank, which offers a risk-free, albeit lower, rate of return. ADS derive three types of equilibria in their model: (i) a 'high' equilibrium, in which institutions are strong, only private banks exist and opportunistic banks honour their deposit contracts; (ii) an 'intermediate' equilibrium in which private banks and the state bank co-exist, in which opportunistic banks find it profitable to breach their deposit contracts, because of relatively weaker contract enforcement and (iii) a 'low' equilibrium, in which only the state bank exists, because contract enforcement is weak and the proportion of opportunistic banks is high. They show that in the intermediate region the proportion of state bank deposits declines when institutional quality increases. They also show that privatisation of the state bank in the low equilibrium region results in financial disintermediation (i.e. no private bank would emerge to fill the gap, as depositors will not trust it). ADS extend their model to allow for politically motivated subsidies to the state bank. They show that the higher the level of these subsidies, the smaller the 'high' equilibrium region. Thus, state banks may feature in equilibrium, even when there are no enforcement problems, because they are able to offer more competitive deposit rates than some private banks. ADS also provide a variety of empirical tests of the relationships predicted by their model, using data from 83 countries. They find that institutional quality indicators, including financial regulation, rule of law and disclosure rules, are much more strongly and robustly correlated to the share of state banks than proxies for politically driven subsidies. They conclude that the privatisation of state banks is, at best, unnecessary, since it is better to build institutions that foster the development of private banks and remove subsidies from state banks. At worse it is detrimental, since when institutions are weak it will almost certainly lead to financial disintermediation.

Legal factors

La Porta, Lopez-de-Silanes and Shleifer (1998), henceforth LLS, examine legal rules covering the protection of (minority) shareholders and creditors, and the quality of their enforcement in 49 countries. They draw on the work of comparative legal scholars, who classify national legal systems into major families of law, even though national differences remain within the same families. These scholars identify two broad legal traditions: civil law and common law. The civil law tradition, which is the oldest and most influential, originates in Roman law. It relies heavily on legal scholars to ascertain and formulate rules, statutes and comprehensive codes, as a primary means of settling disputes. Within the civil law tradition, there are three common families of laws: French, German and Scandinavian. The French Commercial code was written in 1807 and was 'exported' by Napoleon's armies to other countries in central Europe; eventually it was also exported to French colonies in Africa, Asia and the Caribbean. The German Commercial Code, written in 1897, had an influence in central and eastern Europe, Japan, Korea and Taiwan. The Scandinavian family, considered less a derivative of Roman law than French and German law, is considered sufficiently distinct from the other families by legal scholars, but has no influence outside the Nordic countries. The common law family, which originates in the law of England, is formed by judges in the resolution of specific disputes. Precedents from judicial decisions, not contributions by scholars, form the basis of common law. Common law has spread to the former British colonies, including the US, Canada, Australia, India, South Africa, Nigeria, Kenya, Ireland, Hong-Kong and other such countries. LLS find that common-law countries generally have the strongest shareholder protection, while civil-law countries have the weakest. Within the civil law group, French civil law countries offer the worst legal protection to shareholders. Similar results are found for the protection of creditors. French civil law countries compensate for weak investor protection, through mandatory dividend to shareholders and legal reserves. LLS also find that legal origins have a significant influence on legal enforcement, with common law countries and Scandinavian civil law countries having the best quality of law enforcement while French civil law countries having the worst. They do, however, find that the main determinant of legal enforcement is GDP per capita: richer countries have higher quality of law enforcement. Thus, rich countries within the French civil law group, such as France and Belgium, could well offer better law enforcement than poor common law countries.

La Porta, Lopez-de-Silanes, Shleifer and Vishny (1997) examine the influence of legal origins on financial development, mainly focusing on the development of capital markets. They use the same sample of 49 countries as La Porta *et al.* (1998) and find that French civil law countries have the least developed capital markets, especially as compared to common law countries. Their indicators of financial development include: stock market capitalisation/GNP, number of firms relative to population size, initial public offerings (IPOs) relative to population and debt/GDP. Their empirical findings suggest that civil law countries have lower levels of capital market development than common law countries. However, there are no significant differences in relation to banking sector development. In the regressions that use debt/GDP as the dependent variable, once the authors control for creditor rights, only the Scandinavian civil law dummy is negative and statistically significant at conventional levels.

What could be concluded from La Porta *et al.* (1997, 1998) is that civil-law countries, which seem to offer less legal protection to minority shareholders and creditors, have less developed capital markets and greater concentration of ownership at both industry and firm level. However, the implications of legal origins for the development of the banking system, which is perhaps the most important part of the financial system for many developing countries, are less clear cut. Indeed, Rajan and Zingales (2003) find that French civil code countries were no less financially developed in 1913 and 1929 than common law countries, and only started to lag behind after the Second World War. Moreover, legal traditions may themselves be determined by historical, cultural, socio-economic and political factors, so it is not easy to draw out any policy implications from these results. Legal origins are, in fact, highly correlated with a number of other institutional quality indicators, including the efficiency of the judiciary, bureaucratic quality, generalised level of trust and other such, so it is difficult to disentangle the effect of legal origins on financial development from those of other institutions (Zingales 2003). Finally, even if we were to accept that it is the legal system that determines financial development and ultimately growth, there remains the question of how to transform a legal system from the supposedly inferior French Civil Code to the supposedly superior Common Law one. There are, therefore, many unanswered questions as regards the relationship between law and finance, offering fertile ground for more research.

Political economy factors

In the light of the previous discussion of the positive relationship between finance and growth, it is, perhaps, surprising that some countries appear unable or unwilling to harness financial development. It may be plausible to conjecture that efficiency considerations – for example, limited scope for scale economies necessary for efficiency of financial markets – may preclude or slow down the development of financial markets in poorer countries. However, the retarded growth of the financial sector, or, indeed, the variability of the level of financial development in industrialised nations at the same stage of economic development, as documented in an important paper by Rajan and Zingales (2003), remains a puzzle.[12] The key to solving this puzzle, according to Rajan and Zingales, is the lack of political will, or capture of politicians by interest groups opposed to financial openness. In other words, financial development comes about only if the ruling elite welcomes it.

The economic argument constructed by Rajan and Zingales in support of this conjecture proceeds as follows. Openness to either international trade or international capital, while beneficial for the country's welfare in stimulating the development of its financial and product markets, breeds competition and thus threatens the rents of incumbents. When financial markets are underdeveloped, two types of incumbents enjoy rents and therefore may oppose openness and financial development. Established industrial firms, or 'industrial incumbents', are in a privileged position when obtaining external finance due to their reputational capital and their ability to provide collateral. Their rents are generated because new firms with profitable business projects have to team up with an industrial incumbent in order to obtain financing. 'Financial incumbents', in turn, capitalise on their informational advantage which stems from relation-based financing, and become monopolists in providing loans to firms when problems of poor disclosure and weak contract enforcement raise fixed costs of new financial entrants. Financial development improves transparency and enforcement thus reducing the barriers to entry and undermining not just the profits of incumbents who have to operate in a more competitive environment, but the source of their rents since entrants are able to effectively operate without any help from incumbents. Despite the benefits it brings (after all, better disclosure rules improve operating conditions for all – existing and new – firms), financial development threatens both the profits and the positional rents of the incumbents.

The way to remove incumbents' opposition to financial development, Rajan and Zingales argue, is to simultaneously open product and capital markets. More intense competition from foreign entrants, following liberalisation of either trade or capital flows alone, will only intensify incumbents' opposition to financial development. For example, trade liberalisation under protected capital markets would reduce industrial incumbents' competitiveness and profits and thus increase their demand for cheaper and larger loans to defend their domestic market position. Their opposition to financial development – which, if it comes about, would further undermine incumbents' competitiveness, this time vis-à-vis the domestic entrants – would now be even stronger. Incumbent financiers' resistance to financial development, when capital markets are protected while product markets are liberalised, is likely to remain the same: after all, relation-based financing favours dealing with existing large clients and these are incumbent industrialists. Similarly, protected product markets in combination with free international capital flows, create a stronger resistance to financial development from the incumbent financiers (who are forced now to compete for their best and largest industrial clients with foreign financial institutions) while leaving industrial incumbents' incentives for financial development unchanged (there is little use in additional external finance available from tapping international capital markets when the economy is closed to trade). In contrast, trade liberalisation accompanied by freeing of capital flows, forces the incumbent industrialists and financiers to make the best of the liberalised markets in order to cope with the competitive pressure from foreign and domestic entrants. Lower profits of the industrial incumbents and their greater need for external finance now force them to explore possibilities of tapping the international capital markets. If unsuccessful, these industrialists would in fact now support financial innovations that aid greater transparency and thus improve their own access to finance. Incumbent financiers, being forced to lose some of their best clients to foreign competition and at the same time to accept lower profitability of their remaining clientele, are now forced to seek new lending opportunities among young industrial firms which are less known and possibly more risky. Financing these new firms is likely to be unattractive to foreign financiers, but would create incentives for domestic incumbent financiers to support the improvements in, and development of, domestic financial markets. In sum, trade and capital liberalisation aligns the interests of industrial and financial incumbents with those of the rest of the economy and financial development becomes possible.

The empirical evidence provided by Rajan and Zingales focuses on a variety of relationships which suggest that the combination of trade and capital openness are, indeed, correlated with greater financial development. Their findings, while consistent with their conceptual arguments, provide, at best, indirect evidence about the importance played by interest-group politics in financial development. Moreover, their sample of countries, driven by data availability in the pre-Second World War period, is rather limited and in some of the regressions the sample size is as low as 17 observations. Thus, while the ideas in Rajan and Zingales (2003) by themselves undoubtedly advance our understanding of political economy factors, the empirical evidence that is provided is less convincing, which clearly leaves ample scope for further empirical research. Further questions that need to be addressed, both theoretically and empirically, include the following. How do special interest groups come into existence? What institutions and policies – 'political preconditions' for institutions and financial development – moderate the influence of interest groups? If the most effective way to curb incumbents' opposition to financial development is by means of increased openness and competitiveness, then what is the best combination of policies that could pave the way for rapid institutional development? What is the role of the state for shaping the institutional infrastructure in a way that limits the power of the interest groups and the scope for capture of the government policies by special interests? These are all exciting questions that await researchers' attention.

4 Concluding remarks

It is now widely acknowledged that institutions have a first-order effect on financial development and growth, and that the strength of these institutions may determine the success or failure of policies like bank privatisation and financial liberalisation. Financial regulation, the legal system and related institutions, by enhancing investor confidence, play a key role in the functioning of financial markets and institutions, and seem, therefore, to hold the key to both financial development and economic growth. The critical issue, now at the frontier of the literature, is to advance our understanding of the obstacles to financial development, including institutional, legal and political economy constraints. There is no doubt that, while we now know a lot more about financial development than we did even ten years ago, pushing the frontier further will require new and imaginative, possibly trans-disciplinary, approaches.

Notes

1. This is sometimes known as the 'Modigliani-Miller' theorem, which states that the capital structure of the firm is irrelevant. Principal-agent approach and incomplete contracts (for a recent survey, see Hart (2001)), which fall outside of the fold of neoclassical economics but within the 'theory of the firm' part of modern economics, help explain why the Modigliani-Miller neutrality result is invalidated in reality.
2. The first theorem of welfare economics is the twentieth-century analogue of Adam Smith's 'invisible hand': the notion that free markets will achieve a socially optimal outcome if left to their own devices.
3. This literature can be traced back to Akerlof's analysis of the 'lemons' problem in the second hand car market (1970). Akerlof showed that the market can collapse as a result of adverse selection. One of the most important earlier applications to finance is the paper by Stiglitz and Weiss (1981), which explains how adverse selection in the credit market can result in arbitrary rationing of credit among identical borrowers.
4. See Fry (1995) for an extensive survey of earlier literature. There are, however, important exceptions, for example, De Gregorio and Guidotti (1995), on which see below.
5. Rousseau and Wachtel (2001), for example, report that in high inflation countries the effect of finance on growth weakens.
6. Ideally, one would need at least 100 years of data to carry out such tests with a high degree of confidence. However, such data are available for very few countries and, even then, because of changing statistical procedures may not be strictly comparable across time. It is nonetheless now possible to use quarterly data for many developing countries for 25 years or more, which means that samples could exceed 100 observations, increasing the reliability of estimates.
7. Zhu, Ash and Pollin (2002) show that the Levine-Zervos results are driven by the 'East-Asian tigers': once these countries are excluded from the sample or their influence is controlled statistically, the main result that stock market liquidity is positively associated with long-run economic growth becomes statistically insignificant.
8. Broadly speaking, dynamic heterogeneity refers to a situation in which different countries exhibit different business cycle characteristics, such as different speeds of adjustment to shocks.

9. For a flavour of this literature, known as 'unit root literature', see, for example, Durlauf (1989).

10. An alternative explanation why 'repressive' policies, such as deposit rate ceilings, may appear to have a positive effect on financial development is that they may help to reduce moral hazard behaviour by banks, which may in turn reduce the riskiness of bank deposits. See, for example, Arestis and Demetriades (1997) or Hellmann *et al.* (2000).

11. Knack and Keefer (1995), Mauro (1995), Svensson (1998) and Acemoglu *et al.* (2001) provide macroeconomic evidence that suggests a negative impact of insecure property rights on economic growth and investment. Using survey data from transition economies, Johnson *et al.* (2002) find that weak property rights dominate limited access to external finance as a constraint on entrepreneurs' investment decisions.

12. Rajan and Zingales (2003) find that 'by most measures, countries were more financially developed in 1913 than in 1980 and only recently have they surpassed their 1913 levels'.

References

Acemoglu, D., Johnson, S., and Robinson, J. (2001), 'The Colonial origins of comparative development: An empirical investigation', *American Economic Review* 91 (5): 1369–1401.

Akerlof, G. (1970), 'The market for "Lemons": Quality uncertainty and the market Mechanism', *Quarterly Journal of Economics* 84, 488–500.

Andrianova, S., Demetriades, P.O., and Shortland, A. (2002 updated September 2003), 'State banks, institutions and financial development'. Discussion Paper in Economics, Leicester University, 02/13.

Arestis, P. and Demetriades, P.O., 'Financial development and economic growth: Assessing the evidence', *Economic Journal*, May 1997, 107, 783–99.

—— and —— (1999), 'Financial liberalization: The experience of developing economies', *Eastern Economic Journal* 25 (4): 441–57.

——, ——, and Luintel, K.B. (2001), 'Financial development and economic growth: The role of stock markets', *Journal of Money, Credit, and Banking* 33 (1): 16–41.

Beck, T. and Levine, R. 'Stock markets, banks, and growth: Panel evidence', *Journal of Banking and Finance*, March 2004, 28 (3): 423–42.

Bekaert, G. and Harvey, C. (2000), 'Foreign speculators and emerging equity markets', *Journal of Finance* 55, 565–614.

—— and —— (2003), 'Emerging markets finance', *Journal of Empirical Finance* 10, 3–55.

Bencivenga, V.R. and Smith, B.D. (2000), 'Financial intermediation and endogenous growth', *Review of Economic Studies* 58, 195–209.

Caporale, G.M., Cipollini, A., and Demetriades, P.O. 'Monetary policy and the exchange rate during the asian crisis: Identification through heteroskedasticity', *Journal of International Money and Finance*, forthcoming.

De Gregorio, J. and Guidotti, P. (1995), 'Financial development and economic growth', *World Development* 23 (3): 433–48.

Demetriades, P.O. and Luintel, K.B. (1997), 'The direct costs of financial repression: Evidence from India', *Review of Economics and Statistics* 79 (2): 311–20.

Demetriades, P.O. and Luintel, K.B. (2001), 'Financial restraints in the South Korean miracle', *Journal of Development Economics* 64 (2): 459–79.
—— and Hussein, K. (1996), 'Does financial development cause economic growth? Time-series evidence from 16 countries', *Journal of Development Economics* 51, 387–411.
Demirgüç-Kunt, A. and Detragiache, E. 'Financial liberalization and financial fragility', in Pleskovic, B. and Stiglitz, J. (eds), *Annual World Bank Conference on Development Economics 1998*, Washington DC: World Bank: Reuters, Pearson Education, 1999, pp. 303–31.
Diaz-Alejandro, C. (1985), 'Good-bye financial repression, hello financial crash', *Journal of Development Economics* 19 (1): 1–24.
Durham, J.B. (2000), 'Emerging stock market liberalization, total returns, and real effects: Some sensitivity analyses', Queen Elizabeth House, University of Oxford, Working paper No. 48.
Durlauf, S. (1989), 'Output persistence, economic structure, and the choice of stabilization Policy', *Brookings Papers on Economic Activity* 2, 69–137.
Fry, M.J. (1995), *Money, Interest and Banking in Economic Development*, 2nd edition. Baltimore: Johns Hopkins University Press.
Hart, O. (2001), 'Financial contracting', *Journal of Economic Literature* 39 (4).
Hellmann, T.F., Murdock, K.C., and Stiglitz, J.E. (2000), 'Liberalization, moral hazard in banking, and prudential regulation: Are capital requirements enough?', *American Economic Review* 90 (1): 147–65.
Johnson, S., McMillan, J., and Woodruff, C. (2002), 'Property rights and finance', *American Economic Review* 92 (5): 1335–56.
Kaminsky, G.L. and Reinhart, C.M. (1999), 'The twin crises: The causes of banking and balance-of-payments problems', *American Economic Review* 89 (3): 473–500.
King, R.G. and Levine, R. (1993), 'Finance and growth: Schumpeter might be right', *Quarterly Journal of Economics* 108, 717–37.
Knack, S. and Keefer, P. (1995), 'Institutions and economic performance', *Economics and Politics* 7 (3): 207–28.
La Porta, R., Lopez-de-Silanes, F., Shleifer, A., and Vishny, R. (1997), 'Legal determinants of external finance', *Journal of Finance* 52, 1131–50.
——, ——, and —— (1998), 'Law and finance', *Journal of Political Economy* 106 (6): 1113–55.
——, ——, and —— (2002), 'Government ownership of banks', *Journal of Finance* 57 (1): 265–301.
Levine, R. (2003), 'More on finance and growth: More finance, more growth?', *Federal Reserve Bank of St. Louis Review* 85 (4): 31–46.
—— and Zervos, S. (1998), 'Stock markets, banks and economic growth', *American Economic Review* 88, 537–58.
Llewellyn, D. (1999), 'The economic rationale for financial regulation', Financial Services Authority Occasional Paper # 1.
Mauro, P. (1995), 'Corruption and growth', *Quarterly Journal of Economics* 110 (3): 681–712.
McKinnon, R.I. (1973), *Money and Capital in Economic Development*, Washington, DC: Brookings Institution.
—— (1991), *The Order of Economic Liberalization: Financial Control in the Transition to a Market Economy*, Baltimore: Johns Hopkins University Press.

Odedokun, M.O. (1996), 'Alternative econometric approaches for analyzing the role of the financial sector in economic growth: Time series evidence from LDC's', *Journal of Development Economics* 50 (1): 119–46.

Pesaran, M.H. and Smith, R.P. (1995), 'Estimating long-run relationships from dynamic heterogeneous panels', *Journal of Econometrics* 68, 79–113.

Rajan, R. and Zingales, L. (2003), 'The great reversals: The politics of financial development in the 20th century', *Journal of Financial Economics* 69 (1): 5–50.

Rioja, F. and Valev, N., 'Does one size fit all?: A re-examination of the finance and growth relationship', *Journal of Development Economics*, forthcoming.

Rousseau, P.L. and Wachtel, P. (2001), 'Inflation, financial development and growth', in Negishi, T., Ramachandran, R., and Mino, K. (eds), *Economic Theory, Dynamics and Markets: Essays in Honor of Ryuzo Sato*, Boston: Kluwer, pp. 309–24.

Shaw, E.S. (1973), *Financial Deepening in Economic Development*, New York: Oxford University Press.

Singh, A. (1997), 'Stock markets, financial liberalisation and economic development', *Economic Journal* 107, 771–82.

Stiglitz, J. (1999), 'Interest rates, risk, and imperfect markets: Puzzles and policies', *Oxford Review of Economic Policy* 15 (2): 59–76.

—— (2000), 'Capital market liberalization, economic growth and instability', *World Development* 28 (6): 1075–86.

—— and Weiss, A. (1981), 'Credit rationing in markets with imperfect information', *American Economic Review* 71 (3): 393–410.

Svensson, J. (1998), 'Investment, property rights and political instability', *European Economic Review* 42 (7): 1317–42.

Villanueva, D. and Mirakhor, A. (1990), 'Strategies for financial reforms: interest rate policies, stabilization, and bank supervision in developing countries', *IMF Staff Papers* 37 (3): 509–36.

World Bank (1993), *The East Asian Miracle*, Oxford: Oxford University Press.

Zhu, A., Ash, M., and Pollin, R. (2002), 'Stock market liquidity and economic growth: A critical appraisal of the Levine-Zervos Model', University of Massachusetts at Amherst, Political Economy Research Institute, Working Paper # 47.

Zingales, L. (2003), 'The weak links', *Federal Reserve Bank of St. Louis Review* 85 (4): 47–52.

3
Competition in the Financial Sector and Growth: A Cross-Country Perspective

*Stijn Claessens and Luc Laeven**

1 Introduction

Competition in the financial sector matters for a number of reasons. As in other industries, the degree of competition in the financial sector can affect the efficiency of the production of financial services. Also, again as in other industries, it can affect the quality of financial products and the degree of innovation in the sector. Specific to the financial sector is the link between competition and stability that has long been recognized in theoretical and empirical research and, most importantly, in the actual conduct of prudential policy towards banks. Importantly, it has also been shown, theoretically as well as empirically, that the degree of competition in the financial sector can effect the access of firms and households to financial services and external financing. The direction of the latter relationship is, however, unclear. Less competitive systems may lead to more access to external financing since banks are more inclined to invest in information acquisition and relationships with borrowers. When banking systems are less competitive, however, hold-up problems may lead borrowers to be less willing to enter such relationships. Furthermore, less competitive banking systems can be more costly and exhibit a lower quality of services thus providing less financing and encouraging less growth. These effects may further vary by the degree of a country's financial sector development.

Although some of these relationships between competition and banking system performance have been analyzed in the theoretical literature and in some country studies, cross-country empirical research on the issue of and effects of competition in banking systems is still at an early stage. While there have been a number of recent cross-country studies on the effects of banking structure on stability, access to financing and growth, the interpretation of this empirical work is not always clear since some theoretical issues have not always been taken into account. In particular, the long-existing theory of industrial organization has shown that the competitiveness of an industry cannot be measured by market structure indicators alone (such as the number of institutions, Herfindahl or other concentration indexes, ownership structures, such as the degree of foreign or state ownership). Rather, testing for the degree of effective competition needs a structural, contestability approach. To date, however, most papers have not investigated the degree of competition in the banking system using a specific structural model. As such, the results on the effect of market structure on banking system performance, firm financing and growth could reflect factors other than competition. Furthermore, there have been rapid changes in financial services industries worldwide, such as increased substitutability among various types of financial services, more inter-industry competition, greater securitization and larger use of capital markets' instruments and rapid deregulation, making the structure of banking markets a potentially less relevant measure of market conduct.

A more industrial organization-based approach to assessing the degree of competition in the financial sector allows one to overcome the concerns raised by the contestability literature. An additional measure will also allow a comparison of results to other approaches of measuring the impact of competition using banking system structures. In an earlier paper, Claessens and Laeven (2004), applied such a structural competition test (the Panzar-Rosse (1987) methodology) to 50 countries' banking systems. In addition to documenting this measure of competition for a large cross section of countries, the market structure, the role of entry and activity regulations and the role of foreign banks in affecting the competitive conditions of banking systems were analyzed. The finding was that besides the share of foreign banks, measures of banking system structure did not provide any indication of markets' competitiveness, at least not as expected (we actually found that more concentrated systems were more competitive). In this chapter, this measure of the degree of competition in countries' banking systems to economic growth is related. One manner of clarifying the theoretically ambiguous relationships between banking system competition and the provision of external financing is by investigating how the degree of competition affects the growth in value added of sectors that vary in their external financial dependence. This can be done using the empirical set up developed by Rajan and Zingales (1998, RZ hereafter). RZ assess the relationship between financial development and growth using sectoral growth data for a large sample of countries. This methodology has been used in a number of tests, for example, to assess the impact of banking system concentration, the development of trade finance and the strength of property rights on industrial growth.[1] This chapter further adopts the methodology to explore the relationships between banking system competition and growth.

We find that our competitiveness measure is negatively associated with countries' growth, suggesting that less competitive banking systems are better at providing financing to financially dependent firms. We find evidence, however, that the effects of banking system competitiveness on growth vary with the level of countries' financial sector development. In particular, we find that in only countries with less developed financial systems do financially dependent industries grow faster if the financial system is less competitive while in more developed financial systems they grow faster when the financial system is more competitive. Our findings suggest that the trade-off between competition and firm access to external financing arises only in financially less developed countries; in these countries, less competition may be desirable since this leads banks to provide more financing to informationally more opaque borrowers. Yet, in more developed financial systems, more competition may allow for more growth.

The results come with some caveats. We did not control for all other factors that have been found to affect financial sector development. Our results may, for example, capture the fact that less developed financial systems have worse property rights, making it harder to lend if competition is high, or that less developed financial markets are informationally more opaque. While less competition may then be a second best response to enhancing access to firm external financing, the first best response may be to improve property rights and transparency while allowing for more competition. Furthermore, it might be the case that some market power increases financial stability although this effect is not necessarily captured in the industrial growth measure we use since our sample is relatively short. Regardless, the results suggest that competition policy in the financial sector is complicated and can not be evaluated independently from the overall development of the financial system.

In this chapter, Section 1 provides a review of related literature on the theoretical effects of competition in the financial sector, on measuring competition in general and in the financial sector specifically and on the effects of market structure on economic outcomes. In Section 2, the methodology used to measure the degree of competition in the banking market of a particular country and the empirical setup we use for the growth regressions is discussed and the data used in this chapter is presented. The main empirical results regarding banking system competition and industrial growth are provided in Section 3. The conclusions are presented in Section 4.

2 Literature review

Several, related strands of literature are reviewed here. To begin, a short review of the growing theoretical literature on the effects of competition in the financial sector is presented. Next, we briefly review the general theory on measuring competition and examine some of the empirical papers that have applied structural competition tests to the financial sector. Finally, we review the empirical literature that has investigated the relationships between structural and regulatory factors and performance and access to financing and growth, all as they relate to the (competitive) structure of the banking systems, although these papers have mostly not attempted to test a specific structural competition model.

Theory on effects of competition in finance

As a first-order effect, one would expect increased competition in the financial sector to lead to lower costs and enhanced efficiency of financial intermediation, greater product innovation and improved quality. One channel of how one could expect more competitive banking systems to be associated with higher growth is that competition leads to lower costs of financial intermediation, similar to other industries. This could be expected even though financial services have some special properties. In a theoretical model, Besanko and Thakor (1992), for example, analyze the allocational consequences of the relaxing of entry barriers and find, even allowing for the fact that financial products are heterogeneous, that equilibrium loan rates decline and deposit interest rates increase, even when allowing for differentiated competition. In turn, by lowering the costs of financial intermediation and thus lowering the cost of capital for non-financial firms, more competitive banking systems would lead to higher growth rates.

Recent research, however, has highlighted that the relationships between competition and banking system performance, access to financing, technology and growth are more complex. Market power in banking may be, to a degree, beneficial for access to financing. A bank and a borrower establish relationships to overcome information problems and to facilitate lending over time; charging lower rates initially, when firms are young and risky, and higher rates later, when firms are less risky, to recover costs. The higher its market power, the more likely the bank invests in information gathering about firms, especially to information-ally opaque firms, and the more likely it provides credit (Rajan 1992). Indeed, Petersen and Rajan (1995) find, for the United States, that loan rates are lower for young firms and higher for old firms in more concentrated banking markets than for comparable firms in more competitive markets. Importantly, they also find a greater availability of credit for firms in more concentrated markets. The implication is that more competition can undermine the incentives of banks to invest in a relationship. As banking markets are deregulated and become more competitive, that would imply that access to financing could decline.

Yet, such a relationship between a bank and a borrower involves sunk costs and leads to a hold-up problem: the incumbent bank has more information about the borrower than its competitors do. This increases the switching costs for the borrower, especially for better quality borrowers, since they will face adverse conditions when trying to look for financing from another bank (i.e., they will be perceived as a poor credit). Borrowers will be more willing to enter a relationship with a bank if they are less likely to be subject to a hold-up problem, for example, when the market for external financing is more competitive. As such, more competitive markets may see greater access. On the bank side, if faced with a less competitive market, the bank may have less of an incentive to make an (or additional) investment in a relationship as the bank knows that the borrower is (more) captive anyway. With less investment in information acquisition, the supply of loans may be less with less competitive markets. The net effect of these hold-up and other problems is that the degree of lending by banks can rather increase with the overall competitive environment. Boot and Thakor (2000) show, for example, that increased interbank competition may induce banks to make not less but more relationship loans. There can also be effects from the type of information problem back to the scope for potential competition; that is, competition may be endogenous. Dell'Ariccia *et al.* (1999), for example, show that the presence of information asymmetries in lending relationships can become a barrier to entry in the banking system.

These benefits and gains from closer bank–firm relationships and less competition can relate to the general development of the financial system and the economic benefits of internal financial markets (among firms) compared to external financial markets. The benefits and gains of internal markets have been discussed as far back as Coase (1960) and more recently by Williamson (1985). They highlight the role organizations play in reducing transaction costs in various markets. This also applies to financial markets. In particular, when frictions in financial markets are severe, internal financial markets and close relationships can provide benefits in allocating capital more efficiently (Stein, 1997). This role of internal markets can include providing funds to firms that have growth potential but which are financially constrained or in temporary financial distress. One can expect these types of internal markets and informal relationships to be more important when countries and their financial systems are less developed. For more developed countries, external financial markets are more important thus making it imperative to have a more competitive financial system. This, in turn, suggests that the effects of competition in the financial system can vary by a country's financial sector development.

Another channel where competition could be expected to be important for financial services provision would be through the acquisition of technology, thereby increasing the access to and improving the terms of external financing. On one hand, with less competitive market structures, banks might be more willing to invest in technology which, in turn, can help extend the set of borrowers against which banks can lend. On the other hand, technological progress can increase competition from other banks and non-bank financial institutions by lowering production or distribution costs for all financial services providers. With a more competitive structure of existing markets, incumbent financial services providers may be more inclined to invest in technological progress to maintain market share. Again, the net of these effects is unclear. Endogenizing competition, Hauswald and Marquez (2003), for example, analyze the impact of technological progress on competition in financial services. While better information technology may lead to improved information processing and lower costs of financial intermediation, it may also lead to lower costs of information or even free access to information. Better access to information can decrease interest rates, however, Hauswald and Marquez (2003) show that an improved ability to process information can increase interest rates. The net effects on lending rates and access to financing hinge on the overall effect ascribed to technological progress and the existing market structures.

Technological progress can also affect market structures. Marquez (2002) analyzes how information generated through the process of lending can impact the structure of the banking industry to the extent that this information is proprietary to the banks. He shows that, in markets where new entrants have specific expertise in evaluating credit risks or in markets with high borrower turnover, entry should be easier so that incumbents' bank information advantages are reduced. Again, the preferred market structure in terms of access may depend upon the degree of information asymmetries and the ownership and control structures for information.

Apart from its effects on access, terms of financing and market structures, the relationships between competition and stability are not obvious. Many academics and especially policy makers have stressed the importance of franchise value for banks in maintaining incentives for prudent behavior. In turn, this has led banking system regulators to carefully balance entry and exit. This has often been, however, a static view. Perotti and Suarez (2002), for example, draw attention to the importance of the dynamic pattern of entry and exit regulation in driving current actions of banks. They show in a formal model that the behavior of banks today will be affected by both current and future concentration and the degree to which authorities will allow for a contestable system in the future. In a dynamic model, current concentration does not necessarily reduce risky lending but an expected increase in future market concentration can make banks choose to pursue safer lending today. More generally, there may not be a tradeoff between stability and increased competition, in contrast to what is often argued by many policy makers. This has been shown, among others, by Allen and Gale (2000) and reviewed recently by Allen and Gale (2004). Furthermore, Allen and Gale (1998) show that banking system crises, possibly related to the degree of competition, are not necessarily harmful for growth.

In the end, the view that competition in banking is unambiguously good for growth is more naive than in other industries and vigorous rivalry may not be the first-best for financial sector performance. (For a recent, broader review of the theoretical literature on competition and banking see Vives 2001.) Deregulation and technological progress would not necessarily improve financial sector competitiveness and lead to more or better access to external financing and more growth. Nor would a more restrictive competition environment necessarily lead to more financial system stability and growth. Regardless of these theoretical ambiguities on the effects of competition on financial sector functioning, one needs a measure of the effective degree of competition in a banking system to empirically analyze the validity of any of these theoretical predictions. Therefore, we next review the general theory on empirical testing for competition and its application to banking. We then review the empirical literature on the relationship between market structure and economic outcomes although the papers may not use the measure of competition suggested by the industrial organization literature to assess these effects.

Competition testing: theory and empirical results for banking systems

The general contestability literature has suggested specific ways on how to go about testing for the degree of competition. Klein (1971), Baumol *et al.* (1982) were the first to develop a formal theory of contestable markets. They draw attention to the fact that there are several sets of conditions that can yield competitive outcomes, even in concentrated systems. Conversely, they showed that collusive actions could be sustained even in the presence of many firms. Their work has spanned a large empirical literature covering many industries.

Two types of empirical tests for competition can be distinguished since they have been applied to financial sector (and other industries). The model of Bresnahan (1982) and Lau (1982), as expanded in Bresnahan (1989), uses the condition of general market equilibrium. (i) The basic idea is that profit-maximizing firms in equilibrium will choose prices and quantities such that marginal costs equal their (perceived) marginal revenue, which coincides with the demand price under perfect competition or with the industry's marginal revenue under perfect collusion. The alternative approach is Rosse and Panzar (1977), expanded by Panzar and Rosse (1982) and Panzar and Rosse (1987). This methodology uses firm (or bank)-level data. It investigates the extent to which a change in factor input prices is reflected in (equilibrium) revenues earned by a specific bank. Under perfect competition, an increase in input prices raises both marginal costs and total revenues by the same amount as the rise in costs. Under a monopoly, an increase in input prices will increase marginal costs, reduce equilibrium output and, consequently, reduce total revenues.

A number of papers have applied either the Bresnahan or the Panzar and Rosse (PR) methodology to the issue of competition in the financial sector, although mostly specific to the banking system.[2] One of the first papers using the Bresnahan methodology for banks is by Shaffer (1989). He applies the methodology to a sample of U.S. banks and finds results that strongly reject collusive conduct but are consistent with perfect competition. Using the same model, Shaffer (1993) studies the competition conditions in Canada and finds that the Canadian banking system was competitive over the period 1965–89 although being relatively concentrated. He also finds that the degree of competition in Canada was generally stable following regulatory changes in 1980. Gruben and McComb (2003) applied the Bresnahan methodology to Mexico before 1995 and found that the Mexican banking system was super-competitive; that is, marginal prices were set below marginal costs. One of the few studies that uses the Bresnahan model with a relatively large sample of countries is Shaffer (2001). For 15 countries in North America, Europe and Asia during 1979–91, he finds significant market power in five markets and excess capacity in one market. Estimates were consistent with either contestability or Cournot type oligopoly in most of these countries, while five countries were significantly more competitive than Cournot. Since the data refer to the period before the European single banking license was adopted, the result may, however, not be reflective of the current situation.

Shaffer (1982) was also one of the first to apply the PR model to banks. He estimated it for New York banks using data for 1979 and found monopolistic competition. Nathan and Neave (1989) study Canadian banks using the PR methodology. The results for Canada are consistent with the results of Shaffer (1989) using the Bresnahan methodology in that they can also reject monopoly power for the Canadian banking system. (Nathan and Neave found perfect competition for 1982 and monopolistic competition for 1983–84.) Some other studies have applied the PR methodology to some non-North American and non-European banking systems. For Japan, for example, Molyneux *et al.* (1996) find evidence of a monopoly situation in 1986–88.

A number of papers have applied the PR methodology to European banking systems. These papers include Molyneux *et al.* (1994), Vesala (1995), Molyneux *et al.* (1996), Coccorese (1998), Bikker and Groeneveld (2000), Bikker and Haaf (2001), De Bandt and Davis (2000) and Hempel (2002). The countries covered, the time periods and some of the assumptions used vary between the studies. Although the findings varied somewhat, generally, the papers reject both perfect collusion as well as perfect competition and mostly find evidence of monopolistic competition. (Bikker and Haaf (2001) summarize the results of some ten studies.) Bikker and Groeneveld (2000), for example, find monopolistic competition in all of the 15 EU-countries they study.

To date, tests on the competitiveness of banking systems for developing countries and transition economies using these models are few. Using the PR approach, Belaisch (2003) finds evidence of a non-monopolistic market structure in Brazil. Gelos and Roldos (2002) analyze a number of banking markets using the PR methodology, including those in some developing countries. They report that overall banking markets in their sample of eight European and Latin American countries have not become less competitive although concentration has increased. They conclude that lowered barriers to entry, such as allowing increased entry by foreign banks, appeared to have prevented a decline in competitive pressures associated with consolidation. Levy *et al.* (2003) find similar results using the PR methodology for their sample of Latin America countries and find that the process of consolidation in the 1990s, if anything, may have led to more, rather than less, competition. Philippatos and Yildirim (2002) investigate 14 Central and Eastern European banking systems using bank-level data and the PR methodology. They find, except for Latvia, Macedonia and Lithuania, that these banking systems can neither be characterized as perfectly competitive nor monopolistic. They also conclude that large banks in transition economies operate in a relatively more competitive environment compared to small banks.

A broad cross-country study using the PR methodology is that by Claessens and Laeven (2004). Using bank-level data, they estimate the extent to which changes in input prices are reflected in revenues earned by specific banks in 50 countries' banking systems. They then relate this competitiveness measure to indicators of countries' banking system structures and regulatory regimes. They find systems with greater foreign bank entry, and fewer entry and activity restrictions to be more competitive. Importantly, and consistent with some of the other studies, they find no evidence that their competitiveness measure negatively relates to banking system concentration or number of banks in the market. Their findings suggest that measures of market structures do not translate in measure of effective competition, consistent with contestability determining effective competition.

Differences between assessments of the competitiveness of banking systems using the Bresnahan and the PR methodologies appear small, as already noted for Canada. In a broad comparison, Bikker and Haaf (2001) use the PR model and the Bresnahan model, with the latter applied to the market for deposit and loan facilities. They first apply the PR model to 17 European and six non-European (US, Japan, Korea, New Zealand and Canada) markets. They reject both perfect competition and perfect cartel for all markets when including all banks, but cannot reject perfect collusion for Australia and Greece when analyzing only small banks. They find some evidence that smaller banks operate in less competitive environments than larger banks do, suggesting that local markets are less competitive than national or international markets are. They also find that in general, competition appears to be less in non-European countries. Using the Bresnahan model for nine EU-countries in their sample of 17 EU-countries, they find that the markets for deposit and loan facilities are probably highly competitive, a result in line with their results of the PR model, suggesting that the two methodologies lead to similar assessments.

Empirical competition tests using other than the Bresnahan and PR models have also been conducted, although few so far. Kessidis (1991) has developed a model of contestability which focuses on sunk costs. A recent study using this model on the EU-banking markets is Corvoisier and Gropp (2002). They focus on the effects of advances in information technology, given its effects on sunk costs, on competition. They find evidence for an increase in contestability in deposit markets and more moderate effects for loan markets, which they conjecture is because technology has reduced sunk costs more in deposit than in loan markets.

General empirical studies on the effects of banking system structure on banking system performance and economic growth

A number of papers have investigated the effects of market structure, as presumed to relate to competitive conditions in banking systems. The focus of these papers has been varied, but has included trying to establish the impact of competition (or lack thereof) on bank efficiency, firm access to financing, stability and growth. While many of these papers are not formal structure–performance–conduct tests, their results have been interpreted as indicative of the degree of competition and/or its causes and consequences in the financial sector.

For the United States and some other markets, there is some empirical evidence regarding the effects of concentration in the financial system on access to and costs of external financing and growth. For the United States, Petersen and Rajan (1995) offer empirical evidence that firms are less credit constrained and face cheaper credit the more concentrated the credit market is. Collender and Shaffer (2001) document how in the United States, non-metropolitan employment grew faster in areas where there was a more concentrated initial banking structure and where there were locally owned bank offices. Degryse and Ongena (2002) show in the case of Belgium that loan rates increase in the distance between the firm and competing banks and decrease in the distance from the lender and the firm, suggesting that increased distance relaxes price competition.

In many countries, changes in market structures have been driven by consolidation. The effect of consolidation on bank lending terms and access has been a much-researched topic and is too large a literature to review here. (Gilbert (1984) reviews the earlier studies, while Berger, Demsetz and Strahan (1999) review more recent studies on the effects of consolidation, mainly for the United States.) A very recent, but more policy-oriented review on the effects of consolidation is G-10 (2001). It concluded that higher concentration in banking markets may lead to less favorable conditions for consumers, especially in markets for small business loans, retail deposits and payment services, but results were weaker for the 1990s than for the previous decade. It also mentioned that studies on small business lending for Italy and the United States suggest that banks reduce the percentage of their portfolio invested in small business loans after consolidation. Other banks and new entrants, however, tend to offset the reduction in the supply of credit, in both the United States and Italy, although for Italy a shift away from the worst borrowers did exist.

More recently, technological progress and its effects on the banking industry have been much researched. Berger (2003) reviews this literature and finds improvements in costs and lending capacity as well as consumer benefits. The research also suggests significant overall productivity increases in terms of improved quality and variety of banking services and it appears that technological progress may have helped facilitate consolidation. The effects of technology on access are unclear. Research suggests that banks have been able to make small business loans at greater distances (Petersen and Rajan, 1995) and that affiliate banks suffered fewer profit and cost diseconomies associated with the distance to headquarters in recent years. At the same time, there is some evidence that, in part due to technology and more formal internal management, banks have relied less on soft information, making for less access to financing by small firms (Berger, Miller, Petersen, Rajan and Scharfstein, 2002).

Many of these studies pertain to developed countries and are mostly not of a cross-country nature. There are a number of papers, however, investigating across countries the effects of specific structures or other factors presumed to relate to the competitive environment on banking performance. Claessens *et al.* (2001) investigate the role of foreign banks in a cross-country study and show that entry by foreign banks makes domestic banking systems more efficient by reducing their margins. There is also ample evidence indicating that those countries with a larger share of state ownership in banking experience worse outcomes on average. Barth Caprio and Levine (2004) and La Porta *et al.* (2002)

find uniformly negative results for the impact of state ownership on overall banking sector development and banking sector efficiency. Berger, Hasan and Klapper (2004) investigate the effects of community banks on growth in 49 nations for 1993–2000. They find that greater market shares and efficiency ranks of small, private, domestically owned banks are associated with better economic performance, and that the marginal benefits of higher shares are greater when the banks are more efficient. Only mixed support is found for improved financing for Small and Medium Enterprises (SMEs) or greater overall bank credit flows.

These cross-country studies on structure have been complemented with studies on regulations governing entry and exit rules for banking systems. In a broad survey of rules governing banking systems, Barth *et al.* (2001) document for 107 countries various regulatory restrictions in place in 1999 (or around that time) on commercial banks, including various entry and exit restrictions and practices. Using this data, Barth *et al.* (2003), among others, empirically investigate the cost and benefits of these restrictions. They find that tighter entry requirements are negatively linked with bank efficiency, leading to higher interest rate margins and overhead expenditures, while restricting foreign bank participation tends to increase bank fragility. These results are consistent with the view that tighter entry restrictions tend to limit competition and emphasize that it is not the actual level of foreign presence or bank concentration, but the contestability of a market that is positively linked with bank efficiency and stability.

Additionally, a number of recent studies have investigated the combined impact of structure and regulations. Using bank level data for 77 countries, Demirgüç-Kunt *et al.* (2004) investigate the impact of bank concentration and regulations on bank efficiency. They find that bank concentration has a negative and significant effect on the efficiency of the banking system except in rich countries with well-developed financial systems and more economic freedoms. Furthermore, they find empirical support using bank-level data that regulatory restrictions on entry of the new banks, particularly concerning foreign banks, and implicit and explicit restrictions on bank activities, are associated with lower levels of bank efficiency. Also using a cross-country approach, but with firm-level data, Beck *et al.*, (2004) Demirgüç-Kunt and Maksimovic (2004) investigate the effects of bank competition on firm financing constraints and access to credit. They find that bank concentration increases financing constraints and decreases the likelihood of receiving bank financing for small- and medium-size firms, but not for large firms. The relation of bank concentration and financing constraints is reduced in countries with an efficient legal system, good property rights protection, less corruption, better developed credit registries and a larger market share of foreign banks, while a greater extent of public bank ownership exacerbates the relation. Further, a lower degree of contestability and restrictions on banks' activities exacerbate the relation, while high entry and capital requirements alleviate it.

Some papers have analyzed the relationship between banking concentration and banking crises. Beck, Demirgüç-Kunt and Levine (2002), for example, show, using data on 79 countries over the period 1980–97, that crises are less likely (i) in more concentrated banking systems, (ii) in countries with fewer regulatory restrictions on bank competition and activities, and (iii) in economies with better institutions, i.e. institutions that encourage more competition and support private property rights. If there is a link between banking crisis and growth, this could imply that more concentrated banking systems have higher growth.

Finally, there have been a number of cross-country papers studying the impact of banking system structure on growth. Using the empirical methodology of Rajan and Zingales (1998), Cetorelli and Gambera (2001) document, in a cross-section study, that banking sector concentration exerts a depressing effect on overall economic growth, though it promotes the growth of industries that depend heavily on external finance. Using the same data and similar methodology, Deiida and Fatouh (2002) find that banking concentration is negatively associated with per capita growth and industrial growth only in low-income countries, while there is no significant relationship between banking concentration and growth in high-income countries. Dell'Ariccia and Bonaccorsi di Patti (forthcoming) also employ this approach and find that bank competition has a positive effect on firm creation. They also find, however, that the degree of information asymmetries in the country limits the overall positive effects of bank competition on firm credit, consistent with theories that competition may reduce credit to informationally opaque firms. Cetorelli (2001) also uses this methodology and finds that banking concentration enhances industry concentration, especially in sectors highly dependent on external finance, although these effects are less strong in countries with well-developed financial systems. Finally, using a different approach, Eschenbach and Francois (2002) investigate, using a dynamic, simultaneous system approach, the relationship between financial sector openness, competition and growth. Using a panel estimation of 130 countries, they report a strong relationship between financial sector competition/performance and financial sector openness and between growth and financial sector openness/competition. They also find evidence of the presence of economies of scale in the financial sector.

3   Methodology and data

We are interested in studying the effects of banking system competition on growth. As indicated in the review, theoretical work suggests an ambiguous relationship between degree of competition and access to financing and, in turn, growth. While existing empirical work has shown some relationships between market structure and growth, the link from structure to degree of competition is not clear. Thus, to properly investigate the effects of competition on growth we need to use a good measure of competition. Furthermore, we need to control for other country circumstances, which may be correlated with competition but that, in effect, determine the growth effects. Otherwise, the incorrect conclusion that competition is (or is not) important could be reached. Therefore, for our empirical tests on the effects of competition in the banking system on economic growth, we use the setup of Rajan and Zingales (1998, RZ hereafter), which has been used in a number of tests, some of which have been reviewed above.

The RZ model relates the growth in real value added in a sector in a particular country to a number of country- and industry-specific variables. In the case of RZ, the specific test focuses on financial development. The argument of RZ is that financially dependent firms can be expected to grow more in countries with a higher level of financial development. RZ uses U.S. firm data as proxies at the industry level to derive the typical external dependence for a particular industrial sector. Their presumption is that the well-developed financial markets in the United States should allow U.S. firms to achieve the desired financing for their respective industrial sector. This approach offers a way to identify the desired extent of external dependence anywhere in the world.[3] In their regressions, RZ also include the industry's market share in total manufacturing in the specific country to control for differences in growth potential across industries. Industries with large market shares may have less growth potential than industries with small initial market shares when there is an industry-specific convergence. The initial share may also help to control for other variations between countries, such as in their initial comparative advantage among certain industries based on factors other than financial development and banking system competition. Finally, RZ use country and industry dummies to control for country- and industry-specific factors.

The innovation of the RZ approach is that it overcomes some of the identification problems encountered in standard cross-country growth regressions. It does this by interacting a country characteristic (financial development of a particular country) with the external financial dependence of a particular industry. This approach is less subject to criticism regarding an omitted variable bias or model specification than traditional approaches that relate financial sector development directly to economic growth, even when considering other country characteristics. It allows them to isolate the impact of financial development on growth. Furthermore, in addition to including country indicators and industry indicators, they explicitly conduct tests for the importance of other country characteristics. In the regression results explaining sectoral growth, RZ find a positive sign for the interaction between the external financial dependence ratio and the level of financial development.

The results of RZ provide support for the importance of financial system development for growth. We expand the RZ model to test for the effect of competition in the banking system on growth and the specific channels through which competition policy may affect growth. Specifically, we add to their model a variable capturing the degree of competitiveness of the country's banking system interacted with variables of financial dependence and financial sector development as well as entering the competitiveness measure directly. We do this in two different sets of regressions, one with country dummies and one with country control variables.

First variable is the interaction of each industrial sector's external financing dependence and the index of the degree of competition in banking system of the country. With this interaction variable, we test whether industrial sectors that typically use more external financing grow faster (slower) in countries with less (more) competition in their banking systems. As noted, the theoretical prediction of this effect is unclear. On one hand, if more competitive banking systems channel less financing to firms, as they have less incentives to invest in relationships with firms, then especially those firms and sectors heavily dependent on external financing should grow slower. If, conversely, more competitive banking systems lead to more access – as the hold-up problems are less or as firms are more willing to enter relationships – then especially those firms heavily dependent on external financing should grow faster. The test of whether external financially dependent sectors grow faster (slower) in countries with less (greater) competition, then provides evidence that the less (more) banking system competition positively (negatively) affects firms' ability to attract financing and, consequently, through that channel, growth.

(ii)   Second, we explore whether the effects of banking system competitiveness differ by the development of the country's financial system. As noted, the argument has often been made that less developed countries benefit more from closer bank–firm relationships and, indeed, some papers have found some support for this argument. We use the size of the banking system as our measure of financial development. We then create a triple interaction variable by interacting the competitiveness measures with both the size of the country's banking system and each industrial sector's external financing dependence. If smaller, less competitive banking systems function relatively better in providing financing to financially dependent firms, than the coefficient for this triple interaction variable would be positive. Additionally, if more competitive banking systems function better when the financial sector is smaller, then this variable would be negative. Analyzing the signs and magnitudes of the coefficients for the first and second interactive variables will then provide an indication of the effects of competition for financially dependent firms by degree of financial sector development.

(iii)   Third, the effects of the degree of competition in the banking system need not go through the financing angle only. Competitiveness can be important because it leads to a better general development of the banking system in terms of allocating resources, providing new or better quality financial instruments and having lower costs of financial intermediation. If so, then the effects on industrial growth of the degree of competition in the banking system would not need to differ by the degree of the firm's external financial dependence. Some papers have found, however, that the effects of banking system structure (and possibly competition) can vary by the level of development of the country, with well-developed countries, for example, less affected by banking system concentration. Therefore, in a separate set of regressions, we test for the importance of banking system competition by level of financial sector development through including an interaction variable between our measure of banking system competitiveness and the size of the banking system.

(iv)   Fourth, it could be that the competitiveness of the banking system is an indicator of the development of the economy at large, rather than the functioning of the banking system specifically. Therefore, in some specifications, we also include the competitiveness measures directly, without any interactions. We also include other control variables that have been found to correlate with growth, which would help pick up the country, rather than banking system effect. Finally, we perform some robustness tests on the importance of controlling for country-specific factors and using instrumental variables to control for the possible (residual) endogeneity of some variables. As a sign of robustness, it is noteworthy that some of our specifications are similar to those of Cetorelli and Gambera (2001), Deiida and Fatouh (2002), Dell'Ariccia and Bonaccorsi di Patti (forthcoming), except that they use banking sector concentration as a measure of bank competition or structure.

Regression specification and data

The full specification for our regressions is as follows:

$$
\begin{aligned}
\text{Growth}_{j,k} = {}& \text{Constant} + \Psi_1 \cdot \text{Industry dummies}_j \\
& + \Psi_2 \cdot \text{Country controls}_k \\
& + \psi_3 \cdot \text{Industry share of manufacturing value added}_{j,k} \\
& + \psi_4 \cdot \text{External dependence}_j \cdot \text{Financial development}_k \\
& + \psi_5 \cdot \text{External dependence}_j \cdot \text{Competition Index}_k \\
& + \psi_6 \cdot \text{External dependence}_j \cdot \text{Competition Index}_k \cdot \text{Financial development}_k \\
& + \varepsilon_{j,k},
\end{aligned}
\tag{1}
$$

where each industry is indicated by index j and each country by index k. Uppercase Greek letters indicate vectors of coefficients, indexed by industry j or country k. Growth is the average annual real growth rate of value added in industry j in country k.

We use industry-specific and country-specific data from a variety of sources. Table 3.1 presents an overview of the variables used in our empirical analysis and their sources. Most of the variables are self-explanatory and have been used in other cross-country studies of firm financing structures and firm growth. The industry dummies correct for industry-specific effects. In the first set of regressions, we use country dummies to control for country differences. In the second set of regressions, the vector of country control variables differs per specification, with the exact vector of country control variables described in greater detail in the presentation of the specific empirical results. The vector can include the following variables: private credit-to-GDP, stock market capitalization-to-GDP, human capital and the logarithm of per capita GDP.

As a measure of external financial dependence at the sectoral level, data from RZ has been used. RZ construct benchmark data on an industry

Table 3.1   Definition and source of the variables

Variable	Description
Growth	Average annual real growth rate of value added in a particular sector in a particular country over the period 1980–97, if available. The sectors are classified on the basis of ISIC. Source: United Nations Database on Industrial Statistics.
Share in value added	Fraction of ISIC sector in value added of total manufacturing sector in 1980. Source: Rajan and Zingales (1998).
Financial dependence	External financial dependence of U.S. firms by ISIC sector averaged over the period 1980–89. Source: Rajan and Zingales (1998).
Private credit	Private Credit divided by GDP in 1980. Source: Rajan and Zingales (1998) and the International Financial Statistics of the International Monetary Fund.
Concentration	Measure of bank concentration. Sum of the market shares measured in total assets of the three largest banks for the period 1989–96, when available. Source: Cetorelli and Gambera (2001).
Competition	Measure of bank competition. Average *H*-statistic for the period 1994–2001. Source: Claessens and Laeven (2004).
Market cap	Stock market capitalization divided by GDP in 1980. Source: Rajan and Zingales (1998).
Human capital	Human capital is the average for 1980 of the years of schooling attained by the population over 25 years of age. Source: Barro and Lee (1993).
GDP per capita	The logarithm of GDP per capita in 1980. Source: World Development Indicators of the World Bank.
Legal origin	Identifies the legal origin of the Company Law or Commercial Code of each country. There are four possible origins: (1) English Common law; (2) French Commercial Code; (3) German Commercial Code; and (4) Scandinavian Commercial Code. Source: La Porta *et al.* (1999).

Note: This table describes the variables collected for our study. The first column gives the names of the variable as we use it. The second column describes the variable and provides the source from which it was collected.

basis assuming the external financing ratio, that is, the sectors' borrowing needs, for each industry in the United States to form a good benchmark. RZ calculate the external financial dependence ratios by industry using Compustat data on U.S. firms for the years 1980–89, for firms less than ten years old. We simply use their data for this measure. Also in line with RZ, we use the ratio of private credit-to-GDP, as provided by the World Development Indicators, as a proxy for financial development.

As our measure of the degree of competition in the banking system, we rely on Claessens and Laeven (2004, henceforth CL). CL used the Panzar and Rosse (1982, 1987) approach to assess the competitive nature of banking markets around the world. The Panzar and Rosse model provides a measure ('H-statistic') between 0 and 1 of the degree to which input prices are being passed on to output prices in the industry. This H-statistic can be interpreted as follows. $H < 0$ indicates a monopoly; $H = 1$ indicates perfect competition; and $0 < H < 1$ indicates monopolistic competition.[4] CL derive the competitiveness measure using individual bank data for 1994–2001 for some 50 countries. As an alternative measure of countries' banking system competitiveness, we use the banking system concentration ratio (top 3 banks), in which case the specifications are identical to some of those used by Cetorelli and Gambera (2001).

We have data of value added from the UNIDO database. We use the growth in value added over the period 1980–97, but for many countries the database is not complete. For some countries, data are not yet available for the latter part of the period, while some other countries did not have data for the beginning of the period (e.g., some transition economies). Since we use all the data available to us, we therefore end up with a not perfect overlap in terms of periods of dependent and independent variables. Growth may, for example, refer to an earlier period than the competitiveness measure does. Since we always use the average rates of growth over the period available, the sample does, however, remain balanced. The dataset of RZ includes some 45 countries. Since we have a different (larger) time period and we need to merge it with the countries for which we had the CL competitiveness measures, the number of countries included in our dataset drops somewhat and we end up with data on 30 countries. For the growth regressions, as in RZ, we need to drop the benchmark country, the United States, and we are therefore left with 29 countries.

Table 3.2 presents the summary statistics of the country-specific variables (the Annex presents the same statistics, but by individual country). The average sectoral growth real rate is 3 per cent. The average sector requires some 31 per cent of external financing for its investments. Private credit to GDP is on average some 38 per cent, while the average competitiveness measure is 0.66, indicating that some form of monopolistic competition is the most typical of the 29 banking systems.

Table 3.2 Summary statistics

Variable	Mean	Standard deviation	Minimum	Maximum	Number of observations
Growth	0.0305	0.0809	−0.4474	1.0000	1279
Share in value added	0.0157	0.0206	0.0000	0.2244	1263
Financial dependence	0.3135	0.3970	−0.4512	1.4915	1376
Private credit	0.3792	0.1998	0.0686	0.8564	1415
Concentration	0.5476	0.1802	0.2100	0.8700	1415
Competition	0.6586	0.1120	0.4600	0.8600	1043
Private credit × Financial dependence	0.1189	0.1823	−0.3864	1.2773	1376
Concentration × Financial dependence	0.1722	0.2370	−0.3925	1.2976	1376
Competition × Financial dependence	0.2060	0.2685	−0.3880	1.2827	1013
Competition × Private credit	0.2425	0.1281	0.0473	0.5191	1043
Competition × Private credit × Financial dependence	0.0757	0.1162	−0.2342	0.7742	1013

Note: This table reports the summary statistics of the main regression variables. Definitions and data sources of the variables are in Table 3.1.

Table 3.3 Correlation matrix

	Growth	Share in value added	Financial dependence	Private credit	Concentration	Competition
Growth	1					
Share in value added	-0.134	1				
	0.000					
Financial dependence	0.098	-0.076	1			
	0.001	0.008				
Private credit	0.057	0.015	-0.001	1		
	0.040	0.595	0.984			
Concentration	-0.155	0.061	0.006	-0.218	1	
	0.000	0.030	0.813	0		
Competition	-0.211	0.083	-0.006	-0.220	0.333	1
	0.000	0.010	0.848	0	0	

Note: This table reports the correlation matrix of the main regression variables. *p*-values of significance tests are reported below the correlation coefficients. Definitions and data sources of the variables are in Table 3.1.

We also provide the statistics for the interaction variables since those are useful for the comparison of some of the coefficients.

Table 3.3 provides the correlations among the variables. The statistics show that there are some important correlations among the variables. Growth in value added is negatively correlated with the share in value added, indicating the convergence effects. As amply demonstrated, the degree of financial development tends to coincide with the overall level of development of a country. As shown by many as well, there is also a positive correlation between growth in value added and the size of private credit. This is further confirmed by the positive correlation for the interaction variable private credit times financial dependence.

Noteworthy for our analysis, there is a negative correlation between the growth in value added and the competitiveness measure. This suggests that less competitive systems may be better in providing financing. This is not, however, corroborated by the interaction variable since there the correlation coefficient is not statistically significant. This reduced importance of the competitiveness measure may be, in part, because there is a negative relation between the development of the financial system and its level of competitiveness; that is, countries with less developed financial systems have less competitive banking systems. The competitiveness measure and the concentration indexes are statistically significant positively correlated; that is, more concentrated systems are more competitive, in line with what CL have found and in contrast to the belief that more concentrated financial systems are less competitive. As such, analyzing the effects of competition and banking system structure on the level of external financing available and growth could be different exercises. Interestingly, both the concentration and the competitiveness measures are negatively correlated with the private credit variable. All the interaction variables are closely correlated (not reported), as would be expected as the same sectoral financial dependence ratios are used, and the interaction variables are also positively correlated with the simple, non-interacted variables (also not reported).

4   Empirical results

The regression results are presented in this section. In all regressions, the dependent variable is the average annual real growth rate of value added in a particular sector in a particular country over the period 1980–97 (to the extent data is available), with one observation per sector in each country. We first discuss the basic regression specifications, which are estimated using OLS and include country dummies. Industry dummies (not reported) are used in all regressions. The sample varies. In the first two regressions, without the competitiveness measure, we use 40 countries (to replicate the RZ result), while in the other regressions, when we use the competitiveness measure, we have only 29 countries. The results are presented in Table 3.4.

The industry's market share in total manufacturing in the specific country has a negative sign in all regressions, in line with RZ, suggesting that there is some industry-specific convergence. In terms of the original RZ hypothesis, we find that industrial sectors that rely relatively more on external finance develop disproportionately faster in countries with better developed financial markets because the coefficient for the interactive variable private credit-to-GDP times external financial dependence is positive and statistically significant (at the 1 per cent level, column 1). Hence, and although we have a different data period and a somewhat different sample, consistent with the findings of RZ, we find that financial development facilitates economic growth through greater availability of external financing.

In terms of the effect of banking system concentration, we find no statistically significant effect of the interaction between banking system concentration and financial dependence on growth in value added. This contrasts with Cetorelli and Gambera (2001) who do find that more concentrated banking systems have higher growth in value added for financially dependent firms. The difference may be due to the sample and the period covered. To compare the result for the banking system competitiveness variable, we next perform the first two regressions for the smaller sample for which we also have the competitiveness measure (columns 3 and 4). We find that the results are maintained: financial development improves the growth of the more financially dependent sectors, while banking system concentration interacted with financial dependence is still negative, although not significantly related to growth.

In terms of our competitiveness measure, we find that industrial sectors using relatively more external financing develop faster in countries with less competitive banking systems since the coefficient for the interactive variable financial development times the competitiveness measure is statistically significant and negative (column 5). Hence, less competition in the banking system facilitates economic growth as it leads to greater external financing availability. These results show that the view that market power is good for external financially dependent sectors is supported when a more complete measure of competition is used.

Table 3.4 Industry and country-effects

	(1)	(2)	(3)	(4)	(5)	(6)	(7)	(8)
Share in value added	-0.805***	-0.747***	-0.878***	-0.836**	-0.821**	-0.871**	-0.871**	-0.868**
	(0.256)	(0.257)	(0.339)	(0.339)	(0.340)	(0.342)	(0.342)	(0.339)
Private credit × Financial dependence	0.099***		0.080**			0.075*	0.075*	-0.250
	(0.036)		(0.039)			(0.039)	(0.038)	(0.155)
Concentration × Financial dependence		-0.003		-0.054			0.002	
		(0.036)		(0.038)			(0.031)	
Competition × Financial dependence					-0.080*	-0.034	-0.035	-0.220*
					(0.046)	(0.045)	(0.048)	(0.115)
Competition × Private credit × Financial dependence								0.548*
								(0.302)
Industry dummies	Yes	Yes	Yes	Yes	Yes	Yes	Yes	Yes
Country dummies	Yes	Yes	Yes	Yes	Yes	Yes	Yes	Yes
Observations	1190	1190	901	901	901	901	901	901
Number of countries	40	40	29	29	29	29	29	29
R-squared	0.31	0.30	0.28	0.27	0.27	0.28	0.28	0.28

Notes: Dependent variable is real growth in sectoral value added over the period 1980–97, when available. Regressions are estimated using OLS and include industry and country dummies (not reported). Robust standard errors in parentheses. Definitions and data sources of the variables are in Table 3.1. * significant at 10%; ** significant at 5%; *** significant at 1%.

The competition effect on growth appears, however, not to be in addition to the increase in firm growth due to greater external financing availability. This is since, in the regressions where both the interaction variable of external financial dependence with the financial development and the interaction variable of the competitiveness variable with financial development are included (column 6), only the financial development interactive variable is significantly positive. When also including the concentration interaction variable, the coefficients in the regressions on the concentration and the competitiveness measures are both not statistically significant (column 7). The coefficients on the private credit variable remain of similar magnitudes in regressions 6 and 7 as in the earlier regressions (columns 1 and 3), supporting the robustness of this result. The fact that the interaction with the competitiveness variable is no longer significant may be because of the high correlations among the interacted variables. Although the interacted variables – external financial dependence variable interacted with the financial development measure and the external financial dependence measure interacted with the competitiveness index – intend to measure different concepts, the correlation between these variables is very high, 0.77.

As noted, the effects of the competitiveness of the banking system may depend upon the overall development of the system. Therefore, in the regression we also include a triple interaction between financial dependence, the competitiveness measure and the level of private credit to GDP (column 8). This regression leads to the following results: the interaction of financial dependence with the development of the financial sector is no longer statistically significant, the interaction with the competitiveness measure is statistically significant negative and the triple interaction with the competitiveness measure and the private credit is statistically significant positive. Interestingly, the private credit variable interacted with financial dependence is no longer significant in this regression, suggesting that one may need to control for the degree of competitiveness relative to the size of the financial system in order to be able to evaluate the effect of financial sector development on growth.

To interpret all these results, we need to consider the size of the coefficients and the average for the private credit variables. The coefficient for the competitiveness interaction variable is −0.220, while the coefficient for the competitiveness and private credit interaction variable is 0.548. The average credit to GDP ratio is 0.379. Multiplying this with the 0.548 coefficient provides 0.21, or about the same as the negative coefficient on the competitiveness alone interaction, −0.220. This implies that for the average degree of financial sector development, the effect of the degree of competitiveness on growth is about zero. For financially less developed countries, the first interaction is quantitatively more important implying that less competition is better for firm growth for these countries. For more developed financial systems, the second interaction is quantitatively more important and, thus, competition appears to be better for growth of financially dependent firms.

To assess the economic significance of these results, we use the regression estimates to infer the differential impact of financial sector competition on growth of a financially dependent industry in two countries that differ in the level of their financial development. We consider a financially dependent industry that has a score of 0.71 for the financial dependence index, which is exactly one standard deviation above the sample mean. Consider one country that has a well-developed financial system as measured by its level of private credit to GDP of 0.58, which is exactly one standard deviation above the sample mean, and the second country that has a low level of private credit to GDP of 0.18, which is one standard deviation below the sample mean. We now compare the differential impact of the level of financial sector competition on the growth of this industry in these two countries. We consider a high level of competition equal to one standard deviation above the sample mean and a low level of competition equal to one standard deviation below the sample mean of our competition variable. In the financially developed country, the financially dependent industry will grow at a rate of 1.5 per cent per annum more if the country's financial sector is competitive rather than not competitive. Conversely, in the country with an underdeveloped financial sector, this industry will grow at a rate of 1.9 per cent per annum more if the country's financial sector is not competitive. Compared to an average annual growth rate of 3 per cent, these effects are economically significant.

We next conduct some robustness tests. Although the regression results so far all include country dummies, and thus control for any country differences besides the development and competitiveness of the banking system, our effects might still reflect country characteristics. Therefore, we want to control for some variables. In particular, we use some of the variables that have been found to be relatively robust explanatory factors of country growth: the general level of development, as proxied by GDP per capita; the degree of human capital, as proxied by average number of years of schooling; and the degree of development of the stock markets, as proxied by market capitalization to GDP. Furthermore, we directly include the measures of financial sector development and competitiveness to investigate the first order effects of these factors. The results of the various regression specifications are in Table 3.5.

Table 3.5 Country-control variables

	(1)	(2)	(3)	(4)	(5)	(6)	(7)	(8)
Share in value added	-0.790***	-0.829***	-0.694**	-0.728**	-0.708**	-0.839***	-0.827***	-0.820***
	(0.218)	(0.279)	(0.296)	(0.300)	(0.315)	(0.278)	-(0.275)	(0.286)
Private credit	-0.007	-0.008		-0.025	0.015	-0.331***	-0.225***	-0.230**
	(0.017)	(0.019)		(0.019)	(0.018)	(0.065)	(0.081)	(0.092)
Competition			-0.113***	-0.127***	-0.134***	-0.303***	-0.242***	-0.280***
			(0.026)	(0.027)	(0.034)	(0.050)	(0.061)	(0.075)
Private credit × Financial dependence	0.099***	0.083**		0.073*	0.070*	0.079**	-0.273*	-0.258
	(0.037)	(0.039)		(0.039)	(0.039)	(0.038)	(0.165)	(0.161)
Competition × Financial dependence			-0.098**	-0.054	-0.052	-0.049	-0.251**	-0.237**
			(0.049)	(0.051)	(0.050)	(0.049)	(0.118)	(0.119)
Competition × Private credit						0.511***	0.333**	0.409***
						(0.115)	(0.149)	(0.152)

Table 3.5 Continued

	(1)	(2)	(3)	(4)	(5)	(6)	(7)	(8)
Competition × Private credit × Financial dependence							0.594* (0.311)	0.564* (0.306)
Market cap					0.060*** (0.010)			0.067*** (0.010)
Human capital					−0.003 (0.002)			−0.002 (0.002)
Per capita GDP					−0.008 (0.007)			−0.010 (0.006)
Industry dummies	Yes	Yes	Yes	Yes	Yes	Yes	Yes	Yes
Country dummies	No	No	No	No	No	No	No	No
Observations	1190	901	901	901	901	901	901	901
Number of countries	40	29	29	29	29	29	29	29
R-squared	0.11	0.10	0.13	0.14	0.19	0.19	0.19	0.19

Notes: Dependent variable is real growth-in sectoral value added over the period 1980–97, when available. Regressions are estimated using OLS and include industry dummies (not reported). Robust standard errors in parentheses. Definitions and data sources of the variables are in Table 3.1. * significant at 10%; ** significant at 5%; *** significant at 1%.

Columns 1 and 2 show that the key RZ finding is not altered when directly including the measure of financial sector development (as RZ showed as well), both for the larger and smaller sample. In terms of the direct effect of banking system competition, we find that less competitive banking systems have higher growth since the coefficients for the competitiveness measure is statistically significant negative (column 3). The competitiveness interacted with financial dependence is also negative statistically significant, again suggesting that access is improved when the banking system is less competitive. This effect disappears, however, when the interaction between private credit and financial dependence is also included (column 4) or when more country control variables are included (column 5). These results support the view that market power can be good in general, as the competitiveness measure remains statistically significant negative, but not necessarily through the financing needs channel.

As we found, the growth effect of competition may vary by the development of the financial sector. Therefore, we look at the interaction between the competitiveness measure and the banking system development, without considering financial dependence. We find that the interaction between the competitiveness measure and the size of the banking system is also statistically significant positive (column 6). Thus, having a more competitive banking system may be more important when the system is deeper. The positive coefficient of 0.511 for the interaction and the negative 0.303 coefficient for the competitiveness measure alone imply that for the average level of credit, 0.379, less competition is still better. Only for a level of private credit to GDP more than 60 per cent more competition is better for sectoral growth.

Column 7 expands on these results by also including the triple interaction between the competitiveness measure, the size of the private credit in the country and the sectoral financial dependence. This triple interaction variable has a coefficient of 0.594, similar to that of column 8 in Table 3.4, while the competitiveness measures interacted with financial dependence now has a statistically significant coefficient of 0.251, also similar to that of column 8 in Table 3.4. The coefficients imply that the ratio of private credit to GDP for which the effect of competition through the provision of external financing becomes positive is 0.42, close to the average credit to GDP ratio of 38 per cent. As before, this implies that for countries with more than average developed financial systems, the effects of more competition are positive for financially dependent firms, while for less developed financial systems, less competition is better for external financially dependent firms. These results

Table 3.6   Instrumental variables

	(1)	(2)	(3)
Share in value added	−0.788***	−0.859**	−0.800**
	(0.256)	(0.340)	(0.341)
Private credit × Financial dependence	0.070**	0.049*	
	(0.032)	(0.029)	
Competition × Financial dependence			−0.288***
			(0.096)
Observations	1190	901	901
Number of countries	40	29	29
R-squared	0.30	0.28	0.26

Notes: Dependent variable is real growth in sectoral value added over the period 1980–97, when available. Regressions are estimated using instrumental variables and include industry and country dummies (not reported). As instrument for private credit and competition we use the legal origin dummy variables. Robust standard errors in parentheses. Definitions and data sources of the variables are in Table 3.1. * significant at 10%; ** significant at 5%; *** significant at 1%.

remain similar even when including other country control variables (column 8) as the coefficients remain very similar (0.564 and −0.237, respectively).

The effect of competition through the external financing channel need not be the only channel. The regression results of columns 7 and 8 also show negative coefficients for the simple, non-interacted competitiveness measure (−0.242 and −0.280), suggesting that less competition is better. Yet, there is again the effect of the level of financial sector development to consider that in this case is picked up by the interaction between the competitiveness measure and the private credit to GDP ratio, for which the coefficients are positive (0.333 and 0.409). The combination of the two coefficients suggests that for levels of private credit to GDP ratio greater than about 70 per cent, more competition is associated with higher growth, while for lower credit ratios the opposite is the case.[5]

We investigate in Table 3.6 the robustness of our results using instrumental variables techniques, where as instrument we use the country's legal origin. Since we have only one instrumental variable, we are able to run only a few instrumental variables regressions. The first basically confirms the original RZ effects that financially dependent firms grow faster in more developed financial systems, conforming that the effect is not due to an omitted variable (column 1). We also find that more financially dependent firms grow faster in less competitive financial systems (column 2). We cannot investigate the combined effects of the financial development and competitiveness credit for financially dependent industries since we do not have enough instrumental variables.

5 Conclusions

Using a large cross-section of countries, we relate a structural measure of banking system competitiveness to industrial growth. We find that external financial dependent sectors grow faster in less competitive banking systems. We also find that greater competition reduces industrial growth in general. These effects depend, however, upon the state of development of a country's financial system and are reversed when the financial system is larger: in well-developed financial systems more competition helps industrial growth. The view that market power in banking systems is associated with lower competitiveness is good for access to financing thus finds support for less developed financial systems. In more developed systems, competitive pressure may be the best for financial sector functioning. We do not find evidence that market structure, that is, concentration, helps predict industrial sector growth. While it may be, as others have found, that more concentrated banking systems better provide financing to external financially dependent firms, this does not seem to reflect the consequences of market power, or less competitive systems, but might capture other aspects. We find that these results remain using some robustness tests.

These interpretations are tentative, however, since we did not investigate in detail the channels through which increased competition may affect financial sector functioning. In particular, we did not investigate across countries the relationship between direct measures of the cost of financial intermediation, such as net interest margins, and our measure of competition (although our measure of competition does capture the degree to which banks pass input costs on to output costs). We also did not investigate the relationship between direct measures of firms' access to external financing, such as the reported difficulty in obtaining external financing or the degree of other external financing constraints, and our measure of competition. Importantly, while we found that the effects of competition depend on the level of financial sector development, we did not explore other measures of countries' characteristics, including institutional aspects that may explain this effect. It is possible, for example, that the degree of informational opaqueness can both explain a low level of financial sector development and why limited competition is useful for access to financing – through the importance of relationships lending. While this type of omitted variable problem is reduced given our specification, we cannot eliminate the possibility that omitted variables drive the results.

Nevertheless, our results confirm some of the theoretical literature that competition can affect access to external financing. They also suggest that the effects of competition – important for industry functioning, in terms of breadth of services, and costs and quality of products – may vary by the level of financial sector development. The fact that market power matters in providing external finance supports some theory, or even in opposite ways to other findings, might still surprise. At the minimum, it suggests that competition in the financial sector is complicated, while balancing the view that more competition is uniformly good for financial services. While competition may be good in terms of lowering costs and improving the quality of financial services, it need not lead to greater access.

Annex

Country-averages of the main regression variables

Country	Growth	Financial dependence	Private credit	Market cap	Concentration	Competition
Australia	0.0103	0.3187	0.2764	0.3842	0.60	0.80
Austria	0.0286	0.2988	0.7658	0.0285	0.42	0.66
Bangladesh	0.0492	0.3187	0.0686	0.0018	0.62	0.69
Belgium	0.0002	0.2705	0.2901	0.0904	0.49	0.73
Brazil	0.0373	0.2803	0.2331	0.0452	0.40	0.83
Canada	0.0229	0.3187	0.4453	0.4603	0.57	0.67
Chile	0.0656	0.3187	0.3566	0.3447	0.45	0.66
Colombia	0.0362	0.3187	0.1445	0.0520	0.35	0.66
Denmark	0.0205	0.3187	0.4195	0.0865	0.74	0.50
Egypt	0.0628	0.3187	0.2093	0.0104	0.58	
Finland	0.0214	0.3187	0.4824	0.0595	0.85	
France	0.0236	0.2922	0.5444	0.0991	0.28	0.69
Germany	0.0379	0.3250	0.7788	0.0946	0.27	0.58
Greece	0.0165	0.3187	0.4402	0.0760	0.79	0.76
India	0.0709	0.3187	0.2441	0.0486	0.40	0.53
Israel	0.0219	0.3339	0.6694	0.3489	0.79	
Italy	0.0178	0.2861	0.4160	0.0716	0.24	0.60
Japan	0.0464	0.3187	0.8564	0.3017	0.21	0.47
Jordan	0.0562	0.3187	0.5425	0.4959	0.87	
Kenya	−0.0170	0.3347	0.2044	0.0000	0.59	0.58

Annex (Continued)

Country-averages of the main regression variables

Country	Growth	Financial dependence	Private credit	Market cap	Concentration	Competition
Korea	0.1182	0.3187	0.4971	0.0783	0.28	0.68
Malaysia	0.1106	0.3187	0.4837	0.6549	0.44	0.78
Mexico	−0.0112	0.3187	0.1648	0.0676	0.53	
Morocco	0.0714	0.2825	0.1570	0.0242	0.57	
Netherlands	−0.0032	0.3022	0.6036	0.1934	0.77	0.86
New Zealand	0.0239	0.3187	0.1865	0.3321	0.75	
Norway	0.0106	0.3187	0.3429	0.0583	0.60	0.57
Pakistan	0.0738	0.2975	0.2517	0.0285	0.71	0.48
Peru	−0.0341	0.3187	0.1063	0.0595	0.64	0.72
Philippines	0.0401	0.3187	0.2811	0.0969	0.40	0.66
Portugal	0.0176	0.3187	0.5184	0.0075	0.46	0.67
Singapore	0.0742	0.2814	0.5663	1.6240	0.61	
South Africa	0.0219	0.3256	0.2598	1.2031	0.69	0.85
Spain	0.0243	0.3187	0.7552	0.0927	0.34	0.53
Sri Lanka	−0.0222	0.3187	0.2102	0.0616	0.75	
Sweden	−0.0017	0.3187	0.4187	0.1074	0.71	
Turkey	0.0990	0.3187	0.1407	0.0092	0.41	0.46
United Kingdom	−0.0059	0.3187	0.2498	0.3799	0.50	0.74
Venezuela	−0.0228	0.3187	0.3024	0.0488	0.47	0.74
Zimbabwe	−0.0230	0.3087	0.2991	0.4499	0.78	
Total	0.0305	0.3135	0.3792	0.2086	0.55	0.66

Notes: Growth is real growth in sectoral value added for the period 1980–97. Financial dependence is the external financial dependence measure. Private credit is private credit to GDP in 1980. Market cap is stock market capitalization to GDP in 1980. Concentration is the 3-bank concentration ratio for the period 1989–96. Competition is the average *H*-statistic for the period 1994-2001. Definitions and data sources of the variables are in Table 3.1.

Notes

* Claessens is at the University of Amsterdam and a Research Fellow at the CEPR. Laeven is at the World Bank. We would like to thank participants at the money, finance and growth workshop, organized by Charles Goodhart, in Salford on September 8 and 9, and at the University of Amsterdam KAFEE lunch seminar for their comments. We thank Ying Lin for research assistance. The paper's findings, interpretations, and conclusions are entirely those of the authors and do not necessarily represent the views of the World Bank, its executive directors, or the countries they represent.

1. Other papers that use this approach, among others, include Cetorelli and Gambera (2001), which investigates the effects of bank concentration on sectoral growth, Fisman and Love (2003), which investigates the effects of trade credit usage on sectoral growth, and Claessens and Laeven (2003), which investigates the role of property rights on growth, to mention a few.
2. Cetorelli (1999) provides more detail on these formal tests and reviews some of the results of previous empirical banking studies.
3. The advantage of this approach is that one does not need information on the actual external financing dependence for industries in different countries. The comparability of such data would be reduced as accounting practices differ around the world. It does assume that there are technological and economic reasons why some industries depend more on external finance than others do, and that these differences, to a large degree, prevail across countries. This does not mean that the model assumes a sector in two countries with the same degree of financial development to have exactly the same optimal external financing structures. Local conditions such as growth opportunities are allowed to differ between countries. The model only assumes the rank order of optimal external financing needs across industries to be similar across countries.
4. The PR H-statistics is calculated from reduced form bank revenue equations and measures the sum of the elasticities of the total revenue of the banks with respect to the bank's input prices. It can be shown, if the bank faces a demand with constant elasticity and a Cobb-Douglas technology, that the magnitude of H can be interpreted as an inverse measure of the degree of monopoly power, or alternatively, as CL do, as a measure of the degree of competition.
5. Interestingly, the interaction variable of financial dependence with private credit (the original RZ variable) becomes statistically significant negative in regression 7, although it loses significance in regression 8. However, these coefficients should be interpreted together with the positive coefficient on the triple interaction term that also includes the interaction of financial dependence with private credit. The combined effect of the financial dependence and private credit interaction variable on growth is always non-negative, even at low levels of competition, consistent with the RZ result.

References

Allen, Franklin and Douglas Gale (1998) 'Optimal Financial Crises?' *Journal of Finance* 53, 1245–84.

Allen, Franklin and Douglas Gale (2000) *Comparing Financial Systems*, Boston, MA: MIT Press.

Allen, Franklin and Douglas Gale (2004) 'Competition and Financial Stability', *Journal of Money Credit and Banking* 36(2), June.

Barro, Robert and Jong Wha Lee, (1993) 'Educational Attainment', *Journal of Monetary Economics* 32(2), 363–94.

Barth, James R., Gerard Caprio Jr and Ross Levine (2001) 'The regulation and supervision of banks around the world: a new database', in Robert E. Litan and Richard Herring (eds), *Integrating Emerging Market Countries into the Global Financial System*, Brookings-Wharton Papers on Financial Services, Washington, DC: Brookings Institution Press, 183–241.

Barth, J.R., Caprio, G. Jr and Levine, R. (2004) 'Bank supervision and regulation: what works best?' *Journal of Financial Intermediation* forthcoming.

Baumol, William J., John C. Panzar and Robert D. Willig (1982) *Contestable Markets and the Theory of Industry Structure*. San Diego: Harcourt Brace Jovanovich.

Beck, Thorsten, Asli Demirgüç-Kunt and Ross Levine (2002) 'Bank concentration and crises', mimeo, World Bank and University of Minnesota.

Beck, Thorsten, Asli Demirgüç-Kunt and Vojislav Maksimovic (2004) 'Bank competition, financing constraints and access to credit', *Journal of Money Credit and Banking* 36(2), June.

Belaisch, Agnes (2003) 'Do Brazilian banks compete?' IMF Working Paper 03/13, Washington, D.C.

Berger, Allen N. (2003) 'Economic Effects of Technological Progress: Evidence from the Banking Industry,' *Journal fo Money, Credit, and Banking*, 35(2), 141–76.

Berger, Allen N., Rebecca S. Demsetz and Philip E. Strahan (1999) 'The consolidation of the financial services industry: causes, consequences, and implications for the future', *Journal of Banking and Finance* 23 (February), 135–94.

Berger, Allen N. and Timothy H. Hannan (1989) 'The price-concentration relationship in banking', *Review of Economics and Statistics* 71, 291–9.

Berger, Allen N., Iftekhar Hasan and Leora F. Klapper (2004) 'Further evidence on the link between finance and growth: an international analysis of community banking and economic performance', *Journal of Financial Services Research* 25(2), 169–202.

Berger, Allen N., Nathan H. Miller, Mitchell A. Petersen, Raghuram G. Rajan and Jeremy C. Scharfstein (2002) 'Does function follow organizational form? Evidence from the lending practices of large and small banks', National Bureau of Economic Research Working Paper 8752.

Besanko, David A. and Anjan V. Thakor (1992) 'Banking deregulation: allocation consequences of relaxing entry barriers', *Journal of Banking and Finance* 16, 909–32.

Bikker, Jacob A. and Katharina Haaf (2001) 'Competition, concentration and their relationship: an empirical analysis of the banking industry', DNB Staff Report No. 68, De Nederlandsche Bank, July.

Bikker, Jacob A. and Johannes M. Groeneveld (2000) 'competition and concentration in the EU banking industry', *Kredit und Kapital* 33, 62–98.

Boot, Arnoud and Anjan V. Thakor (2000) 'Can relationship banking survive competition?', *Journal of Finance* 55 (2), 679–713.

Bresnahan, Timothy F. (1982) 'The oligopoly solution concept is identified', *Economics Letters* 10, 87–92.

Bresnahan, Timothy F. (1989) 'Studies of industries with market power', in Richard Schmalensee and Robert D. Willig (eds), *Handbook of Industrial Organization, Volume II* (North Holland, New York).

Cetorelli, Nicola (1999) 'Competitive analysis in banking: appraisal of the methodologies', *Economic Perspectives*, Federal Reserve Bank of Chicago, 2–15.

Cetorelli, Nicola (2001) 'Does bank concentration lead to concentration in industrial sectors?' Federal Reserve Bank of Chicago Working Paper 2001–01.

Cetorelli, Nicola and Michele Gambera (2001) 'Banking market structure, financial dependence and growth: international evidence from industry data', *Journal of Finance* 56, 617–48.

Claessens, Stijn, Asli Demirgüç-Kunt and Harry Huizinga (2001) 'How does foreign entry affect domestic banking markets?' *Journal of Banking and Finance* 25, 891–911.

Claessens, Stijn and Luc Laeven (2003) 'Financial development, property rights and growth', *Journal of Finance*, Volume 58 (6) December 2401–36.

Claessens, Stijn and Luc Laeven (2004) 'What drives bank competition? Some international evidence', *Journal of Money Credit and Banking*, 36(2), June.

Coase, Ronald H. (1960) 'The problem of social costs', *Journal of Law and Economics* 3, 1–44.

Collender, Robert N. and Sherrill Shaffer (2001) 'Banking structure and employment growth', mimeo University of Wyoming, and USDA/ERS.

Coccorese, Paolo (1998) 'Assessing the competitive conditions in the Italian banking system: some empirical evidence', *BNL Quarterly Review* 205, 171–91.

Corvoisier, Sandrine and Reint Gropp (2002) 'Contestability, technology and banking', Working Paper, ECB, Frankfurt.

De Bandt, Olivier and E. Philip Davis (2000) 'Competition, contestability and market structure in European banking sectors on the eve of EMU', *Journal of Banking and Finance* 24, 1045–66.

Degryse, Hans and Steven Ongena (2002) 'Distance, lending relationships, and competition', University of Tilburg, Working Paper.

Deiida, L. and B. Fatouh (2002) 'Concentration in banking industry and economic growth', mimeo, University of London.

Dell'Ariccia, Giovanni, Erza Friedman and Robert Marquez (1999) 'Adverse selection as a barrier to entry in the banking industry', *Rand Journal of Economics* 30(3): 515–34, Autumn.

Dell'Ariccia, Giovanni and Emilia Bonaccorsi di Patti 'Bank competition and firm creation', *Journal of Money, Credit, and Banking* forthcoming.

Demirgüç-Kunt, Asli, Luc Laeven and Ross Levine (2004) 'The impact of bank regulations, concentration, and institutions on bank margins', *Journal of Money Credit and Banking*, 36(2), June.

Eschenbach, Felix and Joseph Francois (2002) 'Financial sector competition, services trade and growth', CEPR Discussion Paper No. 3573 (October).

Fisman, Raymond and Inessa Love (2003) 'Trade credit, financial intermediary development, and industry growth', *Journal of Finance* 58, 353–74.

Gelos, R. Gaston and Jorge Roldos (2002) 'Consolidation and market structure in emerging market banking systems', IMF Working Paper No. 02/186, November.

G-10 (2001) 'Report of consolidation in financial sector', Basel, Switzerland: Bank for International Settlements, January.

Gilbert, R. Alton (1984) 'Bank market structure and competition: a survey', *Journal of Money, Credit, and Banking* 16 (November), 617–45.

Gruben, William C. and Robert P. McComb (2003) 'Privatization, competition, and supercompetition in the Mexican commercial banking system', mimeo, Federal Reserve Bank of Dallas *Journal of Banking and Finance* 27, 229–49.

Hempel, S. Hannah (2002) 'Testing for competition among German banks', Discussion Paper 04/02, Economic Research Centre of the Deutsche Bundesbank.

Hauswald, Robert and Robert Marquez (2003) 'Information technology and financial services competition', *Review of Financial Studies* 16, 921–48.

Jappelli, T. and M. Pagano (2000) 'Information sharing in credit markets: a survey', Working Paper No. 36, Centre for Studies in Economics and Finance (CEFS), University of Salerno.

Kessidis, I. (1991) 'Entry and market contestability: the evidence from the United States', in P. Geroski and J. Schwallbach (eds) *Entry and Market Contestability: An International Comparison*, Oxford: Blackwell.

Klein, Michael (1971) 'A theory of the banking firm', *Journal of Money, Credit, and Banking* 7 (February), 205–18.

Lau, Lawrence (1982) 'On identifying the degree of competitiveness from industry price and output data', *Economics Letters* 10, 93–9.

La Porta, R., Lopez-de-Silanes, F., Shleifer, A. (2002) 'Government ownership of commercial banks', *Journal of Finance* 57, 265–301.

Levine, R. (2004) 'Finance and growth: theory, evidence, and mechanisms', in P. Aghion and S. Durlauf (eds), *Handbook of Economic Growth*. Amsterdam: North-Holland Elsevier Publishers, forthcoming.

Levy Yeyati, Eduardo and Alejandro Micco (2003) 'Banking competition in Latin America', mimeo, Inter-American Development Bank, Washington, DC.

Marquez, Robert (2002) 'Competition, adverse selection, and information dispersion in the banking industry', *Review of Financial Studies* 15, 901–26.

Molyneux, Philip, D. Michael Lloyd-Williams and John Thornton (1994) 'Competitive conditions in European banking', *Journal of Banking and Finance* 18 (May), 445–59.

Molyneux, Philip, John Thornton and D. Michael Lloyd-Williams (1996) 'Competition and market contestability in Japanese commercial banking', *Journal of Economics and Business* 48, 33–45.

Nathan, Alli and Edwin H. Neave (1989) 'Competition and contestability in Canada's financial system: empirical results', *Canadian Journal of Economics* 22 (August), 576–94.

Panzar, John C. and James N. Rosse (1982) 'Structure, conduct and comparative statistics', Bell Laboratories Economics Discussion Paper.

Panzar, John C. and James N. Rosse (1987) 'Testing for "Monopoly" equilibrium', *Journal of Industrial Economics* 35, 443–56.

Perotti, Enrico C. and Javier Suarez (2002) 'Last bank standing: what do I gain if you fail?' *European Economic Review* 46 (October), 1599–622.

Petersen, Mitchell A. and Rajan, Raghuram G. (1995) 'The effect of credit market competition on lending relationships', *Quarterly Journal of Economics* 110, 407–43.

Philippatos, George C. and H. Semith Yildirim (2002) 'Competition and contestability in central and eastern European banking markets', mimeo University of Tennessee (February).

Rajan, Raghuram G. (1992) 'Insider and outsiders, the choice between informed and arm's-length debt', *Journal of Finance* 47, 1367–400.

Rajan, Raghuram G. and Luigi Zingales (1998) 'Financial dependence and growth', *American Economic Review* 88, 559–87.

Rosse, James N. and John C. Panzar (1977) 'Chamberlin vs. Robinson: an empirical test for monopoly rents', Bell Laboratories Economics Discussion Paper No. 90.

Shaffer, Sherrill (1982) 'A non-structural test for competition in financial markets', in *Bank Structure and Competition, Conference Proceedings*, Federal Reserve Bank of Chicago, 225–43.

Shaffer, Sherrill (1989) 'Competition in the U.S. banking industry', *Economics Letters* 29, 321–3.

Shaffer, Sherrill (1993) 'A test of competition in Canadian banking', *Journal of Money, Credit, and Banking* 25 (February), 49–61.

Shaffer, Sherrill (2001) 'Banking conduct before the European single banking license: a cross-country comparison', *North American Journal of Economics and Finance* 12, 79–104.

Shaffer, Sherrill and James DiSalvo (1994) 'Conduct in a banking duopoly', *Journal of Banking and Finance* 18, 1063–82.

Stein, Jeremy C. (1997) 'Internal capital markets and the competition for corporate resources', *Journal of Finance* 52, 111–33.

Vesala, Jukka (1995) 'Testing for competition in banking: behavioral evidence from Finland', Bank of Finland Studies, Working Paper No. E:1.

Vives, Xavier (2001) 'Competition in the changing world of banking', *Oxford Review of Economic Policy* 17, 535–45.

Williamson, Oliver E. (1985) *The Economic Institutions of Capitalism*, New York, NY: The Free Press.

4
The Great Divide and Beyond: Financial Architecture in Transition

*Erik Berglof and Patrick Bolton**

A growing and deepening divide has opened up between transition countries where economic development has taken off and those caught in a vicious cycle of institutional backwardness and macroeconomic instability. This "Great Divide" is visible in almost every measure of economic performance: GDP growth, investment, government finances, growth in inequality, general institutional infrastructure and increasingly in measures of financial development. Strategies for financial development have differed dramatically across countries and over time, offering interesting opportunities to study the links between real and financial sector development.

Even in the countries that have made it across the divide, like the Czech Republic, Hungary, Poland, Slovenia and the Baltic states of Estonia, Latvia and Lithuania, a remarkable diversity of policies for financial development has been pursued. Yet, strikingly, today the basic financial architectures of these front-runners are remarkably similar. These financial systems are strongly dominated by commercial banks, which are increasingly foreign owned and which lend primarily to government. Stock markets are highly volatile and illiquid, and their sustainability is in question as the numbers of listed firms are stagnating or even falling. Enterprises rely primarily on internally generated funds, and the bulk of external long-term finance comes from foreign direct investment.

The Great Divide in economic and financial development and the convergence in financial architecture among the successful countries raise fundamental questions about how financial development interacts with economic growth. Is it possible to engineer a development takeoff by creating a modern financial architecture from scratch? Or are financial institutions and markets a reflection of underlying conditions in the real sector? Or are both financial development and economic growth driven by some other underlying variables? Is it possible to leapfrog certain stages of financial development or must all countries go through a phase of bank-oriented financial architecture? The experience of the transition economies represents a unique opportunity to shed new light on these issues.

We start by describing the salient features of financial transition. We will argue that financial development does not explain why a small group of countries developed and grew while the majority of transition economies remained mired in economic stagnation. In general, the financial sector has played a small role in the restructuring of the manufacturing sector in transition economies, and in some cases financial liberalization may have undermined real sector development. We argue that the ability of governments of transition economies to enforce contracts and to achieve fiscal and monetary responsibility, together with a commitment to refrain from excessively bailing out failing banks or loss-making enterprises, determined whether economic *and* financial development took off. Fiscal responsibility promotes both financial development and economic growth through two important channels: it limits the extent of crowding out of private investment by government borrowing, and it makes it credible that the government will be able to maintain the macro stability that is essential for private investment. In addition, it provides some guarantees that the returns from investment are not going to be taxed away in the future by excessively profligate governments desperately seeking tax revenues wherever they can find them. Of course, specific initial conditions and underlying country characteristics facilitate the emergence of fiscally sound governments capable of enforcing the rule of law. We discuss what these conditions might be.

1   The evolution of banking and the emergence of the Great Divide

All banking systems in transition economies have evolved from a single institution, the monobank, which was responsible for both monetary policy and commercial banking. In the monobank system, the overall level of credit was often quite high, with the aim of spurring production along the lines desired by the economic planners, rather than having loans channeled according to conventional standards of creditworthiness.

The monobank was thus not a bank in the sense that it screened and monitored projects nor that it enforced repayment of loans; rather, it was the channel for funds allocated by the plan. Since the planned economy repressed or hid inflation with price ceilings and guaranteed jobs for all, at least nominally, the standard countercyclical tasks of central banking were not especially relevant to the monobank.

The financial sector transition from a planned economy to a market-oriented economy involved transforming the monobank into a decentralized financial system integrated into a market economy. Most Soviet bloc countries started this process by implementing more or less the same measures: by separating the central and commercial banking activities of the monobank and by breaking up the commercial banking activities into multiple smaller units. Most countries also allowed for entry of new banks. A few countries got a head start in separating these two functions and creating a two-tier banking system. The first was Yugoslavia during the 1960s. In the mid-1980s, a few other socialist economies followed: Hungary and, in a less controlled way, the Soviet Union and Poland (Sgard 1996). In parallel, other important reforms were implemented – in particular, price liberalization.

The separation of central and commercial banking brought with it some rudiments of monetary policy, like credit ceilings and refinancing windows. However, central banks had weak incentives to conduct price-stabilizing monetary policy and relatively little power to regulate the commercial banks. Central banks generally attracted highly talented people, but they were often politically weak. The extent of their independence from political influence varied greatly, and actual independence was often less than suggested by formal rules. Moreover, independence from the government did not always protect against influence activities by other lobbying interests.[1]

The new commercial banks formed from the break-up of the monobank faced difficult prospects. For a time, they were little more than accounting constructions, run by segments of the old bureaucratic network and staff. Their inherited balance sheets included household deposits, loans from the central bank and a portfolio of enterprise credits of unknown quality. Bank managers had little genuine banking experience, a generally low quality of assets and little guidance from the poorly developed system of bank regulation. In addition, most of the newly created banks remained under state ownership and their business clients had yet to be privatized, so lending policies were not based on any financial or economic logic. Instead, nonperforming loan losses were automatically rolled over, often with additional loans provided by the central bank (i.e., by printing money). As a number of analysts had expected, lax lending practices to state-owned industry became an important source of inflationary pressure during the early phase of transition.

These fledgling commercial banks were also operating in a difficult macroeconomic situation. Most eastern European economies inherited a massive "monetary overhang": that is, household savings in deposit accounts that had accumulated as a result of the pervasive shortages of consumption goods and distortionary price controls under central planning. Following price liberalization, this money flowed into the economy, and the monetary overhang turned into open inflation. Firms responded to this accelerating inflation with widespread hoarding of goods and by increasingly relying on barter arrangements, even among large businesses. Thus, just at the time when money and credit should have become more central to economic organization and transactions, the new banks found themselves in a macroeconomic environment where rapid disintermediation was occurring.

The first test of the institutional strength of this new constellation of commercial banks came in the early 1990s when central banks made an attempt to control monetary growth, which sharply reduced real credit and created a severe credit crunch (Calvo and Coricelli 1995). In all transition countries, the initial response to the monetary tightening by enterprises was inertia; they reacted to the lower level of credit with mounting unpaid bills to suppliers and, in some cases, to workers. Some countries, however – mostly in central Europe and in the Baltic states – gradually managed to resist the pressures to bail out banks and enterprises. After the initial pain of the credit crunch and several banking crises, the eventual outcome in these countries was a stable monetary and fiscal policy. Some of these countries, like Estonia, went as far as locking in monetary stability through a currency board arrangement. Such restraint in turn laid the foundation for a virtuous spiral of microeconomic restructuring and macroeconomic consolidation. These countries managed gradually to reorient their productive sector and integrate it with world trade, thus restarting the growth process early on (for a survey on the evidence on corporate restructuring, see Djankov and Murrell 2000).

In other transition countries, including most of the former Soviet Union as well as countries in southeast Europe, like Bulgaria and Romania, authorities did not, or could not, resist the pressures for financial relief. Central banks, after only a few months of attempted stabilization, provided additional loans to commercial banks and monetized the rapidly increasing stocks of credit. This pattern of repeated bailouts for both banks and businesses led to a lack of enterprise restructuring, weaker banks, and the need for more inflationary credit bailouts.[2] As a result, these countries have experienced a much more protracted slump than might otherwise have been the case. The Great Divide had opened up.

2   Measuring financial development

Data limitations are a serious constraint for analyzing the interaction between economic and financial development in transition economies. Standard measures of financial development include the assets of financial institutions, the amount of money in circulation and loans to households and enterprises. However, in the early phases of economic transition, real GDP statistics are of dubious quality because of high and variable levels of inflation. Measures of credit as a share of GDP do not adequately correct for inflation in the early years, since initial credit measures were mainly accounting fictions, which did not reflect inflationary expectations. In addition, above-average lending flows to enterprises may have been a symptom of weakness, or softness, during a financial bailout, rather than a reflection of above-average financial development.[3]

With these cautions duly noted, Table 4.1 shows the development of domestic credit to the private sector as a share of GDP during the period 1993–99. (Unfortunately, data for the earlier years of transition are only

Table 4.1   Domestic credit to households and enterprises (percent of GDP)

Country	1993	1994	1995	1996	1997	1998	1999
Czech Republic		51.8	55.3	55.5	60.0	61.5	56.1
Estonia	7.3	11.1	12.5	15.1	20.0	24.4	26.4
Hungary	28.7	24.7	22.3	20.8	21.4	22.7	23.4
Latvia		14.7	11.8	7.0	8.5	12.3	15.7
Lithuania		13.4	14.0	11.5	9.4	10.6	12.3
Poland	10.2	10.5	10.7	13.0	15.6	17.4	20.6
Slovenia		23.1	27.5	28.8	28.6	32.8	35.9
Slovakia		25.8	24.3	28.4	36.1	41.7	39.8
Bulgaria	4.1	3.1	10.6	19.0	15.6	11.4	13.2
Romania					8.3	9.0	9.1
Russia		6.8	7.9	7.0	7.7	10.6	10.2
Ukraine	1.1	1.1	1.5	1.3	1.8	4.8	7.6

Source: IMF International Financial Statistics.

available in a few countries.) The Great Divide is represented in this table, and in the other tables in this paper, by grouping countries that have crossed the Great Divide at the top of the table, while countries who have yet to cross the Great Divide are grouped at the bottom. Only Estonia, Poland, Slovakia and Slovenia saw relatively steady expansion of credit. These countries are also grouped as having crossed the Great Divide, but they are not alone in having done so. The Czech Republic had very high levels of credit already, which reflects the mass privatization of enterprises and extensive bad loans, and thus exaggerates its relative financial development. Hungary had four severe banking crises in four years during the first half of the 1990s, resulting in a sharp drop in credit from 45 percent of GDP in 1990 to 24.7 percent in 1994. But since then, its level of credit has expanded in step with economic growth. Similarly, Latvia and Lithuania first experienced banking crises in the mid-1990s, which reduced the ratio of credit to GDP, followed by a recovery. It is important to stress that in all these countries the real impact of these financial crises was moderate. Most of the problems stemmed from bad stocks rather than flows, and banks had mainly been lending to government and less to households and enterprises.[4] To summarize, the experience of financial transition in the most successful group of countries provides weak evidence at best of a link between financial development (as measured by the domestic credit to GDP ratio) and growth.

The correlation between financial development and economic growth is even weaker in the other countries. Bulgaria experienced rapid growth in credit in the mid-1990s and then a drastic fall in the late 1990s, but its economy declined or showed moderate growth over this time period. In Russia, financial markets developed rapidly, and credit to households and enterprises increased somewhat in the late 1990s, while the economy continued to stagnate. The financial crisis in August 1998 had little long-term impact on Russia's real growth. Some observers even argue that the crisis had a positive effect on economic development by cutting some of the interests blocking reform down to size. While there was a slight fall in credit, the Russian economy subsequently grew rapidly. Ukraine and many other countries that were formerly part of the Soviet Union saw neither financial development nor economic growth. Again, the link between financial development and economic growth does not appear to be very strong during the first decade of transition, at least when one looks at the ratio of domestic credit to GDP.

The differences in development stand out more in measures of financial reform (EBRD 2000) and general institutional quality such as "law on the books" and "law enforcement" indices (Hellman *et al.* 2000;

Table 4.2   Index of banking reform (1991–99)

Country	1991	1992	1993	1994	1995	1996	1997	1998	1999
Czech Republic	2	3	3	3	3	3	3	3	3+
Estonia	1	2	3	3	3	3	3+	3+	4–
Hungary	2	2	3	3	3	3	4	4	4
Latvia	1	2	2	3	3	3	3	2–	3
Lithuania	1	1	2	2	3	3	3	3	3
Poland	2	2	3	3	3	3	3	3+	3+
Slovenia	1	2	3	3	3	3	3	3	3+
Slovakia	2	3–	3–	3–	3–	3–	3–	3–	3–
Bulgaria	1	2–	2	2	2	2	3–	3–	3–
Romania	1	1	1	2	3	3	3–	2+	3–
Russia	1	1	1	2	2	2	2+	2	2–
Ukraine	1	1	1	1	2	2	2	2	2

Note: Index is a scale from 1 to 4+. 1 stands for little progress beyond establishment of two-tier system. 4+ stands for standards and performance norms of advanced industrial economies: full convergence of banking laws and regulations with Bank of International Settlements standards; provision of full set of competitive banking services.

Sources: Various EBRD Transition Reports.

Table 4.3   Index of reforms of non-banking financial institutions (1991–99)

Country	1991	1992	1993	1994	1995	1996	1997	1998	1999
Czech Republic	1	1	2	3–	3–	3–	3–	3	3
Estonia	1	1	2–	2–	2–	2	3	3	3
Hungary	2	2	2	2	3	3	3+	3+	3+
Latvia	1	1	1	2	2	2	2+	2+	2+
Lithuania	1	1	2–	2	2	2	2+	2+	3–
Poland	2	2	2	2	3	3	3+	3+	3+
Slovenia	2	2	2	3–	3–	3–	3–	3–	3–
Slovakia	1	1	2	3–	3–	3–	2+	2+	2+
Bulgaria	1	1	1	1	2	2	2	2	2
Romania	1	1	1	2	2	2	2	2	2
Russia	1	1	2–	2–	2	3	3	2–	2–
Ukraine	1	2–	2–	2–	2	2	2	2	2

Note: Index is a scale from 1 to 4+. 1 stands for little progress. 4+ stands for standards and performance norms of advanced industrial economies: full convergence of securities norms and regulations with International Organization of Securities Commissions standards; fully developed non-bank intermediation.

Sources: Various EBRD Transition Reports.

Pistor *et al.* 2000). While most of the transition countries have adopted increasingly sophisticated legal and regulatory frameworks in the financial area, implementation and enforcement is significantly better in countries on the right side of the divide. Table 4.2 gives an index of banking reforms, and Table 4.3 provides an index of reforms of non-banking financial institutions. All these measures of institutional quality inevitably involve a considerable degree of judgement and should be interpreted with care. Nevertheless, they do highlight the Great Divide; they have also been good predictors of vulnerability during the Asian crisis of 1997–98 (Johnson *et al.* 2000). Obviously, the interesting underlying question is what explains these differences in institutional quality.

3   Beyond the Great Divide: different policies and systemic convergence of financial architecture

The transition experience does not reveal a single magic formula guaranteeing a successful path for financial and economic development. Among the countries that have failed to bridge the Great Divide, a variety of policies have been tried, and several varieties of dysfunctional financial systems have emerged. In Russia and Ukraine, most commercial banks are in private hands, but most of these banks are insolvent and should be closed down. Financial institutions and markets in these two countries were severely hit by the financial crisis in 1998. Corruption, crime and cronyism in these countries undermine enforcement of the legal and regulatory framework. Also, political resistance toward further reforms remains strong.

A second group of less-successful transition countries, including Bulgaria, Romania and Slovakia, have only made partial attempts to reform. The largest banks in these countries are still predominantly state owned. In addition, the presence of a large number of insolvent banks undermines competition. While the regulatory environment is improving, enforcement remains weak.

In the more successful countries in central and eastern Europe, financial architecture is converging despite major differences in policies pursued. After an early boost in stock market activity in the aftermath of mass privatization and different policy responses to the banking crises following price liberalization, bank-based financial systems are emerging. Some examples of these policy differences across the more successful countries include the following: different procedures for restructuring bad loans, different privatization strategies for enterprises and banks, different policies toward foreign entry in the banking sector, different regulatory barriers to entry of new banks and different policies toward stock market development.

The approach to cleaning up bank balance sheets has varied considerably across transition countries, both in the extent to which banks were induced to stop rolling over bad debts to enterprises and in the methods used to recapitalize banks. Some countries, like the Czech Republic, transferred bad debts to specialized "hospital" banks, while others, like Poland, chose to clean up balance sheets within existing institutions.

In an attempt to encourage banks to stop rolling over their bad debts and to deal with the growing problem of payment delays, Hungary adopted a devastatingly effective bankruptcy law. It had an automatic trigger that more or less overnight forced much of Hungary's industry into court-led bankruptcy procedures. The sheer number of cases paralyzed Hungary's courts. Mitchell (2001) characterized it as a "too many to fail" situation. Inevitably, Hungary had to water down its new bankruptcy law and remove the automatic trigger. In a similar attempt, the Czech Republic adopted a bankruptcy code just after its mass privatization program, but suspended its application for two years in response to political pressure from many unprofitable state-owned and privatized firms. Once the Czech bankruptcy law came into force, it led to a wave of takeovers of smaller and not necessarily less efficient firms by large politically connected firms. In a more pragmatic approach, Poland opted for informal workouts outside courts under a moratorium on bankruptcy, with the government offering to give up the seniority of its tax claims to provide incentives for banks and firms to agree to restructure their bad loans.

Countries in transition also opted for very different strategies for privatizing state-owned enterprises. These differences are broad even if one focuses only on those countries that successfully crossed the Great Divide. For example, Hungary started privatization early and followed a case-by-case sales method, while the Czech Republic opted for a mass voucher privatization scheme. A small group of investment funds (tied to large banks) controlling most privatized assets emerged from this mass voucher privatization following the repurchase of most dispersed vouchers from households. Poland dragged its feet in implementing mass privatization, partly out of a concern that the legal and supervisory environment be strengthened first, and partly as a result of resistance to privatization as such. In the meantime, the Polish government proceeded with privatizing a number of individual firms through management buyouts and liquidation schemes.

Bank privatization also followed quite different paths. The Czech Republic included banks in the first wave of voucher privatization.

Poland combined management buyouts, some public offerings and smaller placements with foreign strategic investors. Bank privatization accelerated across central Europe in the second half of the 1990s, but governments often retained strategic stakes. Despite these different privatization strategies, all of these countries ended up with similar bank-based financial systems a decade later. The countries on the "wrong" side of the Great Divide generally have higher shares of banking assets controlled by the state (with Ukraine being an exception).

It was not until foreign banks were allowed to acquire strategic stakes in the domestic banking sectors that private ownership took a firm hold in the banking sector of most countries. By now, several countries have high foreign ownership shares. Hungary was the first country to allow widespread foreign penetration in the banking sector. Foreigners now control more than 40 percent of shares in Hungarian banks, accounting for as much as 80 percent of assets (Abel and Bonin 2000). The Baltic states of Estonia, Latvia and Lithuania also have very high shares of foreign ownership, primarily from banks based in Scandinavian countries. Poland initially took a positive stance toward foreign ownership of banks, then backtracked, before opening the banking sector again to foreign ownership. The Czech government was initially resistant to foreign ownership of banks, but several large failures of domestic banks finally opened up ownership to foreign institutions. Today, the shares of foreign ownership of banks in Poland and the Czech Republic are 52.8 and 50.7 percent, respectively. In the countries on the "wrong" side of the Great Divide, the presence of foreign banks, as well as other foreign direct investment, is much more limited, partly by design and partly by default. Understandably, foreign banks have been reluctant to buy stakes where the regulatory environment is weak.

Most transition countries experienced significant entry of new banks following financial liberalization and the separation of monetary policy and commercial banking (Tang *et al.* 2000). In the Baltic states and in Russia, the number of registered banks increased dramatically in the early years of transition. This wave of new entrants imposed a heavy supervisory burden on central banks with little experience in the task. Most new entrants were small and closely tied to newly privatized enterprises. Most of them quickly became insolvent. Some countries, in particular Romania and Albania but also Russia, even witnessed devastating episodes of frenzied speculation around a small number of unscrupulous banks, which started unsustainable pyramid, or Ponzi schemes, drawing in thousands of inexperienced and gullible households. The inevitable failure of these banks led to severe financial crises and seriously undermined confidence in banking institutions in these countries.

In contrast, in countries of central and eastern Europe, new bank entry has been on a much smaller scale. Hungary has seen only a moderate increase in the number of banks. The number of banks rose somewhat, then fell again in the Czech Republic, declined slightly in Poland and fell sharply in Bulgaria. The number of banks has shrunk following several banking crises, and more consolidation is underway. Foreign-owned banks and banks with stronger capital–asset ratios are growing more rapidly than other banks. On the other hand, larger, more dominant institutions are expanding more slowly (Fries and Taci 2001). Privatized and new private banks have grown at about the same rate as state-owned banks. On the whole, the growth of bank loans has not kept pace with real sector growth.

Table 4.4 provides some data on the banking industry and the official numbers of bad loans, again showing countries that have crossed the Great Divide grouped at the top and others at the bottom. The first column highlights that despite new entry, the banking sector is heavily dominated by the three largest banks in most countries. These banks are not only able to exert monopoly power in deposit and lending activities, but also often yield considerable political influence. The fourth column shows the worst performers in terms of cleaning up bank balance sheets. The Czech Republic, Romania and Slovakia had a bad-loans-to-total-loans ratio between 30 and 40 percent in 1999. This compares with a reported ratio of 7.8 percent for Italy, 1.4 percent for Japan and 0.7 percent for the United States in 1998.[5] The fifth column gives figures for bank spreads. The lower the spread, the better is the banking sector and the legal protection of creditors, other things equal. High spreads reflect higher banking costs, greater monopoly power and greater lending risks.

As hinted at before, many countries pursued a policy of stock market development in the early stages of transition (Claessens *et al.* 2000). One group of countries – including the Czech and Slovak Republics, Lithuania and Romania – made heavy use of stock markets to transfer ownership through mass privatization. The number of firms listed on these stock exchanges increased dramatically, but after an initial phase of high trade volumes, most stocks became and remained illiquid. Over time, many companies have been delisted, and the number of shareholders fell as ownership became increasingly concentrated. Table 4.5 shows the pattern of flat or declining numbers of companies listed on stock markets in a selection of transition economies. Regulation of stock exchanges was minimal. In the Czech Republic, a formal regulator was not even established. A second group of countries – including Estonia, Hungary, Latvia, Poland and Slovenia – developed their stock exchanges

Table 4.4 Indicators of the development of banking sector

Country	Concentration[a] (percentage, 1997)	Number of banks (1999)	Asset share of state-owned banks (percentage, 1999)	Bad loans-total loans (percentage, 1999)	Loan-deposit rate spread[b] (1999)
Czech Republic	74.9	42	23.2	31.4	4.2
Estonia	84.5	7	7.9	3.1	4.5
Hungary	67.4	39	9.1	2.8	3.4
Latvia	53.1	23	8.5[d]	6.3[d]	9.2
Lithuania	69.7	13	41.9	11.9	8.2
Poland	42.3	77	25.0	14.5	5.8
Slovenia	71.7	31	41.7	10.2	5.1
Slovakia	84.5	25	50.7	40.0	6.7
Bulgaria	86.7	28[c]	66[c]	12.9[c]	9.6
Romania	85.0	34	50.3	36.6	—
Russia	53.7	2376	41.9[d]	13.1	26.0
Ukraine	64.4	161	12.5	3.3	34.3

Notes
[a] Defined as the ratio of three largest banks' assets to total banking sector assets.
[b] Loan rate is defined as the average rate charged by commercial banks on outstanding short-term credits to enterprises and individuals, weighted by loan amounts. Weighted average of credits of all maturity is used for Czech Republic, Lithuania and Ukraine. For Poland, only minimum risk loans are considered. Deposit rate is defined as the average rate offered by commercial banks on short-term deposits, weighted by deposit amounts. Weighted average of deposits of all maturity is used for Czech Republic, Estonia, Lithuania and Ukraine.
[c] Data for 1997.
[d] Data for 1998.

Sources: IMF International Financial Statistics, IMF Staff Country report Nr.00/59, WB Database on Financial Development and Structure, EBRD Transition Report 2000.

mainly through a small number of initial public offerings. Trading in most of these shares remained relatively high. A third group of countries that were formerly part of the Soviet Union, including Russia and the Ukraine, developed stock markets through both privatization and initial public offerings. All these countries had mass privatizations, but the exchange of vouchers took place outside the official stock markets. Six transition countries – Albania, Belarus, Bosnia-Herzegovina, Georgia, Tajikistan and Turkmenistan – never established stock markets.

Despite these marked differences in policies with regard to financial architecture, it is a remarkable fact that the financial systems in the more advanced transition countries have converged and now share three key features.

Table 4.5   Number of companies listed on the stock market

Country	1994	1995	1996	1997	1998	1999	2000 (March)
Czech Republic	1024	1635	1588	276	261	164	154
Estonia	0	0	0	22	26	25	23
Hungary	40	42	45	49	55	66	65
Latvia	0	17	34	50	69	70	64
Lithuania	13	357	460	607	60	54	54
Poland	44	65	83	143	198	221	221
Slovenia	25	17	21	26	28	28	34
Slovakia	19	21	816	872	837	845	843
Bulgaria	16	26	15	15	998	828	842
Romania	4	7	17	76	5753	5825	5578
Russia	72	170	73	208	237	207	218
Ukraine	0	96	99	102	113	117	120

Sources: *Emerging Markets Fact Book*, International Finance Corporation; Claessens *et al.* (2000).

First, the financial sector of the successful transition economics is strongly dominated by banks, which lend primarily to governments and other financial institutions. Banks provide some working capital finance to the corporate sector, but so far have played a limited role in financing investments. Investment finance comes almost exclusively from retained earnings, and most external finance comes through foreign direct investment (IMF 2000).

Second, ownership structures in individual firms and banks are concentrated, and turnover of shares is low. Only the stock markets in the Czech Republic, Estonia, Poland and Hungary have capitalization-to-GDP ratios comparable to other emerging markets (23, 37, 36 and 20 percent, respectively). But most exchanges are very illiquid, with trade concentrated in a small number of firms (Claessens *et al.* 2000). The number of listed firms has decreased as a result of foreign acquisitions, domestic mergers and delisting. The best firms show limited interest in listing on local exchanges, preferring instead the quality stamp and liquidity of the international stock markets in Europe and the United States. At the end of 1999, 72 corporations from transition economies were listed on the New York Stock Exchange or Nasdaq, and companies listed in Germany accounted for most of domestic market capitalization in Hungary and the Czech Republic. Turnover is, however, still mostly concentrated in local exchanges. The long-term sustainability of some of these exchanges is in doubt, given the growing integration of financial markets in Europe and the world.

Third, bank spreads – that is, the difference between lending and borrowing rates – have declined significantly in level and volatility in most countries of central and eastern Europe. Nevertheless, they remain high by the standards of developed market economies. For example, compare the spreads in Table 4.4 to the corresponding levels for the United States and Sweden in 1999, which were 2.7 and 3.9 percent, respectively.

To summarize, the countries that find themselves on the prospering side of the Great Divide have now established the basic structure of their financial systems. They all have converged to mainly bank-based financial systems, with a significant fraction of foreign bank ownership. Local equity markets have gradually declined and have been overshadowed by European or US stock exchanges. However, important vulnerabilities remain, and some of the countries still require major, potentially difficult reforms. The countries on the "wrong" side of the Great Divide also have financial systems dominated by banks, but the portfolios of these institutions are in a much worse state and the regulatory environment significantly weaker. As a result, budget constraints of banks and ultimately of governments are more likely to be soft. Stock markets are even less developed. Much of the difficult work of financial development still remains, and most of these countries will only have limited help from the accession process to the European Union, the process that has been so important for the front-runners in central and eastern Europe.

4 Financial transition and financial development: different starting points and moving targets

Transition is a unique historical event, and there are limits to the generality of the lesson that can be drawn from the experience concerning financial development. As the preceding overview of a decade of financial transition highlights, these countries started out with fundamentally imbalanced financial systems supported by powerful institutions. It was inevitable that any development would have to be preceded by an elimination of the monetary overhang and a protracted institutional breakdown. In some cases, this breakdown is not yet complete. On the other hand, many developing countries also have grossly distorted financial systems, often with extensive state intervention, or "crony capitalism", requiring wide-ranging institutional transformation. In the end, the differences between the issues raised in the financial development literature and those of financial transition must be a matter of degree. In particular, the transition experience can shed new light on the difficult question of whether financial development can be engineered to create a financial infrastructure-enhancing economic growth. Certainly, initial hopes were high that a financial infrastructure could be created to help transition economies leapfrog stages of development. These hopes were based partly on the first findings of the emerging financial development literature linking financial development to subsequent growth experience. From a technological point of view, some leapfrogging has taken place. For example, ATM machines are widely available in most countries in central and eastern Europe and in many countries of the former Soviet Union. Some front-runner countries even have high penetration of Internet banking. But when it comes to basic institutions of finance, the hopes that financial development could ignite economic growth appear to have been unrealistic.

Financial development and economic growth

A number of empirical studies based on cross-country regressions have found that financial development at any given point in time – as measured by the ratio of bank lending to GDP and/or the ratio of stock market turnover to GDP – is positively correlated with future per capita economic growth (e.g. King and Levine 1993a,b, Levine and Zervos 1998). The conclusion generally drawn from these studies is that "well-functioning financial intermediaries and markets promote long-run economic growth" (Beck *et al.* 2001, p. 1). The implied prescription for transition economies is to focus on financial reform as one of the ways to achieve economic growth.

Another set of empirical studies have found a statistical relationship between legal investor protection and financial development. These studies have used a country's legal origin as an instrument for resolving the vexing endogeneity question of the interaction between legal protection of investors and investment flows to the corporate sector. Legal origin is typically categorized according to common-law versus civil-law traditions and/or English versus French, German or Scandinavian legal traditions. The theory is that common-law traditions are more investor friendly, and since legal tradition clearly predates investment flows to corporations following the industrial revolution, a clear causal link can be established between the degree of investor protection and the size of outside investment funds to corporations. A common finding of these studies is that countries with a French legal tradition tend to be less financially developed (La Porta *et al.* 1997, 1998, Levine 2000, Beck *et al.* 2001).

The policy implications from these contributions are less clear, as legal traditions are not easy to change. But the findings suggest a link between a country's legal infrastructure (specifically the degree of legal investor protections) and financial development. Indeed, looking beyond legal origin, these studies also find a direct positive relationship between financial development and various indices of investor protection (La Porta *et al.* 1997, 1998). Other studies find a positive relationship between per capita income and various indices of investor protection (Levine 2000, Acemoglu *et al.* 2000). Most intriguingly, these studies also suggest that legal origin has persistent long-run effects on financial development.

A general difficulty in applying the literature on legal origin and financial development to transition economies is that there is little variation in legal origin, since most countries have a civil-law tradition. In addition, most countries have adopted civil-law-type institutions to facilitate accession to the European Union. One exception is Russia, which has had a brief but unfortunate experiment in a common-law approach to corporate law.

More importantly, the view that legal origin has persistent effects on financial development is difficult to reconcile with the observation of Rajan and Zingales (2000) that financial development in 1913 was significantly higher in France than in the United States – apparently, the French legal system was not holding back investment flows to corporations at that time. Rajan and Zingales also observe that around the world, financial development peaked before the First World War, then declined until well after the Second World War, before growing back to a new peak at the turn of the twenty-first century. This financial history suggests that other important factors affect financial development besides legal origin and investor protection.

What might these factors be? Rajan and Zingales (2000) invoke the political power of incumbents. They propose that insiders, primarily incumbent managers or owners and labor unions, are inherently opposed to financial development, as it would bring about greater competition from new entrants. In times of crisis or conflict, these insiders gain more political influence and are able to push through legislation protecting their interests and inhibiting the growth of financial markets. With greater prosperity, however, these interest groups lose their grip on political power, so that eventually new legislation is passed fostering the development of financial markets.

Although this story could explain the U-shaped pattern of financial development of advanced economies in the twentieth century, a deeper analysis is clearly required before one can say with any confidence whether financial development is mainly driven by such a political struggle between insiders and outsiders. A number of other factors could also help to explain the U-shaped pattern of global financial development in the twentieth century, and many of these factors have parallels in the transition economies.

For example, one reason for the decline of global financial development in the 1930s may well involve the stock market crash in 1929, the ensuing banking crises and the general loss of confidence in financial markets and institutions. There are clear parallels to the experience of many transition countries with the repeated collapses of their domestic banks and markets for stocks and bonds.

The decline of private financial development in the middle of the twentieth century may also be related to the rise of the welfare state following the onset of the Great Depression and the Second World War, which had the important effect of removing retirement savings from capital markets. It is only in the 1980s that contribution-based retirement plans have been introduced (mainly in the United States and the United Kingdom). These plans have had a major impact on the growth of the private pension fund industry and on the growth of securities markets in the last two decades. Similar if more limited reforms to build retirement plans based in the private sector are also underway in some of the more advanced transition countries. This should help financial sector development, in particular the growth of securities markets. It is, however, still an open question whether these commitments to privately funded schemes are credible in countries where large segments of the population may end up with very low retirement benefits.

In many European countries in particular, the public sector also expanded dramatically after the Great Depression and the war production effort, with widespread nationalizations of industry following the Second World War in the United Kingdom, France, Italy and elsewhere. A larger public sector meant that a smaller fraction of corporate investments required funding from private sources, thus limiting the extent of the private financial sector. Again, it is only since the beginning of the 1980s that the public sector has been scaled back through large-scale privatization programs (Bortolotti *et al.* 2001). It is still an open question what size of public sector the transition countries will eventually aim for, but the choice could have important ramifications for financial development.

The growth of government debt and the resulting rise in long-term interest rates in recent decades have discouraged private investment. This factor is of particular importance for some transition economies, where extremely high yields on government bonds have discouraged bank lending to the private sector. One piece of evidence consistent with this view is the growth in private lending witnessed in Russia following the default on government bonds in 1998 (e.g. Huang *et al.* 2001).

But with those historical points noted, it does seem that the role of insiders is crucial in understanding patterns of financial development. Indeed, the power of insiders has sometimes been singled out as the key governance problem in transition economies. Again, Rajan and Zingales (2000) propose that insiders get more power in time of economic conflict and use it to suppress financial development. Mancur Olson (1982) has convincingly argued in another context a different story, that insiders become entrenched in good times and that recessions serve to break their hold on critical institutions. Why Olson's story would not apply to financial development in transition economies remains an open question. Privatization in most transition countries resulted in a transfer of control to incumbent management and in some cases to workers. While many firms were looted by their managers initially, and many of them resisted the development of markets for goods and labor, they have later tried to find ways to make commitments to investors that their investments will not be expropriated. However, without effective bonding devices or mechanisms to transfer control to investors, firms have been confined to defensive cost-cutting measures and growth based on internally generated funds.

Bank-based versus financial market-based systems

Most developing economies have bank-based financial systems, and financial markets play a relatively minor role. Only at more advanced stages of development does one see financial markets, including stock and bond markets, play an increasingly important role. Various explanations have been given for this pattern.

One influential view is that when accounting rules and, more generally, regulatory and contractual enforcement institutions are weak, banks are better placed to protect creditor rights (Gerschenkron 1962; Rajan and Zingales 1998). Small investors are deterred from investing in the stock market for fear of being exploited by unscrupulous stock price manipulators and insider traders. They feel that their savings are better protected in deposit or savings accounts at banks, which are generally subject to some form of supervision by the state.

On the corporate side, most firms are too small and risky at early stages of development to be able to issue shares or bonds on an organized exchange at a competitive cost of capital. Only the more advanced economies have a sufficient number of large and stable firms that could get cheaper funds by issuing securities and thus create the thick market externalities necessary to sustain efficient stock markets (Pagano 1993). Stock markets also tend to develop when there is a culture of equity investment and private pension plans, over and above regulatory protections to limit price manipulation and fraud. Finally, stock markets require well-trained professionals, market makers, traders, fund managers and financial regulators, none of which were present at the beginning of transition.

A casual look at financial architecture in developing countries suggests that as the real economy develops, there is a gradual shift from bank-based to market-based corporate finance, but the empirical literature exploring the link between bank-based or market-based financial systems and per capita growth produces mixed evidence. Several studies have found that greater financial intermediation is associated with greater future growth (King and Levine 1993a,b) and that stock market development is also positively related with future growth (Levine and Zervos 1998). More recently, Tadasse (2000) has refined these findings by highlighting that for the less financially developed countries, a greater emphasis on financial intermediation is positively correlated with future growth, while for the more developed countries, there is a negative correlation between financial intermediation and growth. On the other hand, Levine (2000) finds that the relative weight of bank versus market finance is not significantly related to economic growth in cross-country regressions once legal protection is introduced as an additional factor.

The transition experience lends some support to the notion that bank-led finance may be inevitable at certain stages of development and that efforts to develop stock exchanges in some countries may have been premature. On the other hand, the evidence of a link between bank-based development and economic growth is weak. As we have already highlighted, the monetary, fiscal and regulatory environment under which financial institutions and markets had to operate appears to have been as or more important in facilitating both financial and economic development.

Financial development, inequality and instability

While exploring the link between legal infrastructure, investor protection and aggregate investment, some researchers have argued that the legal infrastructure and the extent of investor protection are proxies of broader underlying country characteristics like wealth inequalities, political polarization and macroeconomic instability. For example, Perotti (1996) found that the risk of expropriation of investors is related to political polarization and conflict, which itself is linked to wealth inequalities. Similarly, several empirical studies surveyed in Benabou (1997) have found that protection of property rights is weakened when there is greater income inequality and that greater political instability tends to decrease investment and growth. Also, in a study of financial development in Latin American countries, Padilla and Requejo (2001) have found that macroeconomic stability is a more important factor determining development of lending to the corporate sector than creditor protection.

A systematic analysis for transition countries that explores the link between property rights protection and underlying factors such as political polarization, wealth inequalities and macroeconomic instability remains to be undertaken. However, consistent with the findings of Perotti (1996) and others is the dramatic rise in inequality and poverty rates witnessed by some countries on the wrong side of the Great Divide with particularly weak property rights enforcement, like Russia, Romania and Ukraine. Most transition countries started out with low income inequality as measured by the Gini coefficient, which was around 0.2 on average at the beginning of transition; for comparison, the Gini coefficiencies for Sweden and for the United States at this time are about 0.25 and 0.40, respectively. All of the transition countries have subsequently seen income inequalities rise significantly. But the countries of the Commonwealth of Independent States have experienced much more dramatic increases, with Ukraine and Russia now having extremely skewed income distributions, as shown in Figure 4.1.

5 Explaining the Great Divide and systemic convergence

The emergence of the Great Divide illustrates how difficult it is to implement sustainable financial development and how much underlying country characteristics matter. Indeed, the reason why some countries were able to cross the Great Divide while others did not must be sought to a large extent outside their financial and legal systems.

As we have argued, one leading explanation for the observed variation in financial and economic development across transition countries can be found in the differences in fiscal and monetary discipline and enforcement capacity of governments. Without fiscal and monetary discipline, government borrowing crowds out or discourages investment in

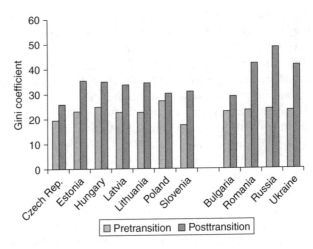

Figure 4.1   Gini coefficients for selected transition economies

Note: Posttransition data refers to 1997, except for Russia, 1998; Ukraine, 1996; Bulgaria, 1996; and Estonia, 1995.

Sources: EBRD *Transition Report 2000*, World Bank *World Development Indicators 2000*, Keane and Prasad (2000).

the private sector and increases macroeconomic uncertainty (for some recent evidence, see Fries and Taci 2001).

As pertinent as this diagnosis may be, it is not all that helpful if one does not also identify why some countries tend to have fiscally irresponsible governments. What determines whether a government will be able to show fiscal and monetary restraint? To address this question, we must return to the situation facing transition countries in the wake of transition, when the first step toward financial development had been taken by breaking up the monobank and ending central economic planning. One heritage of the Soviet past was that governments were locked into financial relationships with a large number of firms facing daunting restructuring tasks. The pressure to keep many loss-making firms afloat through subsidies was tremendous.

One reason why some countries ended up on the wrong side of the Great Divide was that political and economic costs of resisting calls for bailouts were too great. To appreciate the challenge facing some of these countries, particularly those that were formerly part of the Soviet Union, one must look back even further to the Soviet system of production (Berliner 1976, Kornai 1992). This system typically involved production on a very large scale, in many cases only one firm producing or assembling a particular good. It was partly a political decision by Stalin and later Soviet leaders to make regions overspecialized and interdependent, thus increasing the costs of separating a particular republic. In addition, the Soviet economy had a disproportionately large military–industrial sector, where the choice of geographic location of a factory was often made for political reasons rather than comparative advantage. The legacy of these arrangements is visible in today's Russia in the many "one-factory towns" and the large population living in areas that no longer appear economically viable for their current level of population.[6] Following the breakup of the Soviet Union, most newly independent states inherited a highly concentrated and economically nonviable industrial base, which they had little choice but to keep afloat, at least in the short run.

Another factor that affected why some governments were able to impose fiscal and monetary discipline and others not is the coordination of enterprises' lobbying efforts for more subsidies and bailouts (Perotti 1998). In many countries, more or less formalized groups of financial and industrial firms have formed, partly because they were previously connected to the same administrative structure. These groups made it easier for their members to extract benefits from government. Several studies in Russia have shown that such groups were able to relieve credit constraints of individual member firms (Volchkova 2000, Perotti and Gelfer 2001). But they may also have served the purpose of extracting inefficiently large resource transfers from the state.

On the other side of the budget equation, another important factor that has affected government fiscal and monetary discipline was its ability to raise taxes and other revenues. Several countries that have made it across the Great Divide have been able to raise significant revenues through privatization of state assets. But perhaps a more important common denominator of these countries is the considerable legitimacy of their new democratically elected governments. These countries have also had some experience with democracy before the Second World War and have generally a greater respect for "the rule of law." These factors are obviously of critical importance in limiting tax evasion and in facilitating the enforcement of existing rules and regulations. As Pistor *et al.* (2001) have pointed out, an important obstacle toward greater financial development is the lack of enforcement of existing laws, rather than the existence of an inadequate legal framework.

Conversely, for the countries on the wrong side of the Great Divide, one of the main handicaps inherited from the communist past has been the lack of legitimacy of the state, combined with the lack of experience with democratic government. Within the countries that were formerly part of the Soviet Union, only the Baltic states have had a relatively recent experience with democracy. In central and eastern Europe, Bulgaria and Romania have had virtually no experience with democracy, even if they did not live under communism for as long as the Soviet Union.

The ability of governments to implement fiscal and monetary restraint has also undoubtedly been influenced by the country's geographical proximity and likelihood of accession to the European Union. When countries are located close to markets with large and rich populations, the potential benefits from trade are greater and restructuring appears more attractive. Prior experience of trade with the west appears to be an important predictor of whether enterprise restructuring has been undertaken or not. Most of the growth in central and eastern Europe has come from new firms or firms with extensive trade links with the west during the communist era (Walsh and Duffy 2000).

The possibility of joining the European Union has also played an important political role in advancing the reform process in much of central and eastern Europe. The more certain and the sooner the possibility of joining the European Union, the stronger has been the leverage of this outside anchor (Berglof and Roland 2002).

These observations can go a long way toward explaining the emergence of "crony capitalism" in some of the transition countries as well as the lack of fiscal and monetary responsibility of their governments. They also provide a reasonably good fit for which countries made it across the Great Divide. On the other hand, these observations are less useful for understanding the differences in policies pursued among the group of countries that made it across the Great Divide, or the subsequent convergence in the systemic features of their financial architecture.

Financial transition: when will it end?

The task of transforming centrally planned economies into well-functioning market economies appeared to reformers in the early days to be so simple that they proposed several plans to complete transition in fewer than 500 days! A decade or more into transition, it is fair to say that even the front-runners are far from having completed their financial transition. Even though the basic financial architecture of a market economy is now in place in the countries that have crossed the Great Divide, banking and other financial institutions do not yet perform their intended functions of channeling savings into the most productive investments.

Another unexpected development of the past decade is that the financial system of advanced market economies itself has evolved rapidly. Reformers only belatedly realized that the transition process partly involves chasing a moving target. As the Berlin Wall was falling, deep shifts were occurring in the financial systems of the developed market economies, with a greater role for securities and derivatives markets, venture capital financing followed by initial public offerings, and an acceleration in international financial integration to levels not seen since the end of the nineteenth century. With the spread of international finance, policies aimed at developing local stock markets in transition economies became rapidly outdated, even counterproductive. Similarly, the greater financial integration of the European Union and the world at large increased the desirability and sustainability of foreign banks in transition economies.

The ongoing globalization of the financial industry raises the issue of whether it is still meaningful to talk about national financial systems, at least for economies that are small by global standards. The remarkable presence of foreign commercial banks in the transition economies in central and eastern Europe integrates these national financial sectors into the global strategies of a small number of large financial institutions. What is the role of Hansabank and Unibanka, commercial banks active in the Baltic states, in the strategies of their Swedish parent banks? To what extent can we talk about domestic financial intermediation when external finance for investments comes mostly from foreign savings? What influence do domestic regulators and regulation in transition economies have on the behavior of these institutions with global reach? These are some of the new questions for financial development posed by the current trends of world financial integration.

What have we learned?

Perhaps the main lesson of the past decade of financial transition is the importance of fiscal and monetary discipline at the critical point when the Great Divide opens up. It appears to have been a necessary condition for a successful financial transition. Without fiscal discipline, private investment is crowded out or discouraged by the looming threat of macroeconomic instability. Lack of fiscal discipline has also been a symptom of other ills, like a lack of commitment to close down loss-making firms, poor enforcement of property rights and low levels of compliance with taxes. Countries on the wrong side of the Great Divide have been caught in a vicious circle of macro instability and repeated relapses in financial development. Financial development in these countries at best has had little effect on economic growth and may even have been counterproductive by making it easier for firms to receive credit and thereby reducing their incentive to undertake needed restructuring.

In the countries that have crossed the Great Divide, financial architecture appears to have converged to a bank-based system with substantial foreign ownership. On the positive side, the financial sector in these countries has contributed to the hardening of budget constraints. However, banks have not yet begun extending significant long-term finance nor have they actively promoted restructuring in the industrial sector.

Does this mean that Lipton and Sachs (1990, 1992) have been right all along in focusing almost exclusively on issues of macro stability and in neglecting the challenge of creating the institutional foundations for a well-functioning market economy? As we have argued throughout this article, it is not possible to consider the macro and micro aspects of transition separately. There is a basic complementarity between the macroeconomic notion of fiscal and monetary responsibility and the microeconomic foundations of sound financial institutions, protection of property rights and tax compliance. Writing new laws or transferring them more or less wholesale from abroad is a relatively easy task. Enforcement and the creation of functional institutions is much more difficult. Sound government finances create favorable conditions not only for financial development but also for proper enforcement of the law. Conversely, financially disciplined and tax-compliant institutions and households facilitate fiscal and monetary responsibility.

The institution of currency boards provides an instructive illustration of the complementarity of macro and micro aspects of transition. As we have pointed out, several (mostly small) transition countries, for example, Bulgaria and Estonia, have adopted currency boards or equivalent arrangements, essentially fixing the exchange rate in the country's constitution. These arrangements, have been reasonably effective in establishing monetary stability. But a precondition for their feasibility has been a minimum degree of microeconomic enforcement and political stability. Russia, for example, never introduced a currency board, and most economists recommended against doing so, arguing that the commitment may not be sustainable given that contracts were not enforced and the financial sector was fundamentally weak. Bulgaria did introduce a currency board after severe macroeconomic instability and has achieved some moderate success, but so far the microeconomic institutions have been too weak to generate significant positive results. In the Baltics, Estonia in particular, the micro foundations were right, and the currency board arrangement has been a success.

Fiscal and monetary irresponsibility and lack of enforcement emanate from the same underlying political weaknesses. We have argued that the legitimacy of governments and their accountability to the electorate are essential preconditions. Accountability to the outside world through international agreements can also play an important role in helping governments achieve fiscal and monetary restraint. In this respect, the European Union has played an important role in providing outside anchors for the financial and economic development of transition countries. The accession process has removed domestic political constraints in the transition countries of central and eastern Europe. The pressure to meet the criteria for membership in the European Union was essential for the adoption and enforcement of laws and regulations and for building the basic financial infrastructure. Perhaps even more importantly, the widely shared aspiration to "rejoin Europe" has given strong direction to, and strengthened the commitment of, the governments of these countries. Providing such anchors for the countries that have not yet succeeded in crossing the Great Divide remains a major challenge for the future.

Acknowledgments

We are grateful to Philippe Aghion, Mike Burkart, Stijn Claessens, Tore Ellingsen and, in particular, Enrico Perotti for helpful discussions; to Jan Hanousek and participants in the Journal of Economic Perspectives workshop at CERGE-EI, Prague, the Czech Republic; and to colleagues at SITE at the Stockholm School of Economics for comments. Rudolf Bems has provided excellent research assistance.

Notes

* Erik Berglof is Director, Stockholm Institute of Transition Economics (SITE), Stockholm School of Economics, Stockholm, Sweden. Patrick Bolton is Professor of Economics, Princeton University, Princeton, New Jersey, and Research Associate, National Bureau of Economic Research, Cambridge, Massachusetts. Both authors are Research Fellows, Centre for Economic Policy Research, London, United Kingdom.

1. An interesting anomaly is the Central Bank of Russia, which has far-reaching independence, but where the governor is also a cabinet member. For much of the 1990s, Viktor Gerashenko, originally the head of the monobank Gosbank,

occupied this position. During his first tenure under the Yeltsin presidency, he systematically undermined the government's attempt to stabilize the economy by increasing the money supply to bail out ailing banks and firms. In his second tenure after the crisis of 1998, he has pursued a more strict monetary policy, but he also gave in to intense lobbying not to liquidate and restructure the defunct banking sector.

2. After a severe financial crisis, Bulgaria opted for a currency board arrangement, and the country has since enjoyed a period of relative macroeconomic stability and modest growth.

3. Privatization of firms with bank credits is registered as financial development even though nothing has actually changed in terms of the amount of credit extended.

4. A footnote on the Baltic countries may be warranted here. These countries still have lower levels of economic wealth due to lower starting points and deeper and more protracted initial declines. But their institutional development has proceeded much faster than other countries in the former Soviet Union and on par with the lead reformers in central and eastern Europe. This point is illustrated in Tables 4.2 and 4.3.

5. Anyone vaguely familiar with the current situation in the Japanese banking system may question the reliability of these numbers. The uncertainty should be even greater in the countries of central and eastern Europe, in particular in the countries on the "wrong" side of the Great Divide, where regulatory powers are weaker and the incentives to hide bad loans are stronger.

6. In contrast, China relied much more on a strategy of regional decentralization; for an interesting comparison of Chinese and Russian planning, see Qian and Xu (1993).

References

Abel, Istvan and John Bonin. (2000), 'Retail banking in Hungary: a foreign affair?' William Davidson Institute Working Paper 356.

Acemoglu, Daron, Simon Johnson and James A. Robinson. (2000), 'The colonial origins of comparative development: An empirical investigation'. NBER Working Paper No. 7771.

Beck, Thorsten, Asli Demirguč-Kunt and Ross Levine. (2001), 'Law, politics, and finance'. Mimeo, World Bank.

Benabou, Roland. (1997), 'Inequality and growth', in *NBER Macroeconomics Annual 1996*. Ben S. Bernanke and Rotemberg, Julio J. (eds), Cambridge and London: MIT Press, pp. 11–74.

Berglof, Erik and Gérard Roland. (2002), 'From regatta to big bang: The political economy of accession to the European Union'. IMF Working Paper. Forthcoming.

Berliner, Joseph. (1976), *The Innovation Decision in Soviet Industry*. Cambridge, MA.: MIT Press.

Bortolotti, Bernardo, Marcella Fantini and Domenico Siniscalco. (2001), 'Privatization: politics, institutions and financial markets'. FEEM Discussion Paper.

Claessens, Stijn, Simeon Djankov and Daniela Klingebiel. (2000), 'Stock markets in transition economies'. World Bank, Financial Sector Discussion Paper 5.

Djankov, Simeon and Peter Murrell. (2000), 'Enterprise restructuring in transition: A quantitative survey'. Working Paper, SSRN.

EBRD. (2000), *Transition Report*. Washington, DC.: EBRD.

Fries, Steven and Anita Taci. (2001), 'Banking reform and development in transition economies'. Mimeo, European Bank of Reconstruction and Development.

Gerschenkron, Alexander. (1962), *Economic Backwardness in Historical Perspective, A Book of Essays*. Cambridge, MA.: Harvard University Press.

Hellman, Joel *et al.* (2000), 'Measuring governance, corruption, and state capture: How firms and bureaucrats shape the business environment in Transit'. World Bank Working Paper No. 2312.

Huang, Haizhou, Dalia Marin and Chenggang Xu. (2001), 'Financial crisis, economic recovery and banking development in Russia'. Mimeo, Munich University.

IMF. (2000), *World Economic Outlook, Chapter 4*. Washington, DC.: IMF.

Johnson, Simon, Peter Boone and Alasdair Breach. (2000), 'Corporate governance in the asian financial crisis 1997–98'. *Journal of Financial Economics*. October/November, 58(1–2): 141–86.

Keane, M. and Prasad, E. (2000), 'Inequalities, transfers and growth: New evidence from the economic transition in Poland'. IMF Working Paper 00/177, June.

King, Robert and Ross Levine. (1993a), 'Finance, entrepreneurship, and growth: Theory and evidence'. *Journal of Monetary Economics*. December, 32(3): 513–42.

King, Robert and Ross Levine. (1993b), 'Finance and growth: Schumpeter might be Right'. *Quarterly Journal of Economics*. August, 108(3): 717–37.

Kornai, János. (1992), *The Socialist System: The Political Economy of Communism*. Oxford: Oxford University Press.

La Porta, Rafael *et al.* (1997), 'Legal determinants of external finance'. *Journal of Finance*. July, 52(3): 1131–150.

La Porta, Rafael *et al.* (1998), 'Law and finance'. *Journal of Political Economy*. December, 106(6): 1113–155.

Levine, Ross. (2000), 'Bank-based or market-based financial systems: Which is better?' Mimeo, University of Minnesota.

Levine, Ross and Sara Zervos. (1998), 'Stock markets, banks, and economic growth'. *American Economic Review*. June, 88(3): 537–58.

Levine, Ross, Norman Loayza and Thorsten Beck. (2000), 'Financial intermediary development and growth: Causes and causality'. *Journal of Monetary Economics*. 46(1): 31–77.

Lipton, David and Jeffrey Sachs. (1990), 'Creating a market economy in eastern Europe: The case of Poland'. *Brookings Papers of Economic Activity*. 1, 75–133.

Lipton, David and Jeffrey Sachs. (1992), 'Prospects for Russia's Economic Reforms'. *Brookings Papers of Economic Activity*. 2, 213–65.

Mitchell, Janet. (2001), 'Bad debts and the cleaning of banks' balance sheets: An application to transition economies'. *Journal of Financial Intermediation*. January, 10(1): 1–27.

Olson, Mancur. (1982), *The Rise and Decline of Nations*. New Haven, N.J., and London: Yale University Press.

Padilla, Atilano J. and Alejandro Requejo. (2001), 'The costs and benefits of the strict protection of creditor rights: Theory and evidence'. in Marco Pagano, (ed.), *Defusing Default*. Washington: IADB, Chapter 1.

Pagano, Marco. (1993), 'Financial markets and growth: An overview'. *European Economic Review*. April, 37(2–3): 613–22.

Perotti, Enrico. (1998), 'Inertial credit and opportunistic arrears in transition'. *European Economic Review*. November, 42(9): 1703–725.

Perotti, Enrico and Stanislav Gelfer. (2001), 'Red Barons or Robber Barons? Governance and financing in Russian Financial-Industrial groups'. *European Economic Review*. Forthcoming.

Perotti, Roberto. (1996), 'Growth, income distribution and democracy: What the data Say'. *Journal of Economic Growth*. June, 1(2): 149–87.

Pistor, Katharina. (2000), 'Patterns of legal change: Shareholder and creditor rights in transition economics'. EBRD Working Paper 49, London.

Pistor, Katharina, Martin Raiser and Stanislav Gelfer. (2000), 'Law and finance in transition'. *Economics of Transition*. 8(2): 325–68.

Qian, Yingyi and Chenggang Xu. (1993), 'Why China's economic reforms differ: The M-form hierarchy and entry/expansion of the non-state sector'. *Economics of Transition*. June, 1(2): 135–70.

Rajan, Raghuram and Luigi Zingales. (1998), 'Finance dependence and growth'. *American Economic Review*. June, 88(3): 559–86.

Rajan, Raghuram and Luigi Zingales. (2000), 'The great reversal'. NBER Discussion Paper No. 8178.

Sgard, Jerome. (1996), 'Banks during transition: What have we learned?' Mimeo, CEPII.

Tadasse, Solomon. (2000), 'Financial Architecture and economic performance: International evidence'. Mimeo, University of South Carolina.

Tang, Helana, Edda Zoli and Irina Klytchnikova. (2000), 'Banking crises in transition economies: Fiscal costs and related issues'. World Bank Policy Research Working Paper No. 2484, November.

Volchkova, Natalya. (2000), 'Does financial-industrial group membership affect fixed investment: Evidence from Russia'. CEFIR Working Paper No. 4.

Walsh, Patrick Paul and Fiona Duffy. (2000), 'Individual pay and outside options: Evidence from the Polish labour force survey'. William Davidson Institute Working Paper No. 364.

5
Microfinance: Where do we Stand?

Beatriz Armendáriz de Aghion and Jonathan Morduch

1 Introduction

Economies are built upon people buying and selling, lending and borrowing. The beauty of the market is that, when it works well, sellers are matched to buyers and lenders are matched to worthy borrowers. But when the market does not work well, goods go unsold and promising investment projects go unfunded. We understand why markets fail – the economics of information provides rigorous underpinnings for why credit markets, in particular, are so problematic.[1] The challenge has been to move from diagnosis to prescription. The challenge is particularly great in poorer regions, where individuals may have workable ideas and relevant experience but lack collateral. Even a £100 loan can make a difference to a small-scale shopkeeper or craftsperson in countries like Nepal or Uganda, but formal sector banks have steered clear, focusing instead on larger loans to better-established, wealthier clients.

The microfinance movement has aimed to change all that. The hope is that by using innovative new contracts, microlenders can both make profits and serve the under-served. While the full promise is as yet unmet (profits remain hard to squeeze out and the very poor are tough to reach), there are a growing number of success stories and, world wide, nearly 70 million low-income individuals are served by microfinance institutions (Daley-Harris 2003).

In this chapter we first focus on the innovations that have made microfinance possible. We then deliver an overview of recent trends. We argue that the future of microfinance institutions is ultimately in the hands of international donor agencies and local governments, which have been recently promoting competition and stressing financial self-sustainability as a way to maximize the breadth of outreach. The strategy is a major departure from traditional approaches to foreign aid, and it challenges the role of applied welfare economics as the leading framework for policy analysis. In the traditional framework, cost–benefit analyses are used to determine the allocations of subsidies that can do the greatest good for the greatest number. In the new world of microfinance, many eschew subsidies for all but start-up expenses, and the aim is to become fully profitable, independent institutions.

In Section 1 we provide background to the current debate on the role and scope of microfinance institutions. In particular, we deliver a brief explanation of how the innovative "group lending" technique gained donors' attention, and how it captured the imagination of academic economists. In Section 3 we argue that the dissemination of microfinance institutions was facilitated by additional innovations, and we focus on four: the use of "progressive lending", the flexible treatment of collateral, the focus on women as customers, and the promotion of clients' savings. In Section 4 we conclude by spelling out three main areas where the support of international donors and local governments can most effectively help microfinance institutions meet both their self-sustainability and social objectives.

2   Background

Microfinance grew out of experiments in Latin America and South Asia, but the best-known start was in Bangladesh in 1976, following a widespread famine in 1974 and a hard-fought war of liberation in 1971. In the 1970s Henry Kissinger famously called Bangladesh an "international basketcase", but 30 years later Kissinger's prognosis proves to be quite wide of the mark. Bangladesh continues to face economic, political, and social challenges, but it is hardly a basketcase. Fertility rates have dropped from an average of seven births per woman in 1970 to half that today; the economy has slowly moved forward, despite the continuing need for macroeconomic and fiscal reforms; and the microfinance movement has taken root across the nation, with over ten million customers spread across the country's villages. Advocates argue that the microfinance movement has helped to reduce poverty, improved schooling levels, and generated or expanded millions of small businesses (e.g. Khandker 1998). The idea of microfinance has now spread globally, with replications in Africa, Latin America, Asia, and Eastern Europe, as well as in richer economies like Norway, the United States, and England. The latest count includes over 2500 institutions worldwide, each serving on average over 25 000 low-income customers.

No person is more closely associated with microfinance than Muhammad Yunus, an economist who was teaching at Chittagong University in the 1970s. In the midst of the famine, Yunus started looking for ways to improve the lives of the villagers living adjacent to his university. Together with his students, he seized on the credit market as the most direct and effective vehicle for development. Yunus started by lending to villagers from his own pocket and found that not only was he repaid on time but that the villagers were demonstrably benefiting from the new opportunities that the loans opened up. Yunus could not self-finance an initiative that hoped to spread beyond the village, however, and the challenge was to devise a mechanism that could be quickly replicated and that ensured high repayments while containing costs. With the government's blessing, the Grameen Bank was inaugurated in 1976, based on the premise of lending to the very poor at reasonable interest rates and without requiring collateral. In order to keep focused on the poorest clients, the bank instituted a rule (eventually relaxed) that they would only lend to households owning under a half acre of land, a rough indicator for being functionally landless.

The essence of microfinance is to draw ideas from existing "informal sector" credit mechanisms – like intra-family loans, Rotating Savings and Credit Associations (ROSCAs), and local moneylenders – while creating a viable conduit for capital infusions from formal sector banks, donors, and governments.[2] The lack of formal financial institutions in village economies has been long-acknowledged as a barrier to development, and millions of dollars in subsidy were channeled through state-run development banks beginning in the 1950s with the aim of reaching the poor. The initiatives were poorly designed, however, and credit was allocated according to political motives rather than need, management was lax, and repayment rates plummeted. India's Integrated Rural Development Programme (IRDP), for example, ended up with loan repayment rates around 30 per cent before being re-named and reformed. The Grameen Bank managed to persuade donors that it was possible for lending institutions in rural areas to be shielded from political interference and that lending to the poor could yield high repayment rates. For most of its life, Grameen has advertised loan repayment rates around 98 per cent.[3]

How did the Grameen Bank change the equation? The best-known story centers on the group lending methodology. While the Grameen Bank itself has modified many of its features in its new "Grameen Bank II" format (Yunus 2002), replicators worldwide still stay by the older model. The idea is that upon expanding to a new village, the bank holds a meeting and announces that it will soon introduce a new kind of banking operation. The bank will not require collateral and will serve the poorest only; it will make loans to individuals, but in a special way. Individuals interested in borrowing will get loans for their own, independent projects, but they must approach the bank with four others who similarly seek loans. These five-person groups meet with a loan officer from the bank once each week, at which time loans are disbursed and payments are made. To reduce transactions costs, the loan officer meets simultaneously with eight five-person groups, formed as a 40-person "centre"; the meetings take place in the village rather than at the local bank branch.

The loan contract has a twist, and this is what has most interested academic economists. The twist is that should a borrower be unable to repay her loan (about 95 per cent of borrowers are women), she will have to quit her membership of the bank – as will her four fellow group members. While the others are not forced explicitly to repay for the potential defaulter, they have clear incentives to do so if they wish to continue obtaining future loans. The key is that Grameen Bank loans (like loans from other microlenders) are more attractive than loans from other sources like moneylenders. While moneylenders may charge interest rates over 100 per cent per year, the Grameen Bank keeps its official rates at 20 per cent (and even with extra fees, effective rates are below 30 per cent per year).

This methodology has caught the attention of a large number of researchers. Maitreesh Ghatak (2000), and Beatriz Armendáriz de Aghion and Christian Gollier (2000), for example, argue that allowing borrowers to voluntarily form their own groups helps microlenders overcome an "adverse selection" problem. The problem is that a traditional bank has a difficult time distinguishing between inherently "risky" and "safe" borrowers in its pool of loan applicants; if it could, the bank would charge a high interest rate to the risky borrower and a lower one to the safe borrower. But without precise information, the bank must charge the same (high) rates to all potential borrowers, and this can trigger the exit of safe borrowers from the credit market. The outcome is inefficient since, in an ideal world, projects undertaken by both risky and safe borrowers should be financed. Villagers themselves, though, often have quite good information about the relative riskiness of their neighbors, even if the bank is left in the dark. One advantage of the group lending methodology (at least in principle) is that it can put local information to work for the outside lender. Adverse selection is mitigated under the group lending methodology, the argument goes, for two reasons. First, in an economy where all villagers (safe and risky) know each others' types, the group lending contract (specifically the notion of "joint liability") will induce assortative matching: the safe borrowers will form groups among themselves; and risky borrowers will have no choice but to form groups with other risky borrowers. Because by definition members of the latter group are apt to default more often, participants in risky groups will have to repay more often for their defaulting peers. Safer borrowers, by the same token, will have to repay for their peers less often. While all borrowers face exactly the same contracts with exactly the same interest rates, the fact of assortative matching means that safe borrowers pay lower *effective* interest rates: their expected costs (including the cost of repaying for group members in trouble) will be lower. This in turn can induce them to enter the credit market, take loans, and improve efficiency. The very simple contract in effect means that the microlender in practice transfers some of the cost of dealing with risky borrowers back onto the risky borrowers themselves.

From the standpoint of the microlender, bringing the safe borrowers back into the market lowers the average incidence of default and thus lowers costs. With lower costs, the microlenders can in turn reduce interest rates even further. It is most likely to do so if either it faces stiff competition or if, for social reasons, its aim is simply to break even in order to bring about the greatest social gain. Group lending thereby can eliminate adverse selection inefficiencies.[4]

Another strand of argument highlights the fact that the group lending methodology can potentially mitigate *ex ante* moral hazard problems as well. This problem emerges when, after having extended loans, the financial institution cannot effectively monitor borrowers and therefore cannot write a credible contract that enforces prudent behavior. Borrowers are protected by limited liability since they have no collateral to offer (so that, in the case of default the bank cannot seize more than the borrowers' current cash flow). Borrowers may thus be tempted to undertake riskier projects than the bank would like. The gain to the borrowers is that even though such projects may yield a lower return on average, if successful, their returns from such projects can be very high. Since the borrower does not face the full consequences of failure (due to limited liability), tensions emerge. The bank can anticipate this, and will charge relatively high interest rates to compensate for the additional risk – unless a third, well-informed party forces the borrowers not to undertake risky projects.

Joseph Stiglitz (1990) explains that under a group lending methodology, the group plays such a role; since group members agree to shoulder a monetary penalty in the case of default by a peer, the group members have incentives to monitoring each other and can potentially threaten to impose "social sanctions" when risky projects are chosen.[5] In particular, each borrower can denounce her peer's "misbehavior" to the community, and *de facto* prevent her from undertaking risky projects, or they can simply shun the neighbor who deviates, imposing costs that are both economic and social. Because neighbors can monitor each other much more easily than a bank can (because of geographical proximity and trade links) the effective delegation of *ex ante* monitoring from the microlender to the borrowers themselves involves efficiency gains. These gains (again, assuming that the financial institution faces competition or that it is an NGO which merely attempts to break even) will allow interest rates to fall – and they will in turn further mitigate the *ex ante* moral hazard problem.

A third potential benefit of group lending is by reducing *ex post* moral hazard. This problem emerges once project returns have been realized. But assume that the financial institution cannot observe such returns; then, borrowers who are protected by limited liability have incentives to pretend that their returns are "low" or to strategically default on their debt obligations. Group lending with joint responsibility can however lower the incidence of strategic default when project returns can be observed by the borrowers' neighbors. Under the fear of suffering from social sanctions, borrowers will declare their true return realizations and repay when what they can.[6] (While there may be situations in which villagers could instead collude against the bank, collusion has seldom been a problem in practice.) By lowering the incidence of strategic default (and, once more, assuming that the bank faces competition or the simply wishes to break even) group lending can potentially bring interest rates down, and thereby mitigate the *ex post* moral hazard problem as well.

The three arguments rationalize the group lending methodology as a device for overcoming credit market inefficiencies, which are in turn created by informational asymmetries between the financial institution (or the lender) and a group of borrowers. Our description thus far has also helped us understand how social sanctions in village economies or in close-knit societies can serve as an enforcement mechanism that potentially circumvents the limited liability issue.

3 Beyond group lending

The group lending methodology has a great deal to recommend, but it also has problems. In particular, Ashok Rai and Tomas Sjöström (2004) argue that, while the contract can enhance efficiency, it can also diminish it. Consider, for example, a situation in which one borrower cannot repay and the other four partners are then under pressure. They may or may not have the resources and the desire to bail out their neighbor. If they do not, the loan officer is bound by the rules to no longer lend to any of them, even though they may each be exemplary clients and the trouble arose through no fault of their own. When it is costly to find such good clients, the loan officer will be reluctant to abide by the regulations, and often the letter of the law is not implemented. Instead, the customer in trouble is removed from the program, and the other four are allowed to stay on in a group with a replacement member (e.g. Matin 1996). The result is better for everyone, and the new Grameen Bank II introduced by Muhammad Yunus (2002) takes steps toward weakening rules around joint liability.

So, how then are high repayment rates maintained? It turns out that microfinance introduces a series of innovations, none of which have captured the imagination as strongly as group lending but which are, nonetheless, powerful in practice. Early practitioners and social scientists failed to disentangle these elements, and we next set out some of the most important aspects.[7] The features not only help to explain how microfinance works in places like Bangladesh, but also how microfinance can be replicated in places where population densities are lower and local information networks are weaker. Upon arriving in Bangladesh, a visitor is often reminded that this country in square kilometers is as large as the State of Florida, but that instead of having 16 million inhabitants it has 130 million. Many regions of Africa, Latin America, and Eastern Europe are in contrast sparsely populated and that poses a set of challenges. The additional innovations help by not relying on group membership – and the microfinance world is increasingly moving toward traditional bilateral contracts between microlenders and individual clients.

The first additional innovation is "progressive lending". The idea is simple: each borrower is granted a small loan of about £50 in the first period, which is typically repayable over one year in weekly installments. Then, year after year the loan size increases as the borrower demonstrates her reliability and trustworthiness. The scheme has various advantages, one of which is that it enables microlenders to "test" borrowers with small loans at the start in order to screen out the worst prospects before taking additional risks by expanding loan scale.[8] Also, it increases the opportunity cost of nonrepayment in that borrowers become increasingly fearful about being denied access to credit in the future since nonpayment will trigger cut-off from a growing stream of future loans.

There are two reasons why microlenders cannot entirely rely on progressive lending, however. One is that when there is a multiplicity of microlenders, threats to not refinance borrowers lose their teeth because borrowers who default on a loan can always turn to another microlender (assuming that the other microlender has poor information on credit histories, a common situation in the absence of credit bureaux). The other tension is that as the loan size increases, defaults become increasingly attractive, especially if the relationship between the microlender and the borrower has a clear final date. We will come back to remedial measures to these problems in the next section.

Another innovation consists of flexibility with regard to collateral. For banks that require collateral, they can reach a wider group of borrowers by dropping concern with the salvage value of collateral (can the bank sell the asset and cover costs of the defaulted loan?) and instead worrying about "notional" value (is losing the asset enough of a deterrent so that the borrower will behave prudently – even if the salvage value of the asset is negligible?).[9] A case in point is the kind of collateral which is being accepted by microlenders in rural Albania, which include livestock, land, and working tools (selling them is not likely to allow the bank to cover the costs of problem loans through liquidation). One main problem with this innovation, however, is that it still requires some form of collateral and thus can undermine microlenders' efforts to reach very poor borrowers. But it has proven effective when lending to households just below and just above the poverty line, such as those targeted by Bank Rakyat Indonesia, a leading, for-profit lender.

How then to target a population of borrowers which is considered to be both more reliable and poorer? The answer to this question takes us to the next innovation of microfinance: focusing on female customers. According to recent reports, women make up to 80 per cent of the clients of the world's 34 largest microlenders (Priti Mody 2002). This is a major shift for banks working in low-income areas. Historically, banks had targeted farmers, which meant working mainly with men since the decision-makers on farming matters are often men. Yunus, and those who followed him, instead focused on supporting nonfarm enterprises (and often livestock-raising, but seldom crops). This opened up the door for serving women in greater numbers, since women often take the lead in processing (like risk husking) and small enterprise like craft-making.

There are two main reasons for targeting women: one is financial and the other is social. From the financial standpoint, relative to men, women are more conservative in their investment strategies. In an early study from Bangladesh, Mahabub Hossain (1988) found that 81 per cent of women in his sample had no repayment problems versus 74 per cent of men. Similarly, Shahidur Khandker *et al.* (1995) found that 15 per cent of male borrowers had missed payments before the final due date, while all but 1 per cent of women had perfect repayment records. Similar patterns have been found elsewhere: in Malawi, for example, David Hulme (1991) found on-time repayments for women customers to be 92 per cent versus 83 per cent for men, and David Gibbons and S. Kasim (1991) found that in Malaysia the repayment comparison is 95 per cent for women versus 72 per cent for men. The reasons that women are more apt to repay are multiple, but most observers view poor women as having fewer alternative options than their husbands and being more vulnerable to the shame of noncompliance. But, at the same time, we need to stress that the evidence does not condition on other factors and these explanations are anecdotal. Once researchers control for income levels, assets, education, and other socio-economic factors, we suspect that the "advantage" of women will diminish. Banks, though, are most interested in unconditional expectations when targeting, and, for that, simply knowing that women on average are better clients has been a powerful force toward re-orienting programs toward women. Thus, from a purely financial viewpoint, targeting women can make sense.

The other reason for targeting women is that lending to women can be more effective in meeting social objectives. A growing literature in sociology and economics documents both the overrepresentation of women amongst the poorest of the poor and the greater probability that money in the hands of women is spent on children's health and education relative to money in the hands of their husbands. Microlenders such as *ProMujer* in Latin America, have thus turned to microfinance as a way to further their goal of empowering poor women and spreading knowledge on good health, nutrition, and hygiene practices.[10]

A fourth innovation of the microfinance movement concerns savings. Economists have focused sharply on credit market problems in low-income regions, and have left problems with the savings side comparatively neglected. One reason is that it was assumed that poor households have limited demand for saving since surpluses are small given subsistence needs. The second reason for the neglect is that it has been assumed that excess funds could profitably be ploughed into one's farm or small business, so the need for a generic saving account would be minimal. The past two decades of microfinance is showing us that these assumptions have limited appeal. Even very poor households want to save and do save – but must often do it through imperfect informal means, like leaving money with a neighbor, sewing notes into one's clothing or hiding it in the house, and joining rotating savings groups or handing money over to a deposit taker. These means can be costly, provide no hedge against inflation, and offer limited security. One study in Uganda showed that the average loss in savings *per year* was 22 per cent for 99 per cent of households.[11] One source of loss is constant requests for aid from friends, relatives, and, often, husbands.[12] Having a safe, convenient, secure place to save allows poor households to better manage their money, handle large expenses like school fees and religious obligations, and start building up assets that might eventually be used as collateral. Many microfinance institutions, including the Grameen Bank, thus started by creating "voluntary" saving facilities and "compulsory" saving facilities. The former had the objective of meeting individual clients' demand for tiny savings, and deposits were made at weekly meetings. The latter could not be withdrawn without the consent of the group and, in practice, came to act as a form of collateral that could be accessed in times of repayment problems. Thus, introducing savings facilities in tandem with lending further enhanced the lenders' financial self-sustainability objectives.

The push today is to shift from an emphasis on the compulsory deposits and to move toward emphasis on voluntary deposits. One tension is that transactions costs are high since deposits and, with "voluntary" savings accounts, withdrawals are not made in fixed amounts that can be quickly recorded; amounts transacted may also be tiny. Bank Rakyat Indonesia, for example, which has been the pioneer on the saving side, allows clients to open savings accounts with balances of less than £1. Banks also need greater liquidity in order to have funds available for unexpected withdrawals, and this cuts into investment income. Most importantly, institutions that take savings need greater regulation than institutions that only make loans. After all, if the institution collapses, customers with loans outstanding do not suffer (indeed they gain by not having to repay their loans), but a collapsing bank can take customers' lifetime savings and, if unregulated, offer no recourse to the victims. Work is underway to create new regulatory protocols that are effective but not too onerous for microfinance institutions dealing with many small transactions.

4   Recent trends and policy recommendations

Many microfinance institutions initially emphasized high repayment rates, advertising that 95 per cent or more of loans were repaid, a sharp break from the experiences of inefficient state banks that they set out to replace. Making dramatic strides in cutting costs has been harder. The result is that the average microlender has had greater difficulty attaining self-sustainability than donors had hoped. One solution has been to go upmarket, turning from the very poorest to households around the poverty line or just above it. This is the target market, for example, of the affiliates of ACCION International, a network based in Boston, Massachusetts that provides support for microlenders in the United States and Latin America.

ACCION International has been highly influential in shaping donors' minds over the past decade, advocating subsidization for start-up costs only and pushing hard for a commercial orientation. The view is that the best hope to reach the greatest number of poor and near-poor households (if not the poorest) is to get access to commercial capital in amounts that are only possible if institutions transform themselves into fully chartered banks.

Donors have been receptive to the argument and have kept a close eye on the financial statistics of programs. This is clearly a constraint for microfinance enterprises that are operating in increasingly competitive environments, and it poses a high hurdle for programs committed to serving the very poorest. Competition has created trouble in Bolivia and Bangladesh and with the growing successes of microfinance there is apt to be trouble ahead in other regions as well. One priority is thus the creation of credit bureaux that limit the possibility of borrowers getting over their heads in debt and jumping from one microlender to the next without consequence.

Another area that deserves greater consideration is regulation. In the absence of a well-functioning regulatory framework within which microfinance institutions can operate, it will be harder to operate flexible savings accounts and to effectively intermediate finances. The tension, as mentioned in the section above, is that regulation should not overburden the institutions it is trying to help. One middle ground reached in Bangladesh is to impose strict regulations on those programs that seek to create truly flexible savings accounts – but for organizations that form as cooperatives, the government tolerates light regulation as long as the institution has a greater volume of loans outstanding than the amount of deposits taken in. If the institution collapses, the winners (borrowers) will at least outnumber the losers (depositors). The trouble is that with no way of making transfers between the two groups there is still potential for substantial harm.

A final issue involves delivering services that are complementary to finance – in particular health and education services. Programs like

BRAC's Targeting the Ultrapoor ask: how can one expect microfinance to help unhealthy and uneducated individuals to grow out of poverty? In response, BRAC, Bangladesh's NGO, combines credit with training, food subsidies, and other support. It is not possible to expect programs like BRAC to undertake those broader roles while at the same time insisting that they become fully financially self-sustainable, and BRAC's success rests on a partnership with the World Food Programme involving substantial subsidization. Finding the appropriate division of labor is the most difficult but critical step in navigating trade-offs between reaching financial self-sustainability as an institution and helping customers escape poverty and make better lives.

Notes

1. Debraj Ray's (1998) *Development Economics* provides a valuable introduction to arguments. See also Armendáriz de Aghion and Morduch, *The economics of Microfinance* to be published by MIT Press in 2005.
2. There are "random" and "bidding" ROSCAS everywhere, but random ROSCAs are more often observed. In a random ROSCA, a group of individuals meets at pre-determined dates and contributes an amount of cash to a common "pot"; the pot is then given to one member of the group to use to make large purchases. Lucky participants get the pot earlier, but have to continue contributing until everyone in the group has received the pot. Reasons for why ROSCAs do not fail (i.e. why those individuals that get the pot in earlier rounds continue to show up at subsequent meetings), are that individuals in close-knit societies can overcome problems created by informational asymmetries and difficulties enforcing contracts that hobble formal sector institutions. See, chapter 3 of Armendáriz de Aghion and Morduch (2005) for a comprehensive review.
3. See the sources in Armendáriz de Aghion and Morduch (forthcoming) for more on the IRDP. Morduch (1999) provides critical perspectives on the Grameen Bank's repayment rates.
4. Beatriz Armendáriz de Aghion and Christian Gollier (2000) demonstrate, that the bank may be better insured even in urban economies where potential borrowers do not have a great deal of information about each other's types. They show a case in which, although safe borrowers cannot repay the debt of their risky peers, risky ones – when lucky – have high enough returns to repay the loans of their risky peers, which in turn lowers the overall risk faced by the financial institution. This in turn allows the bank to decrease the interest rate, which mitigates the adverse selection problem.
5. Stiglitz (1990) does not make the assumption on social sanctions explicit. Besley and Coate (1995) make this assumption, however, and demonstrate that it is necessary for their results to hold.
6. See, notably, Timothy Besley and Stephen Coate (1995), and Beatriz Armendáriz de Aghion (1999).
7. Armendáriz de Aghion and Morduch (2000).

8. See Parikshit Ghosh and Debraj Ray (1997) for a model that highlights this issue.
9. See Debraj Ray (1998) for more on asymmetries regarding the value that borrowers and lenders attach to collateral.
10. Chapter 7 of our forthcoming book reviews the new economics of gender and implications for microfinance.
11. Graham Wright and Leonard Mutesasira (2000). "Relative Risk to the Savings of Poor People", MicroSave-Africa. Cited in footnote 6 of Hirschland (2003). See Morduch (1999) for more on the hidden costs of informal mechanisms and related inefficiencies.
12. Recent evidence comes from a survey conducted in Nairobi by Anderson and Balland (2002). The authors report that one of the main reasons that women join a ROSCA is that they want to keep their savings away from their husbands' grabbing hands.

References

Anderson, Siwan and Jean-Marie Baland (2002), 'The economics of ROSCAs and intrahousehold allocation', *Quarterly Journal of Economics*, August: 983–95.

Armendáriz de Aghion, Beatriz and Christian Gollier (2000), 'Peer group formation in an adverse selection model', *The Economic Journal*, July.

Armendáriz de Aghion, Beatriz and Jonathan Morduch (2005), *The Economics of Microfinance*, Cambridge, MA: MIT Press.

Armendáriz de Aghion, Beatriz, and Jonathan Morduch (2000), 'Microfinance beyond group lending', *The Economics of Transition* 8 (2): 401–20.

Armendáriz de Aghion, Beatriz (1999), 'On the design of a credit agreement with peer monitoring', *Journal of Development Economics* 60: 79–104.

Besley, Thimothy, and Stephen Coate (1995), 'Group lending, repayment incentives, and social collateral', *Journal of Development Economics* 46.

Daley-Harris, Sam (2003), *The State of the Microcredit Summit Campaign 2003*. Washington, DC: Microcredit Summit.

Ghatak, Maitreesh (2000), 'Joint liability credit contracts and the peer selection effect', *Economic Journal*, July.

Ghosh, Parikshit and Debraj Ray (1997), 'Information and repeated interaction: application to informal credit markets', Texas A&M and Boston University, draft.

Gibbons, David and S. Kasim (1991), *Banking on the rural poor*, Center for Policy Research, Malaysia: University Sains.

Graham, Wright and Leonard Mutesasire (2000), 'Relative risk to the savings of poor people', MicroSave-Africa.

Hirschland, Madeline (2003), 'Serving small depositors: overcoming the obstacles, recognizing the tradeoffs,' *Microbanking Bulletin* 9 (July): 3–8.

Hossain, Mahabub (1988), Credit for alleviation of rural poverty: The Grameen Bank of Bangladesh, Washington, DC: International Food Policy Research Institute Research Report 65, February.

Hulme, David (1991), 'The Malawi Mudzi Fund: daughter of Grameen', *Journal of International Development* 3 (4).

Khandker, Shahidur (1998), *Fighting Poverty with Microcredit*, Washington, DC: World Bank.

Khandker, Shahidur R., Baqui Khalily and Zahed Kahn (1995), Grameen Bank: Performance and Sustainability, World Bank Discussion Paper 306, Washington DC.

Matin, Imran (1996), 'Group credit arrangements with joint liability: Some thoughts and puzzles', *Grassroots* V (20): 44–8.

Mody, Priti (2002), 'Gender empowerment and microfinance', University of Washington, Evans school Working Paper. [Available at www.evans.washington.edu/faculty/cla/599_00pmody.htm.]

Morduch, Jonathan (1999), 'The role of subsidies in microfinance: evidence from the Grameen Bank', *Journal of Development Economics* 60 (1), October: 229–48.

Rai, Ashok and Tomas Sjöström (2004), 'Is Grameen lending efficient? repayment incentives and insurance in village economies', *Review of Economic Studies* 71 (1), January 2004: 217–34.

Ray, Debraj (1998), *Development Economics*. Princeton, NJ: Princeton University Press.

Stiglitz, Joseph E. (1990), 'Peer monitoring and credit markets', *World Bank Economic Review* 4 (3): 351–66.

Yunus, Muhammad (2002), 'Grameen Bank II: Designed to Open New Possibilities', October 2002 [Revision of May 2002 statement]. Available at: http://www.grameen-info.org/bank/bank2.html.

6
Financial Development, Institutional Investors and Economic Performance

E. Philip Davis[1]

Introduction

Institutional investors comprise pension funds, insurance companies and mutual funds. A salient feature of many OECD countries, and some Emerging Market Economies in recent years, is growth of such institutional investors, notably in the wake of pension reform shifting retirement income provision from pay-as-you-go to funding. Table 6.1 shows the size of pension fund sectors in selected countries where radical pension reform has taken place.[2] The ongoing ageing of the population and financing difficulties of pay-as-you-go systems suggests that such reforms will become yet more common in the future. Accordingly, it is important to analyse the impact of institutional investment on the economy.

In this context, this chapter seeks to address the role of institutional investors in financial development, and to trace the effects on economic performance. We first provide background on the stylised facts and economic interpretation of financial development before summarising the results of existing work on financial development and growth, noting the absence of explicit consideration of institutionalisation. We then survey the literature on the specific ways in which institutional investors may assist in economic development before undertaking econometric estimation partly extending earlier work in Davis (2002). The first empirical section uses G-7 plus Australian data to assess the impact of institutional investors on the performance of the corporate sector. The second part seeks to undertake simple growth regressions to assess the effect of institutional investors on growth in 16 OECD countries.

Table 6.1   Characteristics of selected funded pension systems

	Real returns 1970–95	Less average earnings	Less global portfolio	Assets (% of GDP)	Coverage
Chile	13.0 (9.5) (1980–95 only)	+9.8	+4.1	39 (1995)	99% members; 58% contribute
Singapore	1.3 (2.0)	−5.6	−3.8	56 (1996)	90% members, 67% contribute
Malaysia	3.0 (3.9)	−1.4	−3.7	47 (1996)	86% members, 50% contribute
Switzerland	1.7 (7.5)	+0.2	−2.0	73 (1994)	90%
Australia	1.8 (11.4)	+0.8	−4.3	56 (1996)	92%
Netherlands	4.6 (6.0)	+3.2	−0.2	85 (1996)	89%
UK	5.9 (12.8)	+3.1	0.0	76 (1996)	75%

Source: Davis (1998).

1   The evolution of financial structure

There is a widespread perception, backed by empirical observation that financial systems go through stages of development. For example, Rybczinski (1997) suggests that one can distinguish a bank, market and securitised phase. Most Emerging Market Economies (EMEs) are still in the bank-oriented phase, while OECD countries are either in the market or securitised phase (where 'securitised' implies a growing importance of securities finance generally rather than just packaging of loans in the form of securities). Whereas institutional investors are absent at the bank dominated stage, they begin to develop in the market stage and may become dominant in the securitised stage.

Stylised facts drawn from empirical observation suggest a somewhat more complex pattern (see Allen and Gale 2000), although the idea of phases remains helpful. Schmidt et al. (1999, 2001) argue that there is path dependence, meaning that a bank-based system such as Germany will not automatically develop into a market-based system. However, they acknowledge that a financial crisis, perhaps triggered by 'uncoordinated, far-reaching reforms' could lead to that result, because elements such as trust, implicit contracts and mutually consistent expectations which underpin relationship banking would be very difficult to rebuild after such a crisis. We argue in Davis (1993) that pension reform could also have such an effect by developing institutions unwilling to be subordinated to domestic banks.

On average, as shown by Demirguc-Kunt and Levine (2000), banks, nonbanks and stock markets are larger, more active and more efficient in richer countries. Furthermore, in OECD countries, stock markets become more active and efficient relative to banks, and there is some tendency for financial systems to become more market oriented as the countries become richer. Meanwhile, countries with a Common-Law tradition, protection of shareholders' rights, good accounting, low corruption and no explicit deposit insurance tend to be market-based – and have large institutional sectors – whatever their income level, see also La Porta *et al.* (1999). In contrast, countries with a French Civil-Law tradition, poor protection of the rights of shareholders and creditors, poor contract enforcement and accounting standards, restrictive banking regulation, high corruption and inflation tend to have underdeveloped banks and markets – and institutions. The few countries with a German-law tradition, which offers strong protection for creditors, tend to have strong bank-based systems, with small institutional investor sectors.

Rajan and Zingales (2000) show that financial development has not been monotonic. The major OECD countries were on some measures more financially developed in 1913 than in 1980, and a significant reversal in financial development and financial integration took place between 1913 and 1950. A tightening of regulation in that period led to a decline in the size and importance of the financial sector relative to GDP. The imposition of such 'structural regulation' implied that the service provided to the non-financial sector was sub optimal, with for example low deposit rates and rationing of credit to households. It did however prevent banks from taking excessive risks in response to the guarantee provided by the safety net of deposit insurance and the lender of last resort – a factor that has come to the fore in the aftermath of more recent liberalisation in the 1980s. Note that growth of institutional investors tended to precede financial liberalisation but has accelerated in the wake of it.

2   Benefits of large size of the financial system

What of the impact on economic performance of a given size and development of the financial sector? A number of papers have sought to address the relation of financial development to economic growth. King and Levine (1993) used four measures of financial structure, namely the size of liquid liabilities, the role of banks relative to the central bank in allocating credit, credit allocation to private business versus total credit to the non-financial sector and the ratio of credit to private firms to GDP. Across a large sample of countries, the financial variables were found to have a strong relation to three growth variables, namely capital accumulation, economic growth and productivity growth, even controlling for other influences on growth such as education and government expenditure.

Levine and Zervos (1998) found that stock market liquidity (but not size, international integration or volatility) as well as banking development were related to growth. Extensions such as Levine (1999) have additionally allowed for the role of certain legal aspects (linked to creditor and investor rights, contract enforcement and accounting standards) in financial development, and found that these are crucial for economic growth more generally. This influence may operate, inter alia, by influencing the proportion of firms that have access to external finance (Demirguc-Kunt and Maksimovic 1998, 2000). Note that none of these studies looked explicitly at institutional investors, although they may be correlated with stock market liquidity, investor rights and accounting standards.

3   Benefits of market or bank orientation

Since institutional investors are more important in market-oriented countries, it is relevant to probe the comparative advantage of bank- and market-based systems. Several empirical papers in the tradition of those highlighted in Section 2 argue that the overall development of financial services is important to growth and not its bias to bank or market financing (Levine 1997, 2000). On the micro side, research on the best form of corporate finance and governance is also inconclusive (Mayer 1996). Whereas relationship banking systems are good at monitoring and controlling debt exposures, they may also provide such funds beyond the firms' investment opportunities, leading to overinvestment when funds are abundant. In other words, whereas relationship-based systems are good at control and monitoring, arm's length systems are better at governance. In a similar vein, relationship banking systems ease the renegotiation of contracts, which helps overcome liquidity problems but worsens the issue of discipline, leading to so-called soft budget constraints. Arm's length systems can stop unprofitable projects more readily, given lack of long-term monitoring, while liquidity difficulties are worsened.

Taking a broader view, Allen and Gale (1997) suggest that Anglo-American capital markets dominated by institutional investors may have a disadvantage in terms of risk sharing, whereby competition and opportunities for arbitrage constrain financial intermediaries to carry out only cross-sectional risk sharing – exchanges of risk among individuals at a given point in time. This leaves individuals and companies vulnerable to undiversifiable risks arising over time, for example, owing to macroeconomic shocks, which cannot be eliminated by portfolio diversification. Furthermore, in Anglo-American countries, the focus on cross-sectional risk sharing may help to explain the intense focus on risk management via derivatives (Allen and Santomero 1999). In contrast, financial systems in which long-lived banks have some monopoly power over savers facilitate the elimination of such intertemporal risks by accumulation of reserves and smoothing of returns over time. Firms may then obtain rescue finance in recessions, for example.

It may of course be that the benefits of relationship banking in terms of lower agency costs and possibly also costs of bankruptcy are totally offset by higher debt–equity ratios.[3] Again, the benefits of 'time series risk sharing' may be lost as openness to global markets increases via institutional investor growth. Notably, the way the relationship banking system requires that bank margins should widen in a recovery to recoup the 'insurance premia', may not be compatible with a competitive financial system with sizeable institutional investors, where firms can access securities finance. Japan experienced this shift in the 1980s when highly rated firms started to access bond markets, weakening the main bank link. As argued in Davis (1999) EMU together with institutionalisation may lead to eventual shifts to market-based systems in bank dominated countries in Europe. On the other hand, relationship banking applies even in market-based systems such as in the United States to small firms (Berger and Udell 1995), in that small firms for which public information is not available tend to depend on a relationship with a single bank. There are also issues linked to the differing abilities of bank- and market-based systems to finance different types of firm.

Looking at financial stability aspects more widely, collapse of relationship banks may be highly damaging to the economy, given the dependence of the economy on these institutions. The banking crises in relationship banking-based Scandinavia and Japan (Davis 1995a) were certainly highly damaging to the real economy. Davis and Stone (2004) show banking crises have a greater impact on the corporate sector in emerging market economies, which are highly bank dependent. Meanwhile, in Anglo-American countries, the so-called multiple avenues of intermediation are said to cushion the effect of crises in either banks or securities markets on corporate financing (Greenspan (1999), Davis and Ioannidis (2004), Davis and Stone (2004)). Arguably, most securities market crises tended to harm householders' wealth but not the infrastructure underlying securities market functioning. It is market liquidity crises such as the 1998 debacle following Russia/Long Term Capital Management (LTCM) that may be more serious in this regard than price volatility, see Davis and Steil (2001).

A reasonable conclusion may be that of Allen and Gale (2000), who suggested 'since neither markets nor intermediaries work in exactly the way theory suggests, we would do well to exercise some humility in making recommendations about policies to reform our financial systems'.

4   Benefits from the existence of institutional investors

Developing from the survey above, this section outlines more specifically the effects on economic performance of the presence of institutional investors, against the background of the functions the financial system fulfils. These offer material for judging institutions' likely impact on financial development and growth. Following Merton and Bodie (1995), the functions are:

(i) the provision of a mechanism for *pooling of funds* from individual households so as to facilitate large-scale indivisible undertakings, and *the subdivision of shares* in enterprises to facilitate diversification.

(ii) provision of ways to *transfer economic resources* over time, across geographic regions or among industries. By these means, households may optimise their allocation of funds over the life cycle and funds may be optimally allocated to their most efficient use.

(iii) provision of ways to *manage uncertainty and control risk* whereby through securities and through financial intermediaries, risk pooling and risk sharing opportunities are made available to households and companies.

(iv) providing *price information*, thus helping to coordinate decentralised decision making in various sectors of the economy.

(v) *clearing and settling payments* to facilitate exchange of goods, services and assets.

(vi) providing ways to *deal with incentive problems* when one party to a financial transaction has information the other does not, or when one is agent of the other, and when control and enforcement of contracts is costly.

We now go on to assess in detail the consequences of a large institutional investor sector for financial markets,[4] drawing where appropriate on these functions as well as the discussion above to show how their performance is affected. One immediate aspect is *pooling of funds*, where institutional investors' raison d'être is their comparative advantage over direct securities holdings by households in ensuring diversification at low cost (Davis and Steil 2001).

Under the function of transfer of resources across time, there are a number of *mechanisms whereby institutional investment, and notably pension funding may increase personal saving*; imperfect substitution arising, for example, from illiquidity of pension assets may mean that other saving is not reduced one-to-one for an increase in pension wealth; liquidity constraints may imply that any forced saving (such as pension contributions) cannot be offset either by borrowing or reducing discretionary saving (Hubbard 1986);[5] forced saving may reduce myopia of savers in respect of retirement (Morandé 1998); low income workers may not save otherwise (Bernheim and Scholz 1992); the interaction between pensions and retirement behaviour may increase saving in a growing economy, as workers increase saving in order to provide for an earlier planned retirement (Feldstein 1974); tax incentives which raise the rate of return on saving via pension funds may encourage higher aggregate saving;[6] and finally, a cut in social security as part of a shift to funding should increase saving, given the effect on implicit wealth (World Bank 1994). If not offset by higher fiscal deficits, higher personal saving may of course permit higher aggregate investment without recourse to potentially unstable foreign inflows.

On balance, research suggests that growth in funded pension schemes in particular does appear to boost personal saving, subject to a partial offset arising via declines in discretionary saving. Much of the literature, such as Pesando (1992), which is focused on US defined benefit funds, suggest an increase in personal saving of around 0.35 results from every unit increase in pension fund assets, though the cost to the public sector of the tax incentives to pension funds reduces the overall benefit to *national* savings to around 0.2. Effects may be less marked for defined contribution funds, where the worker is more likely to be able to borrow against pension wealth and participation is generally optional. On the other hand, Poterba *et al.* (1996) suggest that 401(k) accounts in the United States have added to aggregate saving, with tax incentives being the main reason. In EMEs, Corsetti and Schmidt-Hebbel (1997) and Morandé (1998) find a positive effect of pension reform on saving in Chile; World Bank (1993) finds similar effects in Singapore. These effects may link to prevalence of credit constraints for low-income households who would not otherwise have saved. Finally, regarding social security Edwards (1995) shows it lowers private saving in EMEs; Feldstein (1995) suggests personal saving rises 0.5 for every unit decrease in social security wealth.

All these estimates abstract from effects on public saving in the transition (e.g. in deficit-financing of existing social security obligations) that may be fully offsetting at a national level. Even tax-financed transitions may according to some authors have at most a small positive effect on saving in the long term (Cifuentes and Valdes Prieto 1997).

The quantitative impact of development of institutional investors on capital markets, abstracting from potential increases in saving, arises mainly from differences in behaviour from the personal sector. Institutional investors in most cases hold a greater proportion of capital-uncertain, long-term assets than households (see portfolios shown in Table 6.2).[7] These differences can be explained partly by time horizons, which for households are relatively short, whereas given the long term nature of liabilities, institutional investors may concentrate portfolios on long-term assets yielding the highest returns. But given their size, institutional investors also have a comparative advantage in compensating for the increased risk by pooling and diversifying across assets whose returns are imperfectly correlated, an advantage linked also to lower transactions costs for large deals and ability to invest in large indivisible assets such as property. Unlike banks, they tend to rely more on public than private information in investment and hence seek relatively liquid assets. However, owing to economies of scale, specialisation, links to investment banks and so on, their information may be typically superior to that of private individuals.

The implication is that even if saving and wealth did not increase, *a switch to funding would increase the supply of long-term funds to capital markets*, thus improving notably the performance of the function of transferring resources. There may be increases in equities, long-term corporate bonds and securitised debt instruments and a reduction in bank deposits, so long as individuals do not adjust the liquidity of their portfolios to fully offset effects of growth of institutional investors – and so long as the macroeconomic environment favours long term financing. A priori, one can argue that full offsetting is unlikely, especially if pension assets are defined benefit and/or implicitly substitute for highly illiquid

Table 6.2 Portfolio distributions of selected funded pension systems

	Bonds	o/w Public	o/w Private	Shares	Property	Loans and mortgages	Short-term assets	Foreign assets
Chile (1994)	45	39	6	33	2	13	6	1
Singapore (1996)	70	70	0	0	0	0	28	0
Malaysia (1996)	55	34	21	16	1	0	30	0
Switzerland (1994)	28	—	—	14	16	41	2	0
Australia (1995)	15	13	2	41	9	0	20	14
UK (1996)	14	n/a	n/a	78	5	0	4	27
Netherlands (1996)	63	n/a	n/a	26	8	n/a	3	23

Note: The Singaporean fund holds undisclosed assets in foreign markets to back the bonds and deposits held by members.

Source: Davis (1998).

implicit social security wealth. Empirical work by King and Dicks-Mireaux (1988) found no such offset for Canada, while Davis (1988) obtained similar results for the G-5. Certainly there seems to be a correlation in OECD countries between equity market capitalisation and the size of the institutional investor sector.[8] Moreover, radical changes in financial structure – inconsistent with full offsetting – have been widely observed to accompany growth of funding, not least in Chile, as discussed below. More generally, the size and activity of equity markets and the number of listed companies differ little between the emerging markets with large institutional sectors and the OECD markets (Table 6.3).

As regards the broader economic benefits of such overall shifts to long term assets, they should tend to reduce the cost and increase the availability of equity and long term debt financing to companies, and hence may raise productive[9] capital formation. Economically efficient capital formation could in turn raise output and 'endogenously', growth itself (Holzmann 1997). Higher growth will of course feed back on saving. 'Endogenous growth' effects of an increase in capital investment on labour productivity, may be particularly powerful in developing countries if a switch from pay-as-you-go to funding induces a shift from the labour-intensive and low productivity 'informal' sector to the capital-intensive and high productivity 'formal' sector (Corsetti and Schmidt-Hebbel 1997).

As noted, equity market development per se has been shown to enhance overall economic development (Demirgüç-Kunt and Levine (1996), Levine and Zervos (1998)).[10] Demirgüç-Kunt and Maksimovic (1998) show that access to an active stock market increases firms' ability to borrow at long maturities, especially in developing financial markets.

Table 6.3   Indicators of financial development

Per cent of GDP	Stock market capitalisation	Stock market turnover	Listed companies (no.)	Bank credit
Chile	149	22	284	63
Singapore	174	71	212	61
Malaysia	255	88	529	129
Switzerland	141	101	233	183
Australia	69	28	1 178	83
Netherlands	90	63	387	118
UK	127	92	2 078	125

Source: IFC Emerging Markets Factbook.

Finally, access to a range of securities in domestic currency should limit the incentive for companies to borrow in foreign currency, which was a feature of the recent Asian crisis. One note of caution is that if governments force institutional investors to absorb the significant issues of bonds that may be needed in a debt-financed transition strategy, or if government issuance crowds out corporate issues, many of the benefits outlined will not be realised.

Besides inducing shifts to longer term assets, funding would also *increase international portfolio investment*, where this is permitted, that is, transfer of resources cross-border, as well as better pooling given the benefits it offers in terms of risk reduction to institutional investors while household activity in this area is low. This has been a particular feature of OECD countries in recent years. Important, and conflicting, issues are raised, notably for developing and transition countries. On the one hand, international investment may be seen as a loss of potential to develop domestic capital markets. It may also be seen as posing a risk of capital flight. On the other, it may be seen as beneficial to institutional investors as volatility of returns could be reduced. In addition, it will forestall the point at which institutional investor investment becomes so large as to face diminishing returns domestically. Also there may be a benefit at a national level if national income is subject to frequent terms-of-trade shocks owing to the position of being largely dependent on commodities for export earnings, while export earnings account for a large proportion of GDP, as is common in developing countries. Hence, holdings of assets offshore can actually help to contribute to greater stability of national income (Fontaine 1997).

Besides the quantitative effects noted above, the development of institutional investors is also likely to trigger *qualitative developments in financial markets*, which will facilitate in particular the functions of managing uncertainty and controlling risk, and providing price information. They are in general subject to positive externalities, as once instituted other investors may also benefit from them. One qualitative improvement is *financial innovation*, which early on in financial development may include equities per se, junior markets, corporate bonds, securitisation, CDs, derivative markets[11] and indexed instruments. In OECD countries, pension funds' need for hedging against shortfalls of assets against liabilities has led to the development of a number of recent financial innovations such as zero coupon bonds and index futures (Bodie 1990). Similarly, immunisation strategies and the development of indexation strategies by and for pension funds have increased demand for futures and options.

Modernisation of the infrastructure of securities markets as required by institutional investors and other institutional investors which should entail improved performance of the function of clearing and settlement on the one hand and provide more sensitive price information on the other, thus improving resource allocation. As a consequence it may help reduce the cost or increase the availability of capital market funds, and hence aid industrial development *per se* as well as facilitating privatisations. In developing countries, their influence may be seen in terms of development of the overall market infrastructure (such as trading and settlement systems) and enhancement of liquidity. In OECD countries, given their focus on liquidity[12] and lesser emphasis on investor protection, institutional investors offer benefits to wholesale equity markets as opposed to heavily regulated retail markets (Steil 1996). They are footloose in their trading, and thus make the business of trading 'contestable' rather than monopolistic, and facilitate its concentration. Increased pension funding would raise the proportion of 'wholesale' trading activity which would be willing to translocate. It would also put pressure on cartels in bond issuance and price fixing in equity trading.

There may be important indirect benefits in this context, as institutional investors press for improvements in what Greenwald and Stiglitz (1990) call the 'architecture of allocative mechanisms', including better accounting, auditing, brokerage and information disclosure. Modern banking and insurance supervision, new securities and corporate laws, junior equity markets and credit rating agencies are also stimulated to develop. Such improvements are crucial for financial development more generally.

An aspect which could weaken the function of providing price information is *institutional investors' direct effect on liquidity and price formation*. Do institutional investors increase or dampen volatility? In normal times institutions, being willing to trade, having good information and facing low transactions costs, should tend to speed the adjustment of prices to fundamentals. It need hardly be added that such market sensitivity generates an efficient allocation of funds and acts as a useful discipline on lax macroeconomic policies. Again, the liquidity that institutional activity generates may dampen volatility, as is suggested by lower average share price volatility in countries with large institutional sectors.[13] And evidence on average day-to-day asset price fluctuations shows no tendency for such volatility to increase (Davis and Steil 2001). (We provide some econometric evidence on this point below.)

Sias (1996) examined directly the relationship between the volatility of securities returns and the level of institutional ownership generally.

He found a positive contemporaneous relation between institutional ownership and securities market volatility after accounting for capitalisation.[14] Possible reasons for a linkage of higher volatility to institutional ownership may include larger average trade size of institutions, which may induce volatility by overwhelming market liquidity and the greater use of program trading by institutional investors. It may also reflect a greater tendency for institutions to engage in noise trading or herding.

Furthermore, some medium term deviations of asset prices from levels consistent with fundamentals – at times affecting global capital markets – may link to institutionalisation. Clearly, these imply a weakening of the financial market function of providing price information. Correction of such situations may involve massive price adjustments or even market liquidity failure. Examples (see Davis 1995c) are the stock market crash of 1987, the ERM crises of 1992–93, the bond markets in 1993–94 and the Mexican crisis of 1994–95. Such events were characterised by features such as heavy involvement of institutional investors in both buying and selling waves; international investment; signs of overreaction to the fundamentals and excessive optimism prior to the crisis; at times, inappropriate monetary policies; a shock to confidence which precipitated the crisis, albeit not necessarily sufficient in itself to explain the scale of the reaction; and rapid and wholesale shifts between markets, often facilitated by financial innovations. Such patterns have been part of the background for renewed discussion of capital controls in recent years. Underlying factors appear to be, crucially, influences on fund managers which induce herding behaviour (notably the prevalence of performance measurement,[15] due in turn to principal–agent incentive problems between the sponsor and the fund manager[16]). In countries such as Chile, 'herding' may also be stimulated by regulations which require institutional investors to obtain similar returns.

By leading to disintermediation, growth of institutional investors is likely to entail increased *competition to the banking sector*. Besides increasing demand for capital market financing generally, disintermediation is facilitated in an institutionalised capital market as the scope of public as opposed to private information and the efficiency of its use by markets may be increased by the development of information technology and the related growth in influence of rating agencies, investment banks and credit assessors covering a wider range of firms. The traditional comparative advantages of banks in this area resulting from economies of scale in information gathering, screening and monitoring (Diamond 1984) may be eroded, even abstracting from price considerations.

Meanwhile on the liabilities side of banks' balance sheets, institutional investors tend to be ready customers for repos, commercial paper and other money-market instruments rather than bank deposits, thus undermining banks' comparative advantage in liquidity provision (Diamond and Dybvig 1983).

On the one hand such competition may lead to heightened efficiency of banks, thus aiding economic development. There are also complementarities in corporate finance between bank and market funding; and banks are essential components of capital market activity *per se* (as providers of collateral, clearing, settlement etc. services). By providing an alternative source of liquidity and long-term finance to banks, institutional and capital market growth helps the economy to diversify against the risks of banking problems ('multiple avenues'). But it may also help to generate them; the lessons of history from OECD countries suggest a need for vigilance, particularly if disintermediation coincides with deregulation and hence heightened competition within the banking sector (Davis 1995a). Banks may respond to the associated pressure on their profits partly by increasing their focus on non-interest income – including asset management income per se, mutual funds and insurance – and reducing excess capacity by merger or branch closure. However, disintermediation historically also led at times to increased risk-taking via aggressive balance sheet expansion (e.g. by lending to property developers) with risk premia which in retrospect proved to be inadequate.[17] Attention to shifts in the riskiness of banks portfolios, focus on capital adequacy and the issue of excess banking capacity are warranted by regulators in this context.

Turning to the *corporate sector*, as outlined, the availability of long-term debt and of equity capital should be increased by a wider investor base as funding develops. These are not independent; as noted, access to long-term finance may also be aided by flotation. Besides equity issues by existing firms, IPOs and privatisations would tend to be facilitated. Particularly for existing firms with small equity bases, there may be important competitive advantages to be reaped from equity issuance in terms of growth potential as well as reducing risks of financial distress in case of economic downturn; long-term debt finance is correlated with higher growth for manufacturing firms (Caprio and Demirgüç-Kunt 1998).

Experience suggest that firms would also need to fulfil certain requirements in order for equity funds to become available from institutional investors, which would improve performance of the financial function of dealing with incentive problems, as well as putting pressure on governments for appropriate legal provisions. The types of adaptation required are clear from the existing 'shareholder value'-based demands made by Anglo-Saxon institutional investors both on their own domestic companies and overseas – demands which would be multiplied by growth of domestic institutions via funding (Davis 1993, 2002). These include pressure for higher and more sustained dividend payments; more-profitable fixed investment; primacy of equity holders as owners of the firm over stakeholders; greater provision of information by firms; removal of underperforming managers; appropriate management structures; equal voting rights for all shares; pre-emption rights; and equal treatment in takeovers. To back up these requirements, institutional investors would demand laws and regulations such as firm takeover codes, insider information restrictions and limits on dual classes of shares, which seek to protect minority shareholders, as well as equal treatment of creditors in bankruptcy, to protect their holdings of corporate bonds.

Such an overall development would have implications not just for balance sheet structure – with potentially lower debt–equity ratios – but also for corporate governance, implying a greater degree of control by capital markets and institutional investors (for a survey see Schleifer and Vishny (1997)). In this context, the 'corporate governance movement' in OECD countries reflects dissatisfaction among institutional investors with costs of the takeover mechanism, and preference for direct influence as equity holders on incumbent management (Davis 1995b, 2002). It also links to indexation by large funds, which seek to improve the performance of firms they have to hold, as well as more generally where institutional investors are very large and cannot readily sell their participations without significant market movements against them. In practice, however, the scope of 'direct influence' is limited in most emerging market countries; Brazil and South Africa are two exceptions.

There is a growing literature on the impact of corporate governance initiatives on performance, albeit mainly focusing on the effects on share prices per se. For example, on the positive side, Wahal (1996), in a sample of forty-three cases, found that efforts by institutions to promote organisational change via negotiation with management (as opposed to proxy proposals) are associated with gains in share prices. Strickland *et al.* (1996) report that firms that were targeted for pressure by the United Shareholders Association[18] experienced positive abnormal stock returns, although corporate governance proposals *per se* had no effect. On the negative side, Del Guercio and Hawkins found no evidence that activism had a significant effect on stock returns over the three years following the proposals. In earlier work, Wahal (1994) had surveyed activism by nine public pension funds over the 1987–93 period and also concluded that there was no evidence of improvement in the long-term stock price performance of targeted firms, which rather continued to decline for three years after targeting. Gillan and Starks (1995) found some positive returns in the short term but no statistically significant positive returns over the long term, leading them to question the overall effectiveness of shareholder activism. Evidence from outside the United States on the effectiveness of corporate governance initiatives is sparse, but Faccio and Lasfer (2000) show that the monitoring role of UK pension funds is concentrated among mature and low-performing firms and that in the long run, the firms in which pension funds have large stakes markedly improve their stock returns.

One can trace a potential transition path for the various types of corporate governance structures that exist when capital markets are rudimentary or absent, as institutional investors become dominant. Family enterprises which seek equity capital from the market may have to reduce their role in governance; privatisation would obviously tend to diminish the role of the state. Meanwhile 'relationship banking' would tend to diminish (Davis 1993). There remain limits to such shifts of corporate finance and corporate governance to capital markets; even in a securitised financial system companies may prefer to incur some bank debt as a signal to capital markets that they are being monitored (James and Wier 1990). In all countries, there would remain a size class of firms too small for even Initial Public Offering (IPO) which would still need a close bank link.

Indeed, there is evidence that institutional investors are reticent in *investing equity in small firms* (i.e. there are limits to potential transfer of resources) despite the fact that their potential for innovation, growth and job creation is widely seen as crucial for economic growth.[19] For example, Revell (1994) shows that in 1989, UK pension funds held 32 per cent of large firms and only 26 per cent of smaller ones. Sias (1996), shows that for the United States institutional holding of the largest firms on average over 1977–91 is over 47 per cent and for the smallest, only 8 per cent. The consequence of neglect of small firms by institutional investors (assuming individual investors do not fill the gap) may be biases in the economy towards sectors with larger firms (for even if small firms can obtain bank loan finance, growth potential via debt is likely to be more restricted than with equity in addition). This may be contrary to the comparative advantage of the economy as a whole.[20] It suggests a need for venture capital funds, junior equity markets and appropriate institutional investor regulation.

As is the case for excess volatility as outlined above, regular performance evaluation of institutional investor managers by trustees is said to underpin *the short-termist hypothesis,* (entailing undervaluation of firms with good earnings prospects and willingness of funds to sell shares in takeover battles). This in turn is held to discourage long-term invest- ment or R&D as opposed to distribution of dividends, which would imply a suboptimal transfer and allocation of resources. Schleifer and Vishny (1990) provide an empirical model suggesting that short time horizons are an equilibrium property of capital markets, owing to the higher cost of long-term than short-term arbitrage.[21] Some recent empir- ical research seems to confirm the existence of short termist effects in the United Kingdom, with overvaluation of profits in the short term (Miles 1993). Evidence from a survey of US CEOs goes in the same direc- tion (Poterba and Summers 1992) Against this, Marsh (1990) notes that in the absence of information relevant to valuations, excessive turnover will hurt performance of asset managers, and reaction to relevant infor- mation on firms' long-term prospects, which itself generates turnover, is a key function of markets. High stock-market ratings of drug companies, with large research expenditures and long product lead times, would seem to tell against the short-termist hypothesis.

5 Developments in Chile

Besides being typical of OECD financial markets with large institutional investor sectors such as the United Kingdom and the United States (Davis and Steil 2001), a number of these phenomena highlighted in the section above are illustrated by the experience of Chile. It provides a test bed for the effects of institutionalisation on a relatively simple financial system.

Holzmann (1997) points to the fact that Chilean pension funds grew from zero in 1980 to 39 per cent of GDP in 1995. They may have played a major role in stimulating the rise in private saving observed over this period (Morandé 1998).[22] This accompanied an expansion of overall financial assets from 28 per cent of GDP in 1980 to 68 per cent in 1993 (Fontaine 1997), with pension assets accounting for a third of this total. Initially funds were invested mainly in debt securities owing to regula- tory prohibition of equity investment, but not solely those of the government – also bank CDs and mortgage bonds. Debt maturities increased as a consequence of the development of pension funds between 12–20 years by 1990. Equity investment was permitted in 1985 and hold- ings have grown to over 30 per cent of assets. This accompanied and encouraged a marked expansion of equity market capitalisation from 32 per cent of GDP in 1988 to 90 per cent in 1993; in the early 1990s, closed companies were encouraged by high P/E ratios to go public and accept standard record keeping and auditing practices, thanks to better access to pension fund financing. In 1991 the pension funds held 1/3 of public bonds, 2/3 of private bonds and 10 per cent of equities.

Holzmann (1997) shows econometrically that the development of financial markets in Chile correlates with strong development of the real side of the economy, via rising total factor productivity and capital accumulation. Holzmann also estimates that long term growth in Chile is 1–3 per cent higher owing to the effects of the pension reform operating via financial markets, although he also points out that the structuring of the transition may have played an important role.[23] As shown in Table 6.4 (EBRD 1996), pension fund growth was accompanied inter alia by rising stocks of corporate bonds, often placed direct by large companies into pension funds, the bond market having been improved by a new risk-classification industry. The life insurance sector grew to provide annuities as well as survivorship and invalidity reinsurance as required by the new system. And other investor groups such as mutual funds and foreign investor funds have emerged, increasing the diversity of market participants.

Fontaine (1997) also notes that pension fund development facilitated internal resource transfers, enabling the Chilean government to service its international debts without extreme fiscal adjustment which was elsewhere damaging to the real economy, by providing a domestic source of borrowing without requiring excessively high interest rates (in fact the debt was generally CPI-indexed). Correspondingly, public sector debt rose from 5 per cent of GDP in 1980 to 28 per cent in 1990. Later, the demand of pension funds enabled debt conversion – by both private and public institutions – to occur smoothly. In addition, the fact that pension funds were not permitted to invest internationally till 1989,

Table 6.4   Developments in the Chilean financial sector

Per cent of GDP	1980	1986	1992
Fixed income instruments	0.2	26	60
Stock market capitalisation	30	24	88
Corporate bonds	0.2	0.4	5
Mutual funds	3	1	2
Foreign capital country funds	0	0	3
Insurance company reserves	n/a	3	7
Pension funds	0	13	32

Source: EBRD (1996).

and then only in a limited way, is considered to explain why the capital markets in Chile grew in size and depth so rapidly. Again, given the existence of domestic long-term institutions and the high domestic saving that pension reform helped to stimulate, Chile is probably better insulated from the shifting behaviour of international investors, as witness the lower correction after the Mexican crisis than for other Latin American markets.

Hansell (1992) suggests development of pension funds has been a major factor behind Chile's bonds being rated investment-grade, the first Latin American country to be so rated since the debt crisis. Disclosure standards are reportedly higher than elsewhere in Latin America. Corporate governance is improved by requirements that pension fund managers vote for independent directors. On the other hand, Chileans have been rather unsuccessful at ownership dispersion, one reason being unwillingness of closely held companies to accept dilution of control. Rating regulations have till recently prevented funds investing in start-up companies and venture capital.

6 Econometric work 1 – institutional investors and corporate sector performance

Section 4 suggests that growth of institutional investors may have major effects on the performance of the corporate sector. Outworkings might include the following:

- The distribution of profits in the form of dividends should be stimulated, rather than their being ploughed back into potentially unremunerative fixed investments.
- Owing to corporate governance pressures, capital accumulation itself may accordingly be lower in the presence of institutional shareholders than would otherwise be the case, other things being equal.
- On the other hand if the efficient use of capital and labour is ensured by governance systems driven by institutional investment, one would anticipate that productivity growth might be improved.
- There may be more research and development, following the suggestion that market based financial systems with large institutional investors may be better placed to finance such investment than banks.
- This could also imply there will be more patent applications if institutional investors are large.
- On the other hand, if institutional holding increases volatility, then the cost of capital could be boosted.

In this section we report on and extend an empirical investigation of these hypotheses at a macro level for the G-7+ countries plus Australia (G-7+ for short), as well as on the subgroups of the Anglo Saxon and CEJ countries (the first three regressions were previously presented in Davis (2002)). We estimate the effects of high and rising levels of institutional ownership of shares, be it domestic or foreign, on aspects of corporate performance, in the presence of variables which capture the 'normal behaviour' of the variables in question. The institutional-share variables, being in the form of proportions, are independent of the level of share prices and purely indicate the changing nature of ownership of the outstanding volume of securities. They are not thus vulnerable to the criticism of purely reflecting share price expectations of dividends, productivity growth and so on, unless institutions behave systematically in relation to such expectations in their asset allocation.

The exercise of course contrasts strongly with the firm level studies typically undertaken in this area and cited in Section 4. However, we would contend that the results are complementary, if the view is taken that the effects of takeovers, institutional activism and other such, are not just apparent in the performance of targeted firms but also in the wider economy. This may plausibly be the case if managers of 'unaffected' firms nonetheless change their behaviour in response to the threat of such action. There remain grounds for caution, for example we only have eight advanced countries (and four Anglo-Saxon ones); deregulation of product markets could also lead to effects on productivity (although it is less likely to affect dividend distribution or investment); and our 'conventional independent variables' cannot perfectly capture the normal developments in the dependent variables in question.

Results in Davis (2002) show that the relevant variables are all 1(1) in levels, except volatility. This result includes the shares of institutional investors in total equity, whereas these could obviously not be trended in the long run. Equally, the real long-term interest rate is non-stationary, probably due to the impact of inflation on real rates in the 1970s. Technically the fact that these variables are difference stationary implies stationarity in variance. This is consistent with them being I(0) about a trend or drifting I(0) variables, which can still be bounded (in the shape of an ogive) over a longer-term sample.

Following these tests, the overall specifications are set in an error-correction format, with normal macroeconomic variables to determine the variable in question, and with the share of foreign and domestic life and pension funds in total equity as additional regressors. As noted, mutual funds are omitted from our general results owing to lack of consistent data; in Davis (2002) we added results including mutual funds as a variant for Canada, the United Kingdom and United States. The drifting I(0) variables, that is, the shares as well as interest rates, can be seen in the long run as shifting the level equilibrium in the long-run cointegrating relation (similarly to the role of unemployment in a wage equation where wages and productivity are cointegrated, and changes in unemployment change the wage/productivity relation). The difference term shows the effect of the drift in the variable over one-time period, which in the long run has no effect.

By this means, we seek to capture the influence of new purchases from other holders and the long run level of institutional holdings, respectively. There is clearly a potential issue of reverse causality, meaning the results need careful interpretation. In other words, there is a need to ensure that we are not merely capturing the investment-response of institutions to aspects of performance already apparent in the outturns. This may in particular affect the difference term; since the level variable is taken with a lag it should be less vulnerable to such misinterpretation.

The estimates were made using a cross section weighted GLS balanced panel, with fixed effects for each country and cross-section weights. The cross-section weights allow for the common disturbances that affect the panel, such as world economic growth, growth in world trade, share prices and global bond yields. We considered this more appropriate than the alternative seemingly unrelated regressions (SUR) given there is a clear relation between equations. The fixed effects should deal with the inevitable heterogeneity between countries in the panel, in terms of levels of the variables concerned. The standard errors are White heteroskedasticity consistent.

We first summarise three sets of results from Davis (2002) in which full details are available, here showing the institutional-share coefficients only (Table 6.5), before detailing new results. One point emphasised above is that institutional investors may seek higher dividend distribution, especially in the case that there is considered to be 'free cash flow' and a lack of profitable investment opportunities. We accordingly estimated for growth of real dividends. Besides institutional shares we included the lagged real dividend flow and lagged GDP as error correction terms as well as the growth of GDP (current and lagged) in order to allow for normal cyclical and trend patterns in dividends. Across the eight countries, the share of foreign institutions has a significant positive coefficient both in the difference and the level terms. This suggests that pressure from foreign institutions for higher real dividend distributions may have played an active role across the G-7+.

Table 6.5   Summary results of panel estimation (institutional share coefficients only)

	G-7+	Anglo-Saxon	CEJ
Dependent Variable: Log difference of real dividends			
DEQLPS	−0.132 (0.075)*	−0.046 (0.124)	1.04 (0.71)
DEQFRS	0.457 (0.229)**	0.032 (0.43)	0.06 (0.43)
EQLPS(−1)	0.038 (0.04)	0.173 (0.064)**	0.606 (0.34)*
EQFRS(−1)	0.43 (0.093)**	0.359 (0.144)**	0.035 (0.41)
Dependent Variable: Log difference of real investment			
DEQLPS	−0.21 (0.21)	−0.23 (0.1)**	−0.088 (0.3)
DEQFRS	00076 (0.11)	0.019 (0.23)	0.09 (0.075)
EQLPS(−1)	0.006 (0.08)	0.008 (0.046)	0.37 (0.17)**
EQFRS(−1)	0.016 (0.072)	−0.135 (0.08)**	0.06 (0.082)
Dependent Variable: Log difference of Total Factor Productivity			
DEQLPS	0.003 (0.017)	−0.037 (0.02)*	0.119 (0.048)**
DEQFRS	−0.04 (0.027)	0.043 (0.08)	−0.062 (0.027)**
EQLPS(−1)	0.034 (0.007)**	0.025 (0.0086)**	0.153 (0.042)**
EQFRS(−1)	−0.054 (0.014)**	−0.045 (0.017)**	−0.044 (0.027)*

Notes: GLS, Fixed effects, cross-section weights, White heteroscedasticity consistent standard errors in parentheses, ** indicates significance at 5% level and * at 10%.

Source: Davis (2002) Key: G-7+ indicates results for Australia, Canada, France, Germany, Italy, Japan, UK and US; Anglo-Saxon indicates results for Australia, Canada, UK and US; CEJ (Continental Europe and Japan) indicates results for France, Germany, Italy and Japan; EQLPS, share of equity held by life and pension funds; EQFRS, share of equity held by foreign shareholders; 'D' indicates first difference operator.

Meanwhile the difference of domestic institutions term is negative. The results for institutional shares in subgroups are different. In the Anglo-Saxon countries, the significant positive effect comes from the lagged level of the domestic institutions and foreign institutions ratios. This implies that institutional pressure is effective in raising real dividends. In the CEJ countries, only the lagged domestic share is positive, suggesting foreign institutions do not exert a strong influence.

The next issue concerns capital accumulation. Do institutions exercise restraint on investment, given the risk that it may become unprofitable? On the right hand side, we had lagged investment, the lagged capital stock and lagged GDP, as well as current and lagged differences of real GDP and a lagged real interest rate as real economy variables. This gives a standard Jorgensen flexible accelerator model (Ashworth and Davis 2001), where the long run ratio of interest is that between invest-ment and GDP. In terms of the share of institutional holdings, the

G-7+ results are insignificant. In Continental Europe and Japan, the level of life and pension holdings has a positive effect. However, in the Anglo-Saxon ones, the significant institutional share terms (difference of domestic and level of foreign) are negative. The implication is that institutional investors exert a strong and consistent negative influence on accumulation in those countries, perhaps disciplining firms inclined to waste free cash flow on unviable projects.

The third estimate is for Total Factor Productivity. Do institutions help to generate higher productivity via corporate governance pressure on firms to maximise profits, efficiency and competitiveness? In this case we simply estimate a distributed lag with GDP together with a partial adjustment term. Note that TFP growth is estimated as $100(\Delta\ln Y - \alpha\Delta\ln L - (1-\alpha)\Delta\ln K)$, where Y is real GDP, L is employment and K the real capital stock. α is set to 2/3, which is approximately labour's income share. The level is the accumulation of this variable. The levels terms show a positive effect from domestic institutions, and a negative effect from foreign ones. This suggests that TFP may be stimulated by domestic institutions' activity and corporate governance pressure, while foreign investors' holdings link to lower TFP growth. For Anglo-Saxon countries, this result again holds, albeit with the coefficient on domestic institutions being only significant at the 90 per cent level. In CEJ, both institutions' share is significant with domestic positive and foreign negative. In CEJ, the difference terms in the institutional share also come through with the same signs as for the levels.

Turning to new results, which we show in detail, the fourth estimate is for the growth of research and development capital (Table 6.6). Although institutions may restrain overall investment, is it the case that institutional shareholding provides a favourable environment for research? Note that this reflects on the 'short termist' hypothesis outlined above which would suggest a negative effect on R and D from impatient institutional investors. The specification is similar to the investment function, with the dependent variable being the second difference of the R and D capital stock. We thus have level and lagged real interest rates, growth rates of GDP, and lagged investment, the capital stock and GDP in levels. For the G-7 there are negative signs on lagged investment and capital, while lagged GDP has a positive sign, suggesting R and D grows with output. There is a negative lagged GDP growth effect and from lagged R and D investment growth. The signs (albeit not always significance) are repeated in the subgroups. Meanwhile at the G-7 level there are offsetting effects of institutional holdings, with a rise in the domestic institutional share accompanying rising R and D investment,

Table 6.6   Results of panel estimation for log-second-difference of research and development capital

	G-7+	Anglo-Saxon	CEJ
DEQLPS	0.018 (0.009)**	0.03 (0.009)**	−0.014 (0.03)
DEQFRS	−0.025 (0.012)**	−0.028 (0.02)	−0.0078 (0.016)
EQLPS(−1)	−0.0056 (0.003)*	−5.38E-05 (0.004)	−0.0033 (0.023)
EQFRS(−1)	−0.0075 (0.005)	−0.0038 (0.006)	−0.011 (0.014)
DDLRDK(−1)	0.26 (0.06)**	0.19 (0.11)*	0.24 (0.08)**
LGDP(−1)	0.021 (0.003)**	0.018 (0.004)**	0.03 (0.006)**
DLRDK(−1)	−0.21 (0.025)**	−0.16 (0.034)**	−0.25 (0.04)**
LRDK(−1)	−0.017 (0.002)**	−0.017 (0.005)**	−0.022 (0.004)**
RLR(−1)	0.00025 (0.0001)**	0.00024 (0.0001)	0.00039 (0.0002)*
DLGDP	−0.0036 (0.008)	0.0074 (0.009)	−0.022 (0.017)
DLGDP(−1)	−0.023 (0.01)**	−0.026 (0.011)**	−0.016 (0.02)
R-bar-2	0.47	0.25	0.53
SE	0.0043	0.0036	0.005
Observations	216	112	108

Notes: See Table 6.5. LGDP, log of real gross domestic product; RLR, real long-term interest rate (long rate less current CPI inflation); VOL, standard deviation of real equity price (equity index deflated by CPI); LRDK, log of R and D capital stock.

while a rise in foreign holdings and the level of the domestic share tend to reduce it. There is less ambiguity at the Anglo-Saxon level where the boost from rising domestic institutional shares is the only significant effect. In CEJ, there are no significant effects. It can be suggested that this evidence tells against 'short termism' in R and D from institutional holdings in the Anglo-Saxon countries.

Complementing the above, we analyse patent applications in Table 6.7. Since there is a trend in the series the dependent variable is the difference of logs. Also, given there was a marked acceleration of patents in most countries after 1995 (making the series I(2) if the last years are included) we truncate the regressions in that year. The Anglo-Saxon countries show no significant coefficients, while in Continental Europe and Japan a restraining influence from foreign shareholdings is detectable. We suggest that patent applications may be less related to institutionalisation than R and D since many patent applications are made by individuals or unquoted firms not subject to institutional pressure.

Table 6.8 looks at the link of institutional shares to equity price volatility. Do institutional shareholdings boost or reduce volatility in the short or long term? Since volatility is an I(0) variable we present the

Table 6.7 Results of panel estimation for log-difference of patent applications (1970–95)

	G-7+	Anglo-Saxon	CEJ
DEQLPS	0.13 (1.3)	−0.009 (0.1)	0.18 (0.5)
DEQFRS	−0.06 (0.5)	0.23 (0.9)	−0.24 (2.1)**
EQLPS(−1)	0.05 (1.1)	0.07 (1.2)	−0.22 (1.5)
EQFRS(−1)	−0.12 (2.4)**	−0.09 (1.0)	−0.3 (3.1)**
DGDP	0.48 (5.0)**	0.5 (3.5)**	0.59 (4.1)**
DGDP(−1)	−0.05 (0.4)	0.24 (1.4)	−0.15 (1.1)
RLR(−1)	0.002 (1.9)*	−0.002 (1.2)	0.003 (1.9)*
LPAT(−1)	−0.12 (4.8)**	−0.09 (2.2)	−0.15 (4.8)**
LGDP(−1)	0.24 (7.1)**	0.26 (4.9)**	0.25 (6.4)**
R-bar-2	0.36	0.4	0.41
SE	0.04	0.04	0.04
Observations	192	96	96

Note: See Table 6.5. LPAT; log of patent applications.

Table 6.8 Results of panel estimation for equity price volatility

	G-7+	Anglo-Saxon	CEJ
DEQLPS	0.53 (0.18)**	0.47 (0.2)**	0.57 (0.49)
DEQFRS	−0.1 (0.19)	0.21 (0.3)	−0.27 (0.24)
EQLPS(−1)	−0.008 (0.08)	−0.09 (0.1)	0.41 (0.13)**
EQFRS(−1)	−0.072 (0.074)	−0.004 (0.08)	−0.08 (0.13)
RLR	−0.005 (0.002)**	−0.005 (0.002)**	−0.003 (0.002)
RLR(−1)	0.002 (0.001)	0.003 (0.002)*	0.0006 (0.002)
DLGDP	−0.124 (0.158)	−0.33 (0.21)	0.21 (0.2)
DLGDP(−1)	0.36 (0.17)**	0.3 (0.25)	0.42 (0.2)**
R-bar-2	0.16	0.22	0.09
SE	0.043	0.04	0.044
Observations	216	112	108

Note: See Table 6.5. VOL; standard deviation of monthly real share price changes.

dependent variable as a level, while lagged dependent variables were insignificant and omitted. (With higher frequency data we could have used a GARCH formulation but this is not feasible with an annual dataset.) We include cyclical variables and bond yields to capture possible macroeconomic effects on volatility. It appears that volatility is higher with a low real interest rate (perhaps reflecting the 1970s experience) as well as when GDP declines after rising in the previous period, as at the turning point of the cycle. Institutional investor effects are found only in differences in the G-7 and Anglo-Saxon countries suggesting it is a shift in sectoral holdings of shares that promotes volatility rather than institutional holdings *per se*. On the other hand in CEJ there is evidence that the level of domestic institutional holdings that accompanies higher volatility.

Table 6.9 summarises the results outlined above. We would argue that this work is consistent with a disciplining role of institutions in the Anglo-Saxon countries, particularly life insurers and pension funds. They exert restraint of investment, and lead to a boost to dividends and to TFP, while they are favourable to R and D. In the Anglo-Saxon countries there is only a short-term effect of domestic institutional holdings on volatility while in the bank dominated countries it may be more persistent. The trend for corporate use of equity to rise, for equity shares of institutions to increase, and for traditional corporate governance structures to break down in CEJ, suggests these results could hold there in the future.

Admittedly, the econometric approach is subject to shortcomings. It is clear that the ownership cannot exceed 100 per cent, as is implied by treating the institutional share as I(1), although similar issues arise in

Table 6.9 Summary of results for institutional shares of equity

Equation	Difference of log real dividends	Difference of log TFP	Difference of fixed investment	Second difference of R and D capital	Difference of log patents	Real share price volatility
G-7+						
DEQLPS	Negative			Positive		Positive
DEQFRS	Positive			Negative		
EQLPS(−1)		Positive		Negative		
EQFRS(−1)	Positive	Negative			Negative	
Anglo Saxon						
DEQLPS		Negative	Negative	Positive		Positive
DEQFRS						
EQLPS(−1)	Positive	Positive				
EQFRS(−1)	Positive	Negative	Negative			
CEJ						
DEQLPS		Positive				
DEQFRS		Negative			Negative	
EQLPS(−1)	Positive	Positive	Positive			Positive
EQFRS(−1)		Negative			Negative	

Note: See Table 6.5.

consumption and investment functions where trends are often detected in variables such as real interest rates, Tobin's Q, and uncertainty. Ideally, a more sophisticated estimation procedure such as Philips Modified estimators should be used. Further work could address these issues, and also include takeovers and profit mark-up as possible dependent variables.

7 Econometric work 2 – institutional investors and economic growth

In this final section we provide some tentative evidence regarding the impact of institutional investment on growth using simple regressions in the tradition of Levine and Zervos (1998). We employ a dataset of 16 OECD countries only.[24] This partly reflects data availability from the OECD Institutional Investors database but also on the basis that mainly among countries in the later stages of financial development will institutional investors become an important component of the financial system. Hence we may discern the contribution to growth and productivity better by excluding lower income countries still at the bank dominated stage. We emphasise that the results should be seen as suggestive rather than conclusive, and a possible basis for further work.

We undertook a set of regressions with growth as the dependent variable. We do not control for the years of schooling and population growth as these are broadly common to OECD countries, as is population growth. A dummy for low-income countries at the start of the sample (Spain) proved insignificant. The OECD database generally covers 1980–2000. Hence there is scope for regressions over 5-year periods. (We note that this may not be long enough to fully smooth out the cycle.) One issue to bear in mind is that since institutional investors hold a large proportion of equity, their significance if detected could relate partly to the forward looking nature of equity markets in anticipating growth.

The results are given in Table 6.10. The results do not favour a strong impact of institutional investor size on overall economic growth, since the coefficients for the ratio to GDP and for the ratio to financial assets (equity plus loans) are not significant, albeit positive. The effect of institutions may be better characterised as contributing to specific aspects of economic performance as set out in the section above than growth *per se*. Some other results are significant. We find that the turnover ratio is frequently significant and positive, as in Levine and Zervos (1998), while the bank loan ratio tends to have a negative sign. This last is intriguing, and it suggests that a large banking sector may limit growth

Table 6.10   Results of growth estimation for OECD countries (1980–2000 5-year period averages)

Equation	1	2	3	4	5
Constant	0.029**	0.033**	0.032**	0.033**	0.03**
Bank lending/GDP	−0.0059	−0.01*	−0.016**	−0.018**	−0.01**
Stock market turnover		0.0046	0.006*	0.006	0.007*
Institutional assets/GDP			0.0053	−0.007	
Equity market capitalisation/GDP				0.023**	
Share of institutions in financial assets					0.004
R-bar squared	0.018	0.052	0.006	0.013	0.031
SE	0.012	0.012	0.012	0.011	0.012
Observations	64	64	59	59	59

Notes: GLS, no weighting, White heteroscedasticity consistent standard errors, ** indicates significance at 5% level and * at 10%.

in a highly advanced country, possibly since it creates macroeconomic volatility (e.g. in commercial property cycles) and is weak at financing innovation. Given the small number of countries, short sample and simple estimation techniques, these suggestions must be accepted with caution at present.

8   Conclusions

In this chapter we have surveyed the work undertaken on the development of institutional investors on economic performance, and undertaken some econometric work to see if positive effects on economic performance and growth are detectable at a macro level. We reviewed the existing literature on finance and growth and found little direct reference to institutions. On the other hand, there is quite a rich literature suggesting that institutional growth – notably after pension reform – may have quantitative or qualitative effects on capital markets detectable at a macroeconomic level, which improve performance of the functions of the financial system. They may also impact on the real economy directly, notably the corporate sector. Consistent with this last point, econometrically, we find that in the G-7 plus Australia, the share of institutional investors in total equities does have a restraining effect on investment, while boosting dividend yields, R and D, and total factor productivity – and in some cases, equity price volatility. On the other hand, using a broader panel, no effect can be detected of the institutional investment/GDP ratio on economic growth.

Notes

1. The author is Professor of Economics and Finance, Brunel University, Uxbridge, Middlesex UB3 4PH (E-mail 'e_philip_davis@msn.com', website www.geocities.com/e_philip_davis). He is also a Visiting Fellow at the National Institute of Social and Economic Research, an Associate Member of the Financial Markets Group at LSE, Associate Fellow of the Royal Institute of International Affairs and Research Fellow of the Pensions Institute at Birkbeck College, London. Views expressed are those of the author and not necessarily those of the institutions to which he is affiliated. The author thanks participants in the British Association conference for helpful comments. The paper draws on material from Davis (1998), (2000), (2002) and (2003) and Davis and Steil (2001).
2. In considering the numbers in Table 6.1, it may be noted that the assets of the Singapore CPF were only 28 per cent of GDP in 1976; the Malaysian fund was 18 per cent in 1980 and the Chilean only 1 per cent in 1981.
3. Certainly, debt–equity ratios are much higher in bank-dominated than market oriented systems, see Byrne and Davis (2003).
4. See also Davis (1999).
5. It might be anticipated that liquidity effects on saving may weaken where credit markets are liberalised and thus access to credit less restricted, or participation in pension funds is optional.
6. On the other hand, one should note that taxation provisions boosting rates of return will only influence saving at the margin for those whose desired saving is below that provided by social security and private pensions; for those whose desired saving exceeds this level, there will be an income effect but no offsetting substitution effect, and saving will tend to decline.
7. Differences in portfolios link to a variety of factors, notably regulation and historical developments.
8. Simple estimation for the EU-15, the United States, Japan and Canada gives a correlation of 0.97. In emerging markets, the activities of foreign investors may be relatively more important.
9. This also requires allocation of funds to their most profitable uses and adequate shareholder-monitoring of the investment projects, which as detailed below should also tend to occur in capital markets dominated by pension funds.
10. Underlying mechanisms include increasing liquidity and thus facilitating financing of long-term, high-return projects; increasing incentives to acquire information about firms; facilitating the tying of management compensation to share prices via stock options; and facilitating takeovers to resolve corporate governance difficulties.
11. On the development of derivatives exchanges in emerging markets see Tsetsekos and Varangis (1997).
12. Liquidity may be less important where pension funds focus on buy-and-hold strategies, as in Chile.

13. This is not to deny that markets may be subject to forms of excess volatility relative to fundamentals, but that the scope of average volatility does not seem to be linked to institutionalisation.
14. The adjustment is needed, since institutions focus on larger stocks; the result is that within each decile of size, the stocks most held by institutions are also the most volatile.
15. It is important to add, however, that the 'cure' (of seeking to reduce performance pressure) may be worse than the 'disease' (potential for herding). An uncompetitive fund management sector without pressure from performance assessment may actually be 'value deducting', investing in securities which do not minimise risk for given return and possibly investing client funds in a way which favours holdings of a parent institution (e.g. 'front running').
16. See Scharfstein and Stein (1990), Froot *et al.* (1992).
17. It may be added that rapid economic growth and at times inappropriate monetary policy also played a role in this typical late 1980s pattern.
18. Note that this is actually a coalition of small investors rather than an institutional investor per se.
19. This tendency may link to illiquidity or lack of marketability of shares, levels of risk which may be difficult to diversify away, difficulty and costs of researching firms without track records and limits on the proportion of a firm's equity that may be held. The development and improvement of stock markets for small company shares is one initiative that may make such holdings more attractive to pension funds.
20. Of course, problems of equity provision to small firms are much more severe with book-reserve pension financing, which tends to preserve the existing industrial structure and not aid equity financing of new firms.
21. It is interesting to add that Von Thadden (1992) has noted that bank monitoring can in theory increase investment time horizons by enabling banks to detect at an early stage whether projects will be viable. This argument implies that a weakening of 'relationship banking' may induce a further shortening of time horizons.
22. However, Holzmann (1997) notes that the initial effect on private saving was low or even negative.
23. The tight fiscal stance may have contributed to economic performance by crowding in of private investment and offering a higher credibility to the reform programme within and outside the country.
24. The countries are Australia, Belgium, Canada, Switzerland, Germany, Denmark, Spain, Italy, Finland, France, Japan, Netherlands, Norway, Sweden, the UK and the US.

References

Allen, F. and Gale, D. (1994), 'A welfare comparison of the German and US financial systems', LSE Financial Markets Group Discussion Paper No. 191.

Allen, F. and Gale, D. (1997), 'Financial markets, intermediaries and intertemporal smoothing', *Journal of Political Economy*, 105, 523–46.

Allen, F. and Gale, D. (2000), '*Comparing Financial Systems*', MIT Press.

Allen, F. and Santomero, A.M. (1999), 'What do financial intermediaries do?', Working Paper No. 99-30-B, Financial Institutions Centre, The Wharton School, University of Pennsylvania.

Ashworth, P. and Davis, E.P. (2001), 'Some evidence on financial factors in the determination of aggregate business investment for the G7 countries', Discussion Paper No. 187, National Institute of Economic and Social Research.

Berger, A. and Udell, G. (1995), 'Relationship banking and lines of credit in small firm finance', *Journal of Business*, 68, 351–81.

Bernheim, B.D. and Scholz, J.K. (1992), 'Private saving and public policy', National Bureau of Economic Research Working Paper No. 4213.

Bodie, Z. (1990), 'Pension funds and financial innovation', *Financial Management*, Autumn 1990, 11–21.

Byrne, J. and Davis, E.P. (2003), 'Financial structure', Cambridge University Press.

Caprio, G. and Demirgüç-Kunt, A. (1998), 'The role of long term finance; theory and evidence', *World Bank Research Observer*, 13, 171–89.

Cifuentes, R. and Valdes Prieto, S. (1997), 'Pension reforms in the presence of credit constraints', in Valdes-Prieto, S. (ed.), *The Economics of Pensions*, Cambridge University Press.

Corsetti, G. and Schmidt-Hebbel, K. (1997), 'Pension reform and growth', in ed. Valdes-Prieto, S. 'The Economics of Pensions', Cambridge University Press.

Davis, E.P. (1988), 'Financial market activity of life insurance companies and pension funds', Economic Paper No. 21. Bank for International Settlements.

Davis, E.P. (1993), 'The development of pension funds, a forthcoming financial revolution for continental Europe', in O'Brien, R. (ed), *'Finance and the International Economy 7, the Amex Essay Awards 1993'*, Oxford University Press.

Davis, E.P. (1995a), *'Debt, Financial Fragility and Systemic Risk, Revised and Expanded Version'*, Oxford University Press.

Davis, E.P. (1995b), *Pension Funds, Retirement-Income Security and Capital Markets, An International Perspective*, Oxford University Press.

Davis, E.P. (1995c), 'Institutional investors, unstable financial markets and monetary policy', in (ed.), Bruni, F., Fair, D. and O'Brien, R. *Risk Management in Volatile Financial Markets*, Dordrecht: Kluwer.

Davis, E.P. (1998), 'Investment of mandatory funded pension schemes', Discussion Paper No. PI-9908, the Pensions Institute, Birkbeck College, London and in Turner, J. and Latulippe, D. (eds) *Funding of Social Security Pensions*, International Labour Office.

Davis, E.P. (1999), 'Institutionalization and EMU; implications for European financial markets', *International Finance*, 2, 33–61.

Davis, E.P. (2000), *Pension Funds, Financial Intermediation and the New Financial Landscape*, Kredit und Kapital, Special Edition on Financial Markets, pp. 229–52.

Davis, E.P. (2002), 'Institutional investors, corporate governance, and the performance of the corporate sector', *Economic Systems*, 26, 203–29.

Davis, E.P. (2003), 'Linkages between pension reform and financial sector development', Asian Development Bank.

Davis, E.P. and Ioannidis, C. (2004), 'Does the availability of bank borrowing and bond issuance smooth overall corporate financing?', forthcoming Brunel University Working Paper.

Davis, E.P. and Steil, B. (2001), *Institutional Investors*, MIT Press.

Davis, E.P. and Stone, M. (2004), 'Corporate financial structure and financial stability', forthcoming IMF Working Paper and in *Journal of Financial Stability*.

Del Guercio, D. and Hawkins, J. (1999), 'The motivation and impact of pension fund activism', *Journal of Financial Economics*, 52, 293–340.

Demirgüç-Kunt, A. and Levine, R. (1996), 'Stock market development and financial intermediaries; stylised facts', *World Bank Economic Review*, 10, 291–321.

Demirgüç Kunt, A. and Levine, R. (2000), 'Bank-based and market-based financial systems; cross-country comparisons', paper presented at the World Bank conference on 'Financial structure and economic development', 10–11 February 2000.

Demirgüç Kunt, A. and Maksimovic, V. (1998), 'Law, finance and firm growth', *Journal of Finance*, 53, 2107–37.

Demirgüç Kunt, A. and Maksimovic, V. (2000), 'Funding growth in bank-based or market-based financial systems, evidence from firm level data', paper presented at the World Bank conference on 'Financial structure and economic development', 10–11 February 2000.

Diamond, D. (1984), 'Financial intermediation and delegated monitoring', *Review of Economic Studies*, 51, 393–414.

Diamond, D. and Dybvig, P. (1983), 'Bank runs, deposit insurance, and liquidity', *Journal of Political Economy*, June, 401–19.

EBRD (1996), *Transition Report 1996*, European Bank for Reconstruction and Development, London.

Edwards, S. (1995), 'Why are saving rates so different across countries?', NBER Working Paper No. 5097.

Faccio, M. and Lasfer, M.A. (2000), 'Do occupational pension funds monitor companies in which they hold large stakes?', *Journal of Corporate Finance*, 6, 71–85.

Feldstein, M. (1974), 'Social security, induced retirement and aggregate capital accumulation', *Journal of Political Economy*, 82, 902–56.

Feldstein, M. (1995), 'Social security and saving, new time series evidence', NBER Working Paper No. 5054.

Fontaine, J.A. (1997), 'Are there good macroeconomic reasons for limiting external investments by pension funds? The Chilean experience', in Valdes-Prieto, S. (ed.), *The Economics of Pensions*, Cambridge University Press.

Froot, K.A., Scharfstein, D.S. and Stein, J.C. (1992), 'Herd on the street: informational inefficiencies in a market with short-term speculation', *The Journal of Finance*, 47, 1461–84.

Gillan, S.L. and Starks, L.T. (1995), 'Relationship investing and shareholder activism by institutional investors', University of Texas Working Paper.

Greenspan, Alan (1999), 'Do efficient financial markets mitigate financial crises?', speech to the Financial Markets Conference of the Federal Reserve Bank of Atlanta, 19 October 1999.

Greenwald, B.C. and Stiglitz, J.E. (1990), 'Information, finance and markets, the architecture of allocative mechanisms', Working Paper No. 3652, National Bureau of Economic Research.

Hansell, S. (1992), 'The new wave in old age pensions', *Institutional Investor*, November 1992, 57–64.

Holzmann, R. (1997), 'On economic benefits and fiscal requirements of moving from unfunded to funded pensions', European Economy Reports and Studies, 4/1997, 121–66.

Hubbard, R.G. (1986), 'Pension wealth and individual saving, some new evidence', *Journal of Money Credit and Banking*, 18, 167–78.

James, C. and Wier, P. (1990), 'Borrowing relationships, intermediation and the cost of issuing public securities', *Journal of Financial Economics*, 28, 149–71.

King, M.A. and Dicks-Mireaux, L. (1988), 'Portfolio composition and pension wealth: an econometric study', in Bodie, Z., Shoven, J.B. and Wise, D.A. (eds), *Pensions in the US economy*, University of Chicago Press.

King, R.G. and Levine, R. (1993), 'Finance and growth, Schumpeter might be right', *Quarterly Journal of Economics*, 108, 713–37.

La Porta, R., Lopez-Silanes, F. and Schleifer, A. (1999), 'Corporate ownership around the world', *Journal of Finance*, 54, 471–517.

Levine, R. (1997), 'Financial development and economic growth: views and agenda', *Journal of Economic Literature*, 35 (June), 688–726.

Levine, R. (1999), 'Law, finance and economic growth', *Journal of Financial Intermediation*, 8–35.

Levine, R. (2000), 'Bank based or market based financial systems – which is better?', paper presented at the World Bank conference on 'Financial structure and economic development', 10–11 February 2000.

Levine, R. and Zervos, S. (1998), 'Stock markets, growth and economic development', *American Economic Review*, 88, 537–58.

Marsh, P. (1990), 'Short-termism on trial', Institutional Fund Managers Association, London.

Mayer, C. (1996), 'Corporate governance, competition and performance', Economics Department Working Paper No. 164, OECD, Paris.

Merton, R.C. and Bodie, Z. (1995), 'A conceptual framework for analysing the financial environment', in Crane, D.B. *et al.* (eds), *The Global Financial System, A Functional Perspective*, Harvard Business School Press.

Miles, D.K. (1993), 'Testing for short termism in the UK stock market', Bank of England Working Paper No. 4.

Morandé, F.G. (1998), 'Savings in Chile; what went right?', *Journal of Development Economics*, 57, 201–28.

Pesando, J.E. (1992), 'The economic effects of private pensions', in *Private Pensions and Public Policy*. Organisation for Economic Co-operation and Development, Paris.

Poterba, J.M. and Summers, L.H. (1992), 'Time horizons of American firms; new evidence from a survey of CEOs', Harvard Business School.

Poterba, J.M., Venti, S.F. and Wise, D.A. (1996), 'Personal retirement saving programmes and asset accumulation; reconciling the evidence', NBER Working Paper No. 5599.

Rajan, R. and Zingales, L. (2000), 'The great reversals; the politics of financial development in the 20th century', Working Paper No. 265, Economics Department, OECD.

Revell, J. (1994), 'Institutional investors and fund managers', *Revue de la Banque*, 2, 55–68.

Rybczynski, T. (1997), 'A new look at the evolution of the financial system', in Revell, J. (ed.) *The Recent Evolution of Financial Systems*, London: MacMillan.

Scharfstein, D.S. and Stein, J.C. (1990), 'Herd behaviour and investment', *American Economic Review*, 80, 465–79.

Schleifer, A. and Vishny, R.W. (1990), 'Equilibrium short time horizons of investors and firms', *American Economic Review*, Papers and Proceedings, 148–53.

Schleifer, A. and Vishny, R.W. (1997), 'A survey of corporate governance', *Journal of Finance*, 52, 737–83.

Schmidt, R.H., Hackethal, A. and Tyrell, M. (1999), 'Disintermediation and the role of banks in Europe, an international comparison', *Journal of Financial Intermediation*, 8, 36–67.

Schmidt, R.H., Hackethal, A. and Tyrell, M. (2001), 'The convergence of financial systems in Europe, main findings of the DFG project', University of Frankfurt.

Sias, R.W. (1996), 'Volatility and the institutional investor', *Financial Analysts Journal*, March/April, 13–20.

Steil, B. (ed.) (1996) 'The European equity markets, the state of the union and an agenda for the millennium', the Royal Institute of International Affairs, London.

Strickland, D., Wiles, K.W. and Zenner, M. (1996), 'A requiem for the USA, is small shareholder monitoring effective?', *Journal of Financial Economics*, 40, 319–38.

Tsestekos, G. and Varangis, P. (1997), 'The structure of derivatives exchanges, lessons for developing and emerging markets', World Bank Policy Research Paper No. 1867.

Von Thadden, E.-L. (1992), 'The commitment of financing, duplicated monitoring and the investment horizon', WWZ Discussion Paper No. 9207, University of Basle.

Wahal, S. (1994), 'Public pension fund activism and firm performance', University of North Carolina Working Paper.

Wahal, S. (1996), 'Public pension fund activism and firm performance', *Journal of Financial and Quantitative Analysis*, 31, 1–23.

World Bank (1993), 'The East Asian miracle; economic growth and public policies', Oxford University Press.

World Bank (1994), 'Averting the old age crisis; policies to protect the old and promote growth', The World Bank, Washington, DC.

7
Money, Stability and Growth

C.A.E. Goodhart

1 Introduction

Let me start with a sweeping assertion. Sustainable growth primarily depends on three main factors; these are good governance, technological development and efficient markets. I put good governance first, because in its absence technological development and markets will be blighted, distorted and misused.

I am not going to discuss technological development further. That is a large and separate subject, outside my own main fields of knowledge and interest.

Two key institutional developments have helped to underpin the achievement both of good governance and of efficient markets. These are the role, or rule, of law and the development of the monetary system. The interaction between respect for the rule of law and good governance is obvious and straightforward. What is being increasingly appreciated, especially since the collapse of communism and the subsequent transition of those countries to a capitalist system, is the essential role that an efficient and effective legal system, involving respect for property rights, contract laws, bankruptcy laws, and so on, plays in the establishment of efficient markets. Professor Erik Berglof discusses this in his companion Chapter 4 in this book.

Let me quote some passages from a recent excellent book by Lars Werin on *Economic Behaviour and Legal Institutions*.

> Most coordination is of an economic nature; hence, it takes place within what is usually called the economic system. But a well-developed economic system can hardly exist unless accompanied by a legal system. Legal rules and arrangements profoundly affect the

possibilities for people to act and the incentives behind the acts. This holds true not only for specific regulatory rules that directly control individuals' economic decisions and dispositions. It also holds true for those parts of the legal system which, at least in democratically-oriented countries, provide the basic framework, such as the general laws of property, contract, tort and crime. But law is not an exogenously given force, operating on human behaviour solely from the outside. It is itself influenced by the pressures of human activity and the wishes and aspirations driving it. There is an all-pervasive interaction between law and economic life. (Preface, p. 5)

Given the importance of law for the structure and performance of the economic system, to what an extent is law a result of endeavors by those who frame it to achieve these effects? This is the second problem, which basically is the opposite of the first problem as it concerns what determines law rather than what are the *effects* of law. It has only recently come under serious attack from a number of economists and legal scholars. Their research provides strong support for the idea that core parts of law and the economic system are evolving in response to one another. If names should be given, perhaps the most important ones are Ronald Coase, Guido Calabresi, Richard Posner, James Buchanan, Gordon Tulloch, Friedrich Hayek, Kenneth Arrow and Douglass North, some of them economists, some legal scholars. (Preface, p. 6)

I myself would add Mancur Olson to that distinguished list. And finally, from chapter 4.

Property rights and rules on rights of transfer instituted by *judge-made law* tend systematically to produce incentives that promote efficiency, that is, encourage wealth-increasing acts and counteract wealth-decreasing acts, with no direct consideration of the consequences for the distribution of wealth. (p. 61)

Similarly, the relationship between money and market efficiency is well understood. Indeed, the standard theory of the emergence of money as an institution is that it developed as a device to reduce transactions costs in market exchanges (Menger 1892, Kiyotaki and Wright 1989). There is, however, an alternative theory, and one that is more firmly based on actual empirical evidence, from anthropology, early history and numismatism, that money came into existence as a social device to limit feuds, which could disrupt society, and to support government.

Let me again provide some supporting extracts.[1]

In any case, the generalized application of monetary values in commodities could scarcely have come about before the appearance of market economies, and monetary valuations were already in existence in what Sir John Hicks has felicitously christened 'customary' and 'command' pre-market societies, *A Theory of Economic History* (1969), pp. 2 ff. (rise of the market), 63–8 (origins of money). He has to some extent telescoped the invention of money and the invention of coinage, and in my view he exaggerates the 'store of value' element in early money. Nor, if my argument that money antedated the development of the market is correct, is it the case that the standard 'should be something that is regularly traded'. In such societies they provide a scale of evaluating personal injuries in the institution which the Anglo-Saxons termed the wergeld, and it is in this institution that the origin of money as a standard of value must, I believe, be sought...

The general object of these laws was simple, that of the provision of a tariff of compensations which in any circumstances their compilers liked to envisage would prevent resort to the bloodfeud and all the inconvenient social consequences that might flow therefrom... The object of the laws is that of preventing retaliation by resort to force, and the principle behind the assessments is less the physical loss or injury suffered, than the need to assuage the anger of the injured party and make good his loss in public reputation.

(And note that the verb 'to pay' derives from the verb 'to pacify' – indicating the original purpose of the payment of wergeld fines or bridewealth.) These 'tariffs' were established in public assemblies, and the common standards were based on objects of some value which a householder might be expected to possess or which he could obtain from his kinsfolk. Note, however, that these schedules did not use, nor did they require, a unit of account since specific payments were required for each type of inflicted injury – and as they were established in public assembly, the required payment would have been widely known.

...

It may not be too far from the truth to argue that our monetary system developed out of the criminal justice system, rather than to replace inefficient barter in markets. While we view justice today as the process that forces criminals to 'pay their debt to society,' in tribal society, justice meant compensation of victims in order to prevent bloodfeuds from developing. In a very interesting book, Innes (1932) argued that tribal justice was gradually replaced by the modern justice system that was designed to maximize payments to 'pacify' the elite. If correct, standardization of fines, fees, tithes, tribute, and later, taxes, in terms of a monetary unit of account was accomplished to reduce the transactions costs of enforcement of 'justice' and centralization of collection rather than to replace inefficient barter. Note that even after the development of capitalism, the crown still relied on fines (levied on almost every conceivable activity) for a substantial portion of state revenues (see Maddox 1769). Above we noted the importance of the imposition of a tax debt in generating a demand for the money issued by the state; taxes are of course just a set of specific fines – a 'fine' for owning property, a 'fine' for earning income, or a 'fine' for importing commodities – although no one today thinks of these activities as 'crimes'. While the modern economy has largely separated the state's fiscal system from its criminal justice system, they were closely intertwined until very recently.[2]

Indeed the contrary story that money evolved from indirect bartering (whereby an object in regular demand would be kept for its use as a bargaining counter, as well as for its own sake), in a process of attempting to reduce transactions costs in a market context, has some patent flaws. For example, one of the world's most widely used commodity moneys has been cattle. Thus, the word pecuniary comes from the Latin root, pecus, a cow. Whereas cattle are perfectly well adapted for clearing social debts, for example, bride-price, murder, and so on, their characteristics (being neither portable, divisible (while alive), durable, nor standardized), are not well geared to normal market transactions.

Nor for that matter are precious metals in their raw state. While the weight of a lump of metal can be easily ascertained, the quality and fine-ness (assay) of any such metal requires great expertise, and considerable extra costs when such expertise has to be purchased. For example, the Japanese developed a metallic means of 'color dressing' Koban coins so that they appeared golden on the outside, but were silver inside, see Ueda, Taguchi and Saito (1996). In practice, the use of precious metals, gold and silver, as money became viable on a large scale only after the establishment of mints when the fine-ness (quality) of the metal could be established and guaranteed by the mint stamp (n.b. until the edges of coins could be milled, the mint stamp could not protect against clipping, sweating, etc., so valuable coins continued to need weighing). Mints were usually run by, and almost invariably owned by, the governing power in the region. Indeed, the power to mint money has historically been one of the main attributes of sovereignty. So, the interrelationship between governance powers and the use of metallic moneys has been intimate and close from the outset. Moreover, the relative value of even the smallest gold and silver coins, relative to the price of objects in regular day-to-day trade, for example, salt, flour, beer, and so on, in mediæval and earlier times, was so high that such coins played little role in standard market conditions.

There are, furthermore, several other examples of primitive 'moneys', the Yap stones being the best known, where the money substance was clearly unsuited to market exchange. In many, perhaps most, of such cases their use was restricted to social (not market) exchanges, for example, tribute, bride price and 'blood money'. But the route from social to market exchange could be, and in several instances was, taken. So the claim that, as a generality, social and governance related exchanges preceded market exchange stands.

This is not to suggest that *none* of the early commodity moneys could have emerged from indirect barter. The use of nails, or otherwise shaped base metals, salt and, particularly, the cocoa bean money of the Aztecs (see Mélitz 1974, pp. 128–30), could have done so. What is argued, instead, is that there were certain crucial developments in the development of money that depended on social and governmental relationships, independently of cost-reducing market transactions, though which could subsequently be applied for that purpose also.

2   Money and government

Thus I contend that the development of the monetary system has close links with that of the legal system (a subject which I am currently pursuing further with Ellen Meade in a study on 'Central Banks and Supreme Courts' (FMG Special Paper No. 153, 2003)), and that both are closely related to governance, though not necessarily to *good* governance.

Werin, for example, distinguishes between judge-made law, which he asserts is efficiency promoting, and politically based laws which, more often than not, are not so. Thus,

> Property rights and restrictions on transfer instituted by politically-based law are of two kinds. They either concern 'constitutional' and 'night watch' matters, basic to any society and which require a purely

political decision process; they then tend to be efficiency-promoting. Or else they are framed so as to promote distributional objectives, with no regard to efficiency. The latter category dominates.

There are numerous ways in which the institution of money supports the conduct of government. We have already described how monetary payments may settle social debts, for example, for crime or bridal dowries, and others. More important, the government of an early economy, without money, such as Egypt,[3] can only obtain resources in two ways, by requiring its population to work (part-time) physically for the State, or to hand over a portion of their crop production.

That is clearly likely to result in inefficiency. Neither the mix of labour services, nor of products, coming forward from such a physical tithe system will necessarily fit the needs of the government closely. This will be particularly so during war time, when there is a temporary, but urgent, need for trained soldiers and war equipment. The maintenance of a large standing army during peace-time is both expensive and also a potential source of danger to the existing government. One solution to this quandary was to buy in mercenaries from abroad, when war occurred, but then by definition the government was not in a position to command them to fight. One of the main purposes, and functions, of early moneys was to provide a war-chest for the purchase of mercenaries, and the payment of tribute, notably in precious metals by vassal, subsidiary states, was, in turn, to help to provide that war-chest.

The close connection between sovereign control over the mint/printing press and the need of governments to maintain access to an immediate source of additional purchasing power during periods of crisis, internal civil strife or external war, has remained over millennia. Thus Glasner, *Free Banking and Monetary Reform* (1989) writes,

This brief survey of the ancient use of the state monopoly over money as an instrument of wartime finance should at least establish the plausibility of my contention that this monopoly was founded on security considerations. Not only is there no evidence that the state established a monopoly over coinage to improve the efficiency of the monetary system, ascribing that monopoly to the desire for monetary efficiency cannot explain why control of the monetary system has been so generally presumed to be an attribute of sovereignty. That feeling, engendered by centuries of historical experience, must stem from a real, if only historical, connection between control over money and the protection of sovereignty. That connection would also explain the otherwise surprising fact that counterfeiting was a treasonable offense under English law. (p. 31)

And,

> If I am correct in attributing the state monopoly over money to the interest of the state in defending its sovereignty, then the govern-ments most likely to relinquish control over the creation of money are ones with no defense responsibilities. That was the American experience. The states, which under the constitution had legal authority over banking but minimal defense responsibilities, often allowed free entry into banking and let banks issue their own notes. However, when some states challenged the political and military supremacy of the federal government, the federal government pre-empted state control over banking. (p. 36)

The state was able to establish a (profitable) monopoly over the issue of currency by its control over the authorised Royal Mint(s), and its severe prosecution of any rivals, as counterfeits. In an earlier article on a some-what similar topic, Goodhart (2003) wrote

> What is remarkable when reading the various histories of minting and currency is the correlation between strong kings (e.g., Charlemagne and Edward I) and successful currency reforms. Naturally, however, the temptation to debase the currency increases when (external) pressures threaten the continuing life of a government. Thus Henry VIII's debase-ment was related to war with France and Scotland at a time when 'The Exchequer's poverty was extreme ... ' (Craig 1953, p. 108). For a splen-did account of how that process (currency debasement) worked in practice, see Sargent and Smith (1995). Glasner (1989 and 1998), emphasises the value to governments facing (military) crises of having control over money creation.

Under the (Chartalist) view of money creation, the collapse of strong government would lead to the cessation, or downgrading of the quality, of minting and a reversion towards barter. Under the Monetary or Mengerian view, once the private sector has established a monetary equilibrium, thereby much reducing transactions costs, there is no con-ceivable mechanism within the model which would lead back to barter. Let us look at history. In Japan, for example, 'Rice and fabrics had been commonly used as a medium of exchange after the government ceased the mintage of coins in 958 AD...' (Seno'o 1996). Also, 'by the end of the tenth century, money circulation ceased and the economy regressed back to a barter economy' (Cargill *et al.* 1997). In any case, when the barbarians submerged Rome, strong government disintegrated. Both governments and mints fragmented into weaker smaller units. MacDonald (1916) describes the process as does Craig (1953), who also notes that amongst the ruling bodies operating mints at this time were Lords Spiritual, as well as Temporal.[4] With the governments being weaker and less secure, their currencies became of lower quality, more likely to be debased, and less acceptable in commerce (much of the minting that occurred was not to finance trade, but for Danegeld and other facets of (military) relationships between power centres). Meanwhile most, but not all, commercial relationships reverted to barter. This decline was halted by Charlemagne and his successor, Louis the Pious.

It is only when a settled and strong government has been established that the authorities can offer both a sufficiently long time horizon and the necessary control to establish a high quality mint. At the same time the creation of money greatly eased and benefited the authorities' fiscal position, as well as much reducing transactions costs for the general public.

In the case of other commodity moneys, such as cattle, salt and cocoa beans, the State had no monopoly in their provision. Sometimes the State tried to force their subject population to shift to using a money which the government did control as a means of raising both seignorage and tax receipts. This Burns (1927) records, that there was reluctance to switch from the use of cattle for certain quasi-monetary purposes. 'The cattle unit [in Rome] died hard, for twenty years later [*c.* 430 bc] it was necessary to order by law (the lex Papiria) that payments in copper should replace payments in cattle' (p. 17).

We shall revert to this later. In other cases, such as the use of cowries in West Africa, there was some degree of state involvement with their use and provision as money, even though they could be gathered by anyone. Mathew Forstater has drawn my attention to some work by Robin Law, who wrote (1978) that 'The apparent preference to the payment of taxes in money – cowries or gold – is especially interesting. It must be assumed that the spread of the use of cowry shells as money in West Africa depended upon state initiative – this was certainly the case with the introduction of the cowry currency in Bornu in the 1840s' (1978, p. 49).

In the same article and again in the The Oyo Empire, c.1600–1836, Law informs us that 'it appears that the issue of 'strung' cowries was a monopoly of the palace' (1978, p. 49). This refers to strings of specific numbers of cowries, and specific numbers of strings collected in a 'head' (1977, p. 209). Also the locations that used cowries were often places where they were not available – far into the mainland, and even areas where cowries were not available even in the sea.

Under normal, peace-time circumstances, when the precious metal coins, gold and silver, remained at their stated fine-ness, the return to the sovereign from seignorage was regular, and good, but not a massive source of revenue. It arose from mint charges, which could be levied since the use-value of coin was generally above that of lumps of precious metal of the same weight. Moreover lower value coin were often exchanged by tale, that is by the stated face value, rather than by a combination of weight and guaranteed fine-ness. So the mint could issue some coins whose value in exchange was above their metallic, input cost.

But the main early route to securing a sudden rush of additional revenue was to de-base the currency, that is to issue coins with the same nominal face value but containing a lower quality of precious metal than previously. Holders of existing coin within the country could be bribed/threatened to hand them back to the mint by a combination of some return from so doing, plus the threat that within the country the government would, after some date, treat the old coins of the same nominal, but higher intrinsic value, exactly the same as the new coin, for example, for the payments of taxes and fines. Of course, in external transactions, where the writ of the government did not run, debasement was, in effect, devaluation (even if, to quote Harold Wilson's claim after the 1967 devaluation 'the coin in your pocket is not devalued'). Accordingly debasement/devaluation led quickly to inflation; debasement could be seen equivalently as providing funds to the government by giving them command over a larger stock of precious metals, by allowing them to increase the nominal monetary base, or as an inflation tax.

Since governments who controlled the mint could always decide on the quality of their coins, why did they not just use that capacity to raise funds to the limit? As Barro (1970) showed, insofar as inflation increasingly drives people to use substitutes for domestic money, for example, foreign money or barter, there will be an interior maximum return to debasement/inflationary money creation. Generally, however, governments sought to commit *not* to use this available access to extra funding under normal conditions, partly in order to leave it available to themselves under special crisis circumstances.

Thus Glasner (1989) writes that

> The national defense rationale for the state monopoly over money implies that governments optimally exploit the monopoly by avoiding inflation in peacetime. If they don't avoid inflation, they risk being left defenceless in wartime. Governments that invest in the monopoly over money by not inflating in peacetime therefore improve their chances of surviving in military competition with other governments. So it would seem that there is a tendency for governments that create inflation in peacetime to be weeded out. (p. 39)

The emergence of banks, and of central banks, by the nineteenth century led to the widespread use of bank notes. The bank notes had value because they were convertible, on demand, into precious metal coins. But the needs of war time or civil emergency (much less frequently some other adverse domestic supply shock), would lead to an external drain of coin, and other forms of precious metal, for example, bars, abroad. This would lead to an inability to meet the convertibility commitment. At such moments governments would react by making the notes of their central bank legal tender for all domestic debts, and unconvertible into precious metals, thereby releasing that stock which had backed the note issue for use in financing the external deficit.

Such a step, also known on the Continent as 'cours forcé,' was perceived as a sign of external weakness in government financing and a prelude to inflation. Throughout the nineteenth century there was a continuous history of governments forced into inconvertibility, legal tender, fiat money, and struggling back thereafter to fiscal retrenchment and restoration of the gold (or silver) standard, see Goodhart, *The Evolution of Central Banks* (1988).

The potential for command over additional resources during crisis periods, and a stable source of seignorage receipts at all times, was by no means the only use governments had for the monetary system.

There is a close relationship between the creation and use of money, as an instrument of state sovereignty, and the ability of the state to raise taxes, a simultaneous two-way relationship. As I wrote in my earlier paper (2003), pp. 7–8

> First, without money, it would be hard to place taxes on anything other than the production, transport and trade of goods, since only goods (or labour time) could be delivered. Once money exists, poll, income and expenditure taxes as well as taxes on the production of

services become easier to levy. When taxes are received in goods or labour, the balance of goods (and labour) obtained will not be that required for public sector expenditures, so money reduces the transactions costs of governments, pari passu with that of the private sector.

By the same token taxes payable in monetary form raise the demand for base money. Since a government obtains seignorage from money creation, this benefits the fiscal position twice over, not only from the taxes levied but also from the seignorage resulting from the induced monetary demand. This was, as Lerner (1954) notes, one of the major reasons for the introduction of Confederate currency by the South in the US Civil War.

Indeed the imposition of taxes, payable only in money (and not in goods or in kind), has been used on numerous occasions in colonial history for the primary purpose of forcing taxpayers out of a (non-monetary) subsistence economy and into a cash economy producing goods for sale in the world economy; the receipt of extra fiscal revenues was in some cases just a subsidiary motive, as recorded by writers such as Ake (1981), Rodney (1981); Amin and Pearce (1976).[5]

There is, indeed, a large literature on the use of taxes, payable in monetary form, as a means of driving peasants into a monetary relationship with a capitalist economy. This is not only to be found in the literature on colonial development, but also in the earlier development of capitalism in Europe, for example, Hoppe and Langton (1994).[6]

In an excellent book, *The Making of National Money: Territorial Currencies in Historical Perspective*, Helleiner (2003) outlines the motives, and (technological) conditions, that led to the development of territorial currencies in the nineteenth and twentieth centuries.

Thus he writes, 'Before the nineteenth century, monetary structures in all parts of the world, including Europe, diverged from the territorial model in three ways: foreign currencies frequently circulated alongside domestic currencies, low-denomination forms of money were not all integrated into the official monetary system, and the official domestically issued currency was far from homogenous and standardised. Only in the nineteenth century did each of these features begin to be overcome in ways that allowed territorial currencies to emerge' (p. 3).

Helleiner identifies four main motives for this development. Two of these have already been adequately noted here. These are, first, the beneficial impact on the fiscal position of the state; indeed Helleiner suggests that this motive can be 'easily overstated' (p. 3). The second was

'The desire to control the domestic money supply for macroeconomic purposes' (p. 9). But this was not originally with the aim of enhancing discretionary control, rather the opposite. 'In the nineteenth and early twentieth centuries, policymakers inspired by classical economic liberalism often created note monopolies because of their desire to manage their country's growing supply of paper money in keeping with the automatic market-based principles of the gold standard. In these instances, ... policymakers hoped a more consolidated national monetary structure would allow them to guarantee that discretionary management of the domestic money supply and exchange rate did *not* happen. Their conception of macroeconomic management, thus, was extremely limited and sought simply to manage the domestic money supply in a way that simulated the automatic macroeconomic adjustment mechanisms of the gold standard' (p. 9).

The two additional motives that Helleiner emphasises are, first the reduction in transactions costs, and second to strengthen national identities. In the first of these, see p. 8 and Chapter 3, Helleiner notes that the conscious policy of reducing transactions costs (nb. by *official* action, not just private market processes) was 'very prominent politically throughout the nineteenth and twentieth centuries. Policymakers were frequently driven by the desire to eliminate domestic transaction costs encountered by merchants operating in newly emerging nationwide markets where no standardised and exclusive currency existed. The emergence of national markets was also a "vertical" [phenomenon] in which the poor began to become incorporated within the larger market economy for the first time. In this context, creators of territorial currencies hoped to eliminate the transaction costs associated with the use of low-denomination money that was both heterogeneous and had an uncertain link to the official monetary systems.'

Finally, as Helleiner notes, p. 11 and Chapter 5, 'territorial currencies were also often constructed to strengthen national identities. Although economists sometimes acknowledge the importance of the link between territorial currencies and national identities, the issue rarely plays any significant role in their analysis of the geography of money. Interestingly, the relationship between territorial currencies and national identities has also received almost no attention from scholars of nationalism or within new literature on the sociocultural dimensions of money. This issue, however, motivated nationalist policymakers throughout the nineteenth and twentieth centuries. They saw the construction of territorial currencies as fostering national identities in several ways. At the level of iconography and naming, policymakers recognised that exclusive and standardised coins and notes might provide an effective vehicle for their project of constructing and bolstering a sense of collective tradition and memory. By reducing transaction costs within the nation, a territorial currency was also seen to facilitate "communication" among citizens. Because trust plays such a large role in the use and acceptance of modern forms of money, it was thought that territorial currencies might encourage identification with the nation-state at a deeper psychological level. And finally, territorial currencies were increasingly associated with national sovereignty both in a symbolic sense and because they could be used to serve the national community as tools for activist national macroeconomic management.'

The analogy to the introduction of the Euro as a conscious attempt to bolster a European identity hardly requires emphasis.

3 Constraints on government misuse of control over the monetary base

Although much of the benefits of their monopoly control over the monetary system goes to the government, for example, fiscal benefits, seignorage, a tool for enhancing national identity, and so on, and governments have managed the monetary system since time immemorial, the existence of money is at the same time an essential part of the infrastructure of the capitalist, market system. Although much of the story about the private sector inventing money, via indirect barter in commodities, is a myth, the benefits in massive reductions in transactions costs in the operation of markets do certainly exist.

The dramatic developments in our market economies over recent centuries simply would not have been possible without the institution of money. The financial intermediaries, which the other chapters in this book discuss, trade money now for money in the future, an inter-temporal trade. Their growth has itself been dependent on the successful operation of a monetary economy. In these other chapters there has been much discussion of when, and whether, a financial system may be successful in sustaining growth.

When one focuses, instead, on the narrower monetary system, there is one overriding criterion for assessing its success; that is its ability to sustain price stability. That criterion alone is not sufficient. By most standards Japan has enjoyed price stability in the last decade, with a low average mean inflation rate and little variance. But few would describe Japan's monetary policy as successful. So there needs to be an additional criterion that monetary policy does not lead to such disturbances that real growth and asset markets are adversely affected.

Nevertheless the monetary system, and markets, do not work efficiently if there is virulent inflation, or anticipated deflation (even on a moderate scale). All this is well known. The point is that there is a tension in this respect between the objectives of the government on the one side, and of the private sector on the other. As a persistent debtor, the government benefits from unanticipated inflation. Even when inflation is correctly anticipated, the government can garner extra revenue from the inflation tax via additional seignorage (up to some internal maximum).

So, there is always a short-term incentive for the government to abuse its monopoly control over monetary creation to extract greater resources for itself. But the more that the government is thereby tempted, the less efficient the monetary system becomes. Ultimately as hyperinflation sets in, flight from the domestic monetary system even erodes any benefits to the government itself.

The standard answer to this problem (of time inconsistency) has been for the government to commit to a monetary regime which would publicly constrain it from (excessive) money creation. Adherence to the gold standard was just such a commitment device. Moreover, it worked extremely well in the late nineteenth and early twentieth centuries, allowing a degree of free movement of goods, labour and capital that has barely been re-attained in recent years (and still far from it for labour).

During this period it was fully appreciated that the abandonment of convertibility to gold, and the adoption of a fiat, legal tender currency system, was usually an indication of fiscal weakness and excess. It was realised that extreme crises (notably wars) could force a temporary abandonment, and governments could be given the benefit of the doubt if they indicated a determination to rejoin the standard.

In his book, *Monetary Regimes and Inflation*, Bernholz (2003) has described the close links between fiscal excess, fiat monetary regimes and hyperinflation. Thus, 'First, all hyperinflations in history occurred after 1914 under discretionary paper money standards except for the French case during the Revolution of 1789–96, when a paper money standard was introduced with assignats' (p. 8).

Next, 'With the inflationary bias of governments, inflation can only be absent in the long run if the hands of the rulers are bound by an adequate monetary regime or constitution' (p. 14).

And, finally, in Section 5.2, 'In this section it will be demonstrated by looking at 12 hyperinflations that they have all been caused by the financing of huge public budget deficits through money creation' (p. 69).

All this was perfectly well known in the nineteenth century. So why was the gold standard abandoned in the inter-war period? A good question!

There are several interacting reasons for the departure from gold in the inter-war years, which have been well recorded by Eichengreen (1992) in his excellent book, *Golden Fetters*. I would propose four such main explanations:-

(i) Decline of wage/price flexibility;
(ii) The First World War shocks and mal-distribution of gold reserves;
(iii) Poor policies, especially, but not only, in the United States;
(iv) Theoretical changes to, and in perceptions of, the responsibilities of government.

One of the mysteries of the inter-war years is how the major developed countries recovered so rapidly from the immediate post-war depression in 1919–20, yet failed to do so from the later slump in 1929–33. One cause of the earlier recovery was the massive decline in wages and prices in the immediate post-war period, perhaps facilitated by an appreciation that the inflation at the end of the First World War had raised wages/prices to 'artificial' and untenable levels, which allowed an expansion in the real monetary base (Meltzer 2003) – though a cessation to the post-war fiscal retrenchment may also have played a large part. Be that as it may, if nominal exchange rates are fixed to gold, it makes it much easier to adjust to relative, and to overall, disequilibria without adverse real effects if wages and prices are extremely flexible. For a variety of reasons, including the rise in unionisation, and political support for the management of economics, willingness to accept wage/price cuts as a remedy for insufficient demand declined sharply thereafter.

Meanwhile the shocks facing the developed world as a result of the First World War, and in its aftermath, were far greater than those earlier. It was no surprise that the main European combatants lost almost all their gold (to the United States) and were forced off gold into a fiat regime, nor that the US sterilised the counterpart inflow to avoid inflation. Nevertheless the resulting concentration of gold reserves in the United States meant that other countries needed to re-peg at levels that gave them a competitive advantage (vis a vis the United States), thereby in effect raising the world price of gold. The French did so; the British did not; and economic policies in Germany were badly distorted by political squabbling over reparations. The result was that gold reserves remained mal-distributed, mainly in the hands of the French and Americans.

When the downturn came in 1929, the US monetary authorities did not shift rapidly or energetically enough to counter it, partly because they saw the downturn as an appropriate cleansing of the previous financial excesses (see Friedman and Schwartz 1963, Meltzer 2003). Given that passive stance, the US downturn put pressure on Austria and Germany. The resulting crisis there then forced the United Kingdom off gold, and so it went on.

Meanwhile Keynes was arguing that the gold standard was a 'barbarous relic' anyhow. Reliance on price/wage flexibility was both dangerous, because Fisherian debt/deflation dynamics could easily outweigh any Pigouvian beneficial real balance effects, and also unlikely to occur in the new politico-economic system with strong unions. Instead the new policy proposal was to manage domestic demand so as to achieve 'full employment' at stable, pre-existing wage/price levels. But, given the historically determined level of the gold standard exchange rate, the level of demand that gave internal equilibrium (i.e. 'full employment') would not necessarily be that giving external equilibrium, that is without persistent and large-scale reserve flows. The Keynesian answer was to abandon the fixed, gold standard, exchange rate, and to allow (and to hope that) exchange rate adjustments that would bring the balance of payments into equilibrium.

In the event, in the late 1930s the developed world did move to floating rates, but were forced into it by default of better alternatives rather than as a chosen policy preference. This floating rate experience was not happy (see Nurkse 1944), but this was probably due as much to the autarchic, protective policies adopted by most countries, and to the worsening political scene and the capital flows that engendered, as to the shortcomings of the floating rate regime itself.

Be that as it may, the pegged exchange rate system, established at Bretton Woods, was primarily meant to rectify the problem of achieving external equilibrium, to avoid the disadvantages of an excessively rigid system, that is, the gold standard, on the one hand and of an excessively unstable system, that is, floating exchange rates on the other. At that time (i.e. 1945) the main problem for domestic price stability was perceived as deflation, rather than inflation. General domestic demand management, using fiscal policy primarily rather than monetary policy, was seen as the cure for any such deflationary pressures.

In practice the Bretton Woods system did also act as a constraint on the inflationary proclivities of some governments, including the United Kingdom. So long as the central country, that is, the United States, maintained price stability, the system worked well, allowing rapid growth, high employment and low, but upwardly creeping, inflation. But the stability of the system was increasingly threatened by rising capital mobility. Meanwhile a combination of pressures from the Vietnam war and of political incentives for domestic expansion led to greater external US deficits and higher domestic US inflation.

The Bretton Woods system in turn buckled, despite serious attempts to preserve it. Once again, the developed countries moved to a floating exchange regime more by default than by intention. But now (the 1970s) the context was of worsening inflation, not deflation (as in the 1930s). The 1970s were a disastrous period. A sharp downwards shift in the trend growth of productivity, occurring around 1973, which was not perceived at the time, led governments to overestimate the extent of slack in the economy, and to expand too much in the early 1970s. That, combined with the 1973 oil shock, led to sharp spikes in inflation, low growth and rising unemployment, that is, stagflation.

Meanwhile theoretical developments had underlined the need for governments to find 'anchors' to enable them to maintain price stability. The demonstration that one could not achieve better growth in the medium and longer term by monetary expansion (variously known as the vertical Phillips curve, long-term monetary neutrality, or the natural rate of unemployment hypothesis), was widely accepted (Friedman 1968, Phelps 1968); as was the argument (time 'inconsistency'), that governments would regularly come under pressure to undertake expansionary monetary policies (Kydland and Prescott 1977, Barro and Gordan 1983). Such theoretical analysis helped to drive the search for monetary 'anchors', or regimes, that would preserve price stability.

Monetary targets were tried, with varying conviction by those in charge, for example, Volcker (1979–82), and then generally abandoned as the relationship between the growth of the monetary aggregates and nominal incomes (velocity) was found to be too unpredictable. Some, for example, Lawson in the United Kingdom, 1988–89, and Cavallo in Argentina, sought to use a fixed peg to another more stable country's currency as their anchor. As in the case of the gold standard itself, this required an extent of wage/price flexibility and fiscal restraint and control that was all too often lacking.

Where we have now reached, of course, is the adoption of a (new) regime of independent Central Banks with a mandate for price stability. The independence of the Central Bank is meant to protect against the pressures felt by government to reflate, while the mandate for price stability comes both from historical experience and modern theory. Will it work? So far it has worked well, since its widespread adoption in the early 1990s. Weaknesses, however, include the fact that stability in goods and services (consumer) prices in the main countries has been accompanied by instability in exchange rates (real as well as nominal) and in other asset prices, for example, houses and equities. Questions remain about how to respond to asset price movements in a system aiming to achieve price stability. There is also some concern, largely driven by Japanese experience, whether the monetary authorities could deal with a shock that drove the economy into price deflation.

Of course, as with the gold standard, any really severe crisis, for example, war or natural disaster, would lead to a government override of the inflation target and of central bank independence. The potentiality for such an override is either implicitly, or in some cases explicitly, written into the institutional arrangements. As with the gold standard, such an override procedure is both inevitable and, on balance, desirable.

Not all countries have opted for the independent Central Bank/ inflation target regime. An alternative is to abandon a separate currency, either by adopting a common currency with a federal central bank and inflation target, as in the euro zone, or by fixing to another currency, for example, by a Currency Board or dollarisation. In the first case monetary policy decisions are shared; in the latter case they remain solely under the control of the central country.

In either case the conditions for success are much the same as required under the gold standard, that is, fiscal restraint and control, and mechanisms for handling problems of external disequilibria other than by exchange rate changes. Wage/price flexibility is usually the most efficacious and best, but labour migration and fiscal adjustments can be of great help. It is obvious that there are countries, and circumstances, where rigidly fixed exchange rates do not work well; Argentina has been just such a case. How well the euro zone will operate remains to be seen, with the stability and growth (fiscal) pact (treaty) under threat, and doubts about the efficacy of its internal adjustment mechanisms.

The more closed the economy (and large economies such as the United States, Japan or the euro zone become relatively closed), the greater the internal wage/price flexibility needed to cure an external disequilibrium (absent exchange rate changes). For such reasons a move towards a single world monetary system is unthinkable at present; and if there was to be any such world system in the future, it would probably be managed (by some world monetary authority) rather than a reversion to the gold standard of yesteryear.

So, as far as can be ascertained now, the present monetary regime of independent central banks, plus inflation targets, will persist into the indefinite future. There has, however, been a question raised whether technological progress might imperil the position of central banks; in particular whether the advent of e-money might provide a complete substitute for cash? If cash, the main liability of central banks, largely disappeared, would central banks still have the wherewithal to fix short-term interest rates for the economy as a whole (B. Friedman 1999)?

In practice, however, cash is unlikely to be superseded by plastic (or other electronic wizardry), as a means of payment. Cash has the advantage of anonymity (for black and grey market purposes), whereas electronic transfers can be traced; cash is a cheap means of payment (unlike cheques which will be superseded); electronic transfers are, at least at present, more subject to fraud than cash is to counterfeit; cash has first mover advantage and is almost universally acceptable (Drehmann *et al.* 2002).

Even if cash was to disappear, though it will not do so, the ability of central banks to fix short-term rates does not depend on the existence of such liabilities, but on the need for those institutions running the payments system, currently the commercial banks, to settle their transactions in, and therefore need to hold reserves of, balances held at the central bank. So long as central banks continue to provide useful services to government, including managing monetary policy and the financial system successfully, then government in turn can make sure that the central bank remains the sole monopoly provider of the high-powered monetary base, and can hence fix interest rates (see the special issue on 'The Future of Monetary Policy', ed. A. Posen, *International Finance* (2000)).

The emphasis in this section has been on the importance of the monetary regime, whereby the access of the government to money creation is constrained. While this is the key determinant of monetary stability in the longer term, there have been instances of monetary instability caused by fluctuations in bank lending to the private sector. Dynamic instability can ensue from the interaction between asset prices and bank lending, and such boom/bust cycles have been common phenomena in capitalist economies. The IT bubble was a case in point, even though central banks were reasonably successful (outside Japan), in preventing that cycle impinging on goods and services price inflation (and limiting its effect on real output growth).

Inflationary expansion of bank lending, and hence of bank deposits, is also more likely if bankers, and possibly even central bankers, come under the control of industrial magnates. Such businesses incur debt in order to grow. So they tend to benefit when credit is cheap and easy.

Accordingly bankers influenced by industrialists are likely to be more willing lenders. Nevertheless there are offsetting advantages, for example, information flows and in the length of planning horizons, in having close links between industry and banks. During the 1980s particularly, the German/Japanese model of banking, where such relationships are maintained, was praised as the superior pattern for all others to follow. The travails of the Japanese banks, and economy, since 1990, and in Germany more recently, has tarnished the reputation of that model, particularly as compared to the Anglo-Saxon market-oriented model.

Given monetary stability, the underlying rationale of the financial sector is the allocation of credit to investors/borrowers and the mobilisation of funds from savers/lenders. This is a key determinant of growth. But this is the main subject of most of the other chapters in this book. So my purpose here has been to maintain a proper balance by emphasising the essential role of the nexus between the government and the monetary system, that is the monetary regime, in the achievement of monetary and price stability, without which financial intermediation would be severely hampered, if not prevented entirely.

4   Conclusion

As Luigi Zingales stated in his 'Commentary' on Ross Levine's survey paper on finance and growth (2003),

> In 1993 many people doubted that there was a relation between finance and growth; now very few do....I will focus, thus, on the weak links in the quest for a reliable relation between finance and growth that policymakers can use in their decisions.... As La Porta *et al.* (1999 and 2002) document, there is a set of countries that seem to be doing the right thing in many dimensions: their legal enforcement is better, their level of generalised trust higher, their judicial system more efficient and independent; they have less corruption, less regulation, more respect for property rights, and better-developed financial markets. Each institution taken individually has a positive effect on economic growth. Yet there are too many (highly correlated) variables and too few countries to be able to reliably identify the effect that one institution has compared with another.
>
> To make the problem worse, all these variables are measured with errors. Thus, a multiple regression may fail to identify which of these variables really matter.

Finally, these characteristics seem to be very persistent. In fact, all are highly correlated with the country from which their legal system originated.

As I claimed at the very outset of the chapter, the most important determinant of growth is good governance. Good governance is linked in turn with the establishment and maintenance of the rule of law, *and* with monetary stability. Indeed, both the rule of law and a well-chosen monetary regime can be perceived as commitment devices whereby the government constrains its use of its own short-term powers in the longer-term interest of all its subjects. By the same token the ability of financial intermediation and development to help general longer-term sustainable growth depends sensitively on these same underlying conditions.

The institution of money has always been intimately connected with the exercise of state power. The nature and usage of each monetary regime has been as much a political, as a purely economic matter, for better or (often) worse. The attempt to air-brush the role of the government out of the history, and out of current analysis of the working, of the monetary system – though commonly done – is a categorical mistake.

If we are to examine the effects of the financial system on growth, we have to remember the essential underlying importance of monetary stability and the rule of law, and both are in turn a function of the governance of the country.

Notes

1. Both extracts come from *The State, The Market and The Euro* (2003), the first originally came from Grierson (1977, 1970) in his pamphlet on 'The Origins of Money', pp. 19–21, but was reproduced in Goodhart 'The two concepts of money: implications for the analysis of optimal currency areas', chapter 1, Appendix A, p. 16; the second from Wray, 'The neo-Chartalist approach to money', chapter 5, pp. 97–8.
2. An article by K. Gattas (2003) appeared in the *Financial Times*, on Wednesday, 6 August, p. 18, under the heading, 'US finds blood money is price of keeping Iraqi peace'. It included the following passage:

   'This compensation money will put an end to attacks against US soldiers by relatives of those killed by Americans,' explains Taha Bdawi, the city's US-backed mayor. 'This is a tribal, traditional society, where the principles of *tha'r* (revenge) and *fidya* (blood money) are still in force.' Tribal custom demands that for every man killed, four men from the enemy tribe must die, or one man if it was an accidental death. But a vendetta can be avoided through financial compensation – the current price is 1m Iraqi dinars (about £388) for an accidental killing and 4m dinars for premeditated murder.

3. The Egyptians had, however, one of the first, and perhaps best, automatic fiscal stabilizer. This was in the form of a graduated well which could accurately measure the height of the annual flood of the Nile. When the flood was high, the harvest rose, and so did the proportionate tithe; and vice versa.
4. Thus Craig (1953, p. 12) writes that, 'Mints run by ecclesiastics on the other hand were proprietary. Only two are known to have survived from the earliest primitive period. The archbishop of Canterbury has two units. ... The single unit of the abbot of St Augustine's was merged in this property in or before the tenure of the See by the patron Saint of Goldsmiths, St Dunstan. The saint's three minters were serfs; he was a hard man of affairs who once shocked his congregation by suspending Easter mass until they hanged certain counterfeiters of his coin, whose trial the people would have delayed till Monday out of respect of the day.'
5. Interestingly some similar policies had preceded the arrival of the colonial powers in West Africa. Thus Paul E. Lovejoy, in his article on 'Interregional Monetary Flows in the Pre-colonial trade of Nigeria' writes:-

   'Dependencies of such emirates as Nupe paid their levies in cowries as well as that the taxation system effectively assured that people participated in the market economy and used the currency, a policy remarkably similar to the one which the later colonial regimes pursued in their efforts to see their own currencies accepted' (1974, p. 581).
6. There are a small number of economists, mostly related to the post-Keynesian school, who perceive the nexus between taxation and money as a way to encourage the unemployed (as well as subsistence peasants), back into the employed labour force. Essentially the policy is to combine a tax (usually a flat rate, poll tax) on all those to be attracted back into the labour force, to be paid in money, while simultaneously offering *everyone* some job, usually in the service sector, for example, looking after old people or sprucing up public parks, whereby they could earn such money (plus enough to live on). The proponents ignore, however, the point that so long as vacancies exist in such jobs, for example, hospital porters (and they usually do), such a policy is in a sense already in being; and the unemployed have chosen, reasonably enough, to opt out. Moreover, the efficiency of trying to pressurise the unemployed into doing jobs that they may not want to do, and may often do badly, and having to administer all that, is questionable. As I grow older, the idea of having some young male layabout press-ganged into looking after me in order to earn enough to pay his poll tax is becoming increasingly uninspiring.

References

Ake, C. (1981), *A Political Economy of Africa*, Harlow: Longman.

Amin, S. and Pearce, B. (1976), *Unequal Development: An Essay on the Social Formations of Peripheral Capitalism* (translated from French by B. Pearce), Hassocks: Harvester Press.

Barro, R.J. (1970), 'Inflation, the Payments Period, and the Demand for Money', *Journal of Political Economy*, 78 (6) (November/December).

Barro, R.J. and Gordon, D.B. (1983), 'A Positive Theory of Monetary Policy in a Natural Rate Model', *Journal of Political Economy*, 91 (4) (August).

Bernholz, P. (2003), *Monetary Regimes and Inflation: History, Economic and Political Relationships*, Cheltenham, UK: Edward Elgar.

Burns, A.R. (1927), *Money and Monetary Policy in Early Times*, New York: Alfred A. Knopf.

Cargill, T., Hutchinson, M. and Ito, T. (1997), *The Political Economy of Japanese Monetary Policy*, Cambridge, MA: MIT Press.

Craig, J. (1953), *The Mint*, Cambridge: Cambridge University Press.

Drehmann, M., Goodhart, C. and Krueger, M. (2002), 'Challenges to Currency', *Economic Policy*, 34 (April): 195–227.

Eichengreen, B. (1992), *Golden Fetters: The Gold Standard and the Great Depression*, Oxford: Oxford University Press.

Friedman, B.M. (1999), 'The future of monetary policy: The central bank as an army with only a signal corps?', NBER Working Paper 7420.

Friedman, M. (1968), 'The role of monetary policy', *American Economic Review*, 58 (March): 1–17.

Friedman, M. and Schwartz, J. (1963), *A Monetary History of the United States, 1867–1960*, Princeton, NJ: Princeton University Press for NBER.

Gattas, K. (2003), 'US finds blood money is price of keeping Iraq peace', *Financial Times*, August 6: 18.

Glasner, D. (1989), *Free Banking and Monetary Reform*, Cambridge: Cambridge University Press.

Glasner, D. (1998), 'An evolutionary theory of the state monopoly over money', in K. Dowd and R.H. Zinbalake (eds), *Money and the Nation State*. London, Transaction Publishers, pp. 21–45.

Goodhart, C.A.E. (1988), *The Evolution of Central Banks*, Cambridge, MA: The MIT Press.

Goodhart, C.A.E. (1998/2003), 'The two concepts of money: implications for the analysis of optimal currency areas', *European Journal of Political Economy*, 14, 407–32, reprinted as Chapter I, in *The State, the Market and the Euro*, Nell, E.J. and Bell, S.A. (eds), Cheltenham, UK: Edward Elgar.

Goodhart, C.A.E. and Meade, E. (2003), 'Central banks and supreme courts', Financial Markets Group, London School of Economics, Special Paper No. 153 (October).

Grierson, P. (1977), 'The origins of money', Creighton Lecture, Cambridge, 1970, reprinted and revised in pamphlet form, University of London: Athlone Press.

Helleiner, E. (2003), *The Making of National Money: Territorial Currencies in Historical Perspective*, Ithaca, NY: Cornell University Press.

Hicks, J.R. (1969), *A Theory of Economic History*, Oxford: Clarendon Press.

Hoppe, G. and Langton J. (1994), *Peasantry to Capitalism*, Cambridge: Cambridge University Press.

Innes, A.M. (1932), *Martyrdom in Our Times: Two Essays on Prisons and Punishments*, London: Williams & Norgate.

Kiyotaki, N. and Wright, R. (1993), 'A search-theoretic approach to monetary economics', *American Economic Review*, 83: 63–77.

Kydland, F.E. and Prescott, E.C. (1977), 'Rules rather than discretion: the inconsistency of optimal plans', *Journal of Political Economy*, 85 (June): 473–91.

La Porta, R., Lopez-de-Silanes, F. and Shleifer, A. (2002), 'Government Ownership of Banks', *Journal of Finance*, 57 (1) (February): 265–301.

La Porta, R., Lopez-de-Silanes, F., Shleifer, A. and Vishny, W. (1999), 'The Quality of Government', *Journal of Law, Economics, and Organization*, March 1999, 15 (1), pp. 222–79.

Law, R. (1977), *The Oyo Empire, c.1600–c.1836: A West African Imperialism in the Era of the Atlantic Slave Trade*, Oxford: Clarendon Press.

Law, R. (1978), 'Slaves, trade, and taxes: the material basis of political power in precolonial West Africa', *Research in Economic Anthropology*, 1: 37–52.

Lerner, E.M. (1954), 'The monetary and fiscal programs of the Confederate Government, 1861–65', *Journal of Political Economy*, 62: 506–22.

Levine, R. (2003), 'More on finance and growth: more finance, more growth', *Federal Reserve Bank of St Louis Review*, 85 (4) (July/August): 31–46.

Lovejoy, P.E. (1974), 'Interregional monetary flows in the precolonial trade of Nigeria', *Journal of African History*, 15 (4): 563–85.

MacDonald, G. (1916), *The Evolution of Coinage*, Cambridge: Cambridge University Press.

Maddox, T. (1969 [1769]), *The History and Antiquities of the Exchequer of the Kings of England, in Two Periods*, Vols I and II, 2nd edn, NY: Greenwood Press.

Mélitz, J. (1974), *Primitive and Modern Money: An Interdisciplinary Approach*, Reading, MA: Addison-Wesley Publishing Co.

Meltzer, A. (2003), *A History of the Federal Reserve: Volume 1, 1913–1951*, Chicago, IL: University of Chicago Press.

Menger, K. (1892), 'On the origin of money' (translated from German by C.A. Foley), *Economic Journal*, 2: 238–55.

Nurkse, R. (1944), *International Currency Experience*, Geneva: League of Nations.

Phelps, E.S. (1968), 'Money wage dynamics and labor market equilibrium', *Journal of Political Economy*, 76 (August): 678–711.

Posen, A. (ed.) (2000), 'The Future of Monetary Policy', Special Issue of *International Finance*, 3 (2) (July).

Rodney, W. (1981), *How Europe Underdeveloped Africa*, Washington, DC: Howard University Press.

Sargent, T.J. and Smith, B. (1995), 'Coinage, debasement and Gresham's Laws', unpublished manuscript (August).

Seno'o, M. (1996), 'Yamada Hagaki and the history of paper currency in Japan', Bank of Japan, Institute for Monetary and Economic Studies, Discussion Paper 96-E-25.

Ueda, M., Taguchi, I. and Saito, T. (1996), 'Non-destructive analysis of the fineness of kobans in the Yedo Period', Bank of Japan, Institute of Monetary and Economic Studies, Discussion Paper 96-E-26.

Werin, L. (2003), *Economic Behavior and Legal Institutions: An Introductory Survey*, Singapore: World Scientific Publishing Co.

Wray, L.R. (2003), 'The neo-Chartalist approach to money', Chapter 5 in *The State, the Market and the Euro* (eds), Nell, E.J. and Bell, S.A. Cheltenham, UK: Edward Elgar.

Zingales, L. (2003), ''Commentary' on Levine's R. paper on 'More on Finance and Growth: More Finance, More Growth'', *Federal Reserve Bank of St Louis Review*, 85 (4) (July/August): 47–52.

Index

causality
  financial development and
    economic growth, 42–3, 45,
    46–7, 48
  Granger causality, 42–3
  see also reverse causality
Cavallo, Domingo, 199
Central Bank of Russia, 131n1
Central Banks, 199–200, 201
central Europe, 106–34
central planning, 107–8, 126, 128
Cetorelli, Nicola, 79, 83, 85, 89
Charlemagne, King of the Franks, 189,
  190
Chartalist view of money creation,
  189
child labour, 7
Chile
  financial development, 158
  institutional investors, 161, 165–7
  pension funds, 150, 156, 157,
    177n12
China
  banking system, 15–17, 27
  decentralization, 132n6
  non-government credit, 8
Cho, Yoon Je, 20
civil law, 57–9, 120, 121, 151
Claessens, Stijn, x, 66–105
Clapham, J.S., xx
Coase, Ronald, 71, 184
Coccorese, Paolo, 74
coins, 186–7, 191, 192
  see also minting
collateral, 142, 144
Collender, Robert N., 76
collusion, 73, 74, 75
commodities, 185
common law, 4–5, 34n21, 57–9, 120,
  121, 151
Commonwealth of Independent
  States, 125
communism, 127–8, 183
compensation, 185, 186, 203n2
competition, x, 66–105
  capital market liberalization, 59, 60
  financial development, 6
  financial liberalization, 49, 51
  incumbents, 59, 60, 61, 121

institutional investors, 161–2
  Marshall, xix
  Pareto efficiency, 40
  perfect, 73
  testing, 73–6
compulsory savings, 144
consolidation, 75, 77, 116
consumer theory, 39–40
consumption
  future, 38
  neoclassical theory, 39, 40
contestability, 67, 72, 73–4, 75–6,
  78–9
contracts
  enforcement, 51, 55, 56, 60, 107,
    123
  incomplete, 64n1
  legal structures, 15
  microfinance, 135, 138, 139, 141
  relationship banking, 152
corporate bonds, 156, 159, 163, 166
  see also bond finance
corporate control, 46
corporate governance, 163–4, 167,
  171, 174
corporate sector, 162–4, 167–75, 176
corruption, 48, 49, 51, 79, 113, 151,
  202
Corsetti, G., 156
Corvoisier, Sandrine, 76
costs
  competition in banking, 69, 71,
    73, 76
  microfinance, 139
  relationship banking, 153
  see also transaction costs
counterfeiting, 189
'cours forcé', 192
Craig, J., 189, 190, 204n4
credit
  adverse selection, 41, 64n4
  banking concentration, 70, 76, 78–9
  booms, 19
  competition in banking, 84–8,
    89–97, 99–100, 101n5
  creditor rights, 24, 34n21, 35n24,
    123
  GDP ratio, 10, 46, 84–8, 89–97,
    111, 152